To Kathy,
"Follow the gleam"
Love,
Marilee

MEDITATIONS OF JAMES ROBERT HARTLAND

In Whose Life I See:

Meditations of James Robert Hartland

Compiled by Marilee Hartland Lake

ISBN: 978-0-9964554-2-8

Library of Congress Control Number: 2016907177
Printed in the United States of America

Marilee A. Lake
Tipp City, Ohio

www.marileelakeauthor.com

This book is dedicated to the Glory of God and to all who were blessed by the life of "Pastor Jim"

I would like to acknowledge the support and help from my family and my fellow performers in LightReaders. This book would not be possible without them.

(Jim and Helen Jane Hartland, Feeding Hills, Massachusetts)

Table of Contents:

Forward: p. 1

Searching For God: p. 3   My Father's World
                                          Life in Such an Age
                                          Roadways to God

Growing in Faith: p. 23   The Marks of Maturity
                                          Facing Forth with Open
                                          Mind
                                          A Signpost and a Seed of
                                          Faith
                                          Creative Thinking

God's Loving Call: p. 49   Love's Destiny
                                          Not Enough Darkness
                                          There's No Hidin' Place
                                          for Love

Palm Sunday: p. 69   We would See Jesus...
                                          Facing Jerusalem
                                          Radiant Heights and
                                          Shadows Dim

Maundy Thursday: Those Who Cross
the Kidron: **p .83**   Neither for These Alone
Life's Wider Vistas

Good Friday: **p. 93**   Love So Amazing
It is Finished…

Easter: **p. 101**   Love Bearer to Mankind
From Tomb to Triumph
Earth's Darkness Turns
to Day

Eastertide: **p. 127**   More than Memory
Of Spring—and Life—
and God!

Christian Family Life: **p. 141**   This Business of Happy
Living
To Have and to Hold
On Making Houses
Home

Mother's Day: **p. 163**   A Smile and a Dream
The Madonna of the Tear
Cupboards and Clasped
Hands

Pentecost: **p. 181**   "…And Pentecost!"
The Power to Become

Through the Valley: **p. 197**   The Call of the Depths
Why Do Good People Suffer, Too?
The Sacredness of Life
The Far Look

Christian Service: **p. 225**   On Walking Crooked Miles
A Complete Offering

Thanksgiving: **p. 241**   Warmth in the Winter Wind
The Mayflower is Still Sailing
The Mayflower Compact

Christmas: **p. 255**   The Abiding Light
The Everlasting Sign
The Enduring Word
The Eternal Miracle

Following Jesus: **p. 277**   This above All
The Value of Venturing Forth
Gleam Following

(Jim and Helen Jane Hartland, Urbana, Ohio)

Forward

In February of 2013, shortly after my father's passing, my brother and I discovered a number of red folders filled with papers. I didn't know what they were, but my brother had still lived at home when my father retired, so he knew right away. "Those are Dad's top sermons!" he informed me. My father had carefully preserved his favorite sermons so that he would be able to easily find something if he was asked to supply a pulpit on short notice.

As I went through these folders, I found several empty, and some contained brief outlines that would only have meaning for my father. But others were written out in almost complete form, and the words fell like poetry on the ear. As I read these, I could hear my father's voice and remembered where our family was, and what we had experienced when he had first delivered them. Recognizing their timeless quality, I knew that they needed to be shared.

Dad had a true heart for mission, so I decided that all proceeds from book sales of his meditations should support Bradley's House of Hope, a therapy center for handicapped children near Managua, Nicaragua. I have personally visited this mission and am amazed with the way this mission brings hope to children and their families in the second poorest country in the Western Hemisphere.

This book is titled, *In Whose Life I See*, because these are words from my father's favorite hymn. They echo how he strived to live his own life, and are an example for us all to follow:

Dear Master, in whose life I see
All that I would but fail to be,
Let thy clear light forever shine,
To shame and guide this life of mine.

Though what I dream and what I do
In my weak days are always two,
Help me, oppressed by things undone,
O thou whose deeds and dreams are one!
(John Hunter)

MEDITATIONS OF JAMES ROBERT HARTLAND

Searching For God

(Mountain Cross, Jumonville, Pennsylvania)

"In the beginning God created the heaven and the earth." Genesis 1:1

My Father's World
Genesis 1: 26-31

August 27, 1944
Armagh-Seward Methodist Church, Armagh, Pennsylvania
First sermon

This is my Father's world, and to my listening ears
All nature sings and 'round me rings the music of the spheres.
This is my Father's world; I rest me in the thought
Of rocks and trees, of skies and seas
His hand the wonders wrought.

This is my Father's world, the birds their carols raise.
The morning light, the lily white, declare their Maker's praise.
This is my Father's world; He shines in all that's fair.
In the rustling grass I hear Him pass.
He speaks to me everywhere.
Maltbie Davenport Babcock

*I*t is so great a thrill to stand on a high place and to look around in every direction to see that on all sides there is the natural beauty of God's world. The towering trees, the rock formations, and the sky all blend into something which awes us. How amazing it is to know that the beauties of nature are here for our pleasure and for our use.

Humanity is the greatest of God's creations, the climax, the crown of this genius in whom is our beginning. And standing there upon the high place, we understand the significance of the psalmist's message:

When I consider Thy heavens, the work of Thy fingers, the moon and the
stars which Thou has ordained,
What is man, that Thou art mindful of him,
And the son of man, that Thou visitest him?
(Psalm 8: 3-4)

And with the view of the distant horizons in our eyes and with the luring quality of the mountain peaks before us, truly we do feel insignificant there upon the high place with God's world before us.

But then, the psalmist moves forward to the prominence of humanity, and thinking deeply about God's creation, we also come to reflection where we understand ourselves as being unique and as being the peak of creation with distinct bodies, wills, and personalities. And so, we too, can understand and cry forth heartily with the psalmist concerning humanity:

> *For Thou has made him a little lower than the angels and has crowned*
> *him with glory and honor.*
> *(Psalm 8:5)*

One of our modern poets has put the thought strikingly and memorably for me as he talks of the marvels of God's world; the lightning, the skies, the streams and flowers and fields, and the miracle of night and dawn. Then as the poet prepares our minds, he too, comes to his great thought in these words:

> *Then—to complete creation's span,*
> *In his own image—God made man,*
> *And signed his name with stroke most sure,*
> *Man is God's greatest signature!*
> *(Anonymous)*

Oh truly, it is a good thing for us to ascend into the high places of earth and to be alone with God—to catch a glimpse first of our own insignificance which deepens our humility, and then to realize our own importance, to restore our dedication to live and to walk in God's way. It is a good thing for us to ascend into the hills and to have our faith enriched there along with God. But the test comes when we come down once again into the ways of humanity and to face the people of our daily living with the same deep faith of humility and of dedication.

We need this strong faith and sincere dedication. For when the crises arise in life—five years ago it was a terrible war, and we knew not when the end of the fighting and the anxious days would come. Today it is the rumors of war that arise from our misunderstandings of other cultures and our lack of compassion for less fortunate beings as we go about smugly content with our own little selves and our little circle of friends.

And other pictures come before our eyes here in the world of man—it was a terrible picture in those days of blackened ruins and loss of homes and families and ways of life, and church spires fallen into the debris of war's destruction. And now, it is the terrible waste of an extravagant way of life in which one society lives in the light of high luxury and another gropes amidst the gloom of poverty. And out of this picture of destruction there arise the cries of men as they question God and God's way and wonder why God allows such destruction to come over God's wonderful world.

So we need again and again to go to our hilltop to catch the vision of the world as God gave it to us and to understand God's goodness and faith in us—that God also gave us the will to choose which way we should go in life, to decide for ourselves what we should do with the beauties and the benefits of this world. For it is when humanity—God's greatest creation, God's autograph—works in conflict with the forces of God's nature, that the economic upheavals occur, and the hatreds and greed arise, and war breaks out over the earth.

So when humanity uses its will against God's natural laws, there is a terrible picture of suffering and deep sorrow.

> *What is man, that Thou are mindful of him*
> *And the son of man that Thou visitest him?*

Such pictures need not be, for when one knows God intimately and serves God zealously, there is the picture of cooperation and of concern for all humanity and for God. Tolstoy, the Russian writer-philosopher, sums up such a picture:

> *He whose aim is his own happiness is bad.*
> *He whose aim is the good opinion of others is weak.*
> *He whose aim is the happiness of others is virtuous.*
> *He whose aim is God—is great!*

And one who ascends into the high place to deepen his humility, and to enrich her faith, will come down again, if the experience there be truly sincere, to strengthen in service to God and to humanity. For in such a world as this, to eliminate from our society the pictures of dark destruction, we must learn to understand one another and to live together in the bonds of God's love.

I have been impressed with this statement of one of our national leaders, Henry A. Wallace:

The world is a neighborhood. We have learned that starvation in China affects our own security—that the jobless in India are related to the unemployed here. The world is one family with one future—a future that will bind our brotherhood with heart and mind and not with chains, which will save and share the cultured past and now aborning—will work out a peace on a level of high and open cooperation, which will make democracy work for mankind by giving everyone a chance to build his own take in it.

Lord Byron puts it, "To have joy, one must share it. Happiness was born a twin."

Alan G. MacDiarmid's words offer us the Jesus vision:

When we lie down, worn out
Other men will stand up young and fresh,
By the steps that we have cut
They will climb.
By the stairs that we have built
They will mount
They will never know the names of the men who made them.
At the clumsy work they will laugh
And when the stones roll,
They will curse us.
But they will mount
And on our work,
They will climb and by our stairs.

And then back once more, to the final stanza of our opening hymn:

This is my Father's world, O let me ne'er forget
That though the wrong seems oft so strong
God is the ruler yet.

IN WHOSE LIFE I SEE

This is my Father's world. Why should my heart be sad?
The Lord is king, Let the heavens ring!
God reigns; Let the earth be glad.
(Maltbie Davenport Babcock)

Life in Such an Age
James 4: 8-14

January 12, 1958
First Methodist Church, Rochester, Pennsylvania

*T*he speakers and the writers of modern times are in accord when they join forces to remind us of the seriousness of our day and of the necessity for wise and wholesome living in such an hour. A contemporary poet has put it importantly:

> *To be alive in such an age*
> *With every year a lightning page*
> *Turned in the world's great wonder-book;*
> *When rail and road and steel and stone*
> *Become avenues of God,*
> *A trump to shout His message through*
> *And crown the work that man can do.*
> *O age of strife! O age of life!*
> *Rise, soul, from thy despairing knees,*
> *Give thanks with all thy flaming heart.*
> *Crave to have in it a part*
> *Arise, and claim thine heritage,*
> *To be alive in such an age.*
> *(Ayanna Ross)*

One of the common interests humanity has had over the centuries is for a longer life. We remember the fabulous story of Ponce de Leon and the Fountain of Youth. Perhaps we have in our times seen bottles of magical elixirs which when drunk restore the vitality and the handsomeness of youth. Perhaps, we too, if we admit it, yearn for an eternal youth and a longer life-span than life ordinarily affords us. But there is something far more important than life's length—what we can do with life while it is ours upon this earth. To what ends we expend our God-given talents, how we consume our energies, how we use all that is given unto us is the important matter for a Christian to consider—not how long did you live, but what did you do with life? James asks it, *"What is your life?" (James 4:14).*

This is a great time to be alive—an important time, a time of opportunity. Lewis Mumford puts it that these past fifty years of history were more significant than the previous thousand years. I exclaim at times over the mobility of humanity that has come about in even my own lifetime—at the changes wrought, at the gadgets invented and put into daily use, at the often baffling and constant progress of life.

Well, in the face of it—the importance of the age—what is your life? What can you do with it?

We need not look far afield to see what many men and women are doing with life in this serious day—they're doing the same thing that Jonah tried—running from life—seeking escape from life's hard responsibilities. You remember how God told him to go east to fulfill life's assignment, but Jonah preferred to go west. The thing is that when we try to run from life—seeking new locations and such, we find that the same old problems or even more or worse ones have preceded us in the westward trek, and stand to greet us with their smug sneers when we arrive at what we thought would be our Utopia.

Ibsen, the dramatist, gives us Peer Gynt—that character who consistently refused to face a difficulty. He sought to go around it, over it, or under it; but he always ran into more difficulty dodging duty than he would have met had he had the courage to face life in the first place. The world is round, and when you try to run away from life, it does seem that you only come back to where you started.

Yet people are devious in their attempts to run away. Some try it by rationalization—that process of getting your system of reason to sustain you in the action you desire to take. It operates when a man reasons with himself rather than with the facts. A fellow figures that he doesn't have time for worship on Sunday because his job is difficult and his frail body needs the seventh day to rest in bed. Now this indeed may be true, but what that fellow tries to do is to salve his own conscience by making the facts in the situation contribute to his own desire. If he were honest, the truth of the matter is that he wanted to stay in bed anyway. It's one often used way of escape from the responsibilities of life.

Another one is romance—to take one's mind away from the realities of life to life's fantasies. There are soap-opera addicts and movie fiends as well as dope and drink intemperates—and perhaps this danger is as keen in its mental effect as the latter is harmful to the body's physical health! In such escape, the child never becomes an adult to put aside the childish things of the play-world. It's fine indeed to dream—but unless the dreams materialize into deeds, the world does not progress through us.

Oh, there are other ways of escape. Some enjoy poor health—who use this method to escape life's demands, who crave the sympathy of the world, who wish the attention of the crowd, so the sickness comes until the responsibility is passed.

What is your life? Not how long, but how lived!

Then there are the thousands who follow the herd instinct, who play "follow-the-leader" in life. They run with life with no consideration for the individuality of their personality. Those who live by herd instinct forget that startling climax of creation whereby a human became a living soul. Some historians have termed Christians a peculiar people—and so we are in a measure. No doubt the easiest way of life is the way of conformity. Yet Christ refused to conform to the world; rather he sought to transform the world. The genius of Christianity is not in its conformity, but in its transforming power. Had Christianity conformed, it would have died in the first century. Those who have stood out above the crowd, who have defied the status quo, who have stood against entrenched greed and injustice, have been the leaders of history. Christians—the militant ones, not those of course who bear the title so lightly—have been a peculiar people. They have refused to run with life. Rather, they have sought to change the very course of life itself. Drifting with the current is the line of least resistance—dead fish always drift downstream. Only the living salmon dare the waterfalls. To drift in one's spiritual life ultimately means death to the soul. One hymn puts it:

> *Dare to be brave, dare to be true:*
> *Don't be a drifter,*
> *Breast the stream,*
> *And struggle for a worthy dream.*
> *Be one of those with standards high,*
> *Who dare to do and dare to try.*
> *Too many merely drift along,*

Hopeless when danger's winds grow strong;
Crushed by rocks they might evade,
Were they not too lightly swayed.
(W. J. Rooper)

What is your life? What do you do with it—how do you live it?

There's a third way of meeting life and expending it. You can run life. You can take hold of it positively—not lie down and let life run over you—but stand up to life and wrestle with it. Our speaker the other evening pointed out that while the disciples were beset by the storm on the sea, our Lord Jesus lay asleep in the boat, unafraid. For He had learned to take life or to lay it down. Fear, frustrations, perplexities did not disturb nor destroy His calm confidence in the goodness of God. Life with its troubles surely was of genuine concern to Him, but it did not overrun Him. He mastered it and ran life without fear and anxiety because of that knowledge of the goodness of God.

It involves purposeful living. If we believe that God lives, we must believe that God has a plan. God is not a capricious being who fluctuates with each momentary whim. There is wisdom and order in the universe; there is divine planning. God would not have toiled in creation without a purpose. Tennyson puts it, "I doubt not through the ages, one increasing purpose runs."

The first novel that Lloyd Douglas wrote bore the title, *One Increasing Purpose*. It's the story of a young man who could not quite understand that his life had a purpose until he found himself in a ministry of healing. Thereafter he bent all his interests in that directions and became a great surgeon. You never fully understand yourself until you discover the purpose life holds for you.

Each year there is published a little booklet by one of our Methodist boards that tells of the needs of the world for people with a purpose. Doctors, nurses, teachers, engineers, agricultural experts, and sociologists—to lift the levels of life for so many. Thrilling possibilities for abundant living—life with a purpose—and the high call to serve so that others may live more comfortably and more abundantly. The holy challenge to tell others the greatest story and lead their lives unto the Lord their Savior.

Such taking hold of life involves discipline. One who wastes life—some say they do not have time for this or that—that's the most commonly heard and about the feeblest reason that people give for their absence at holy worship. But it's not true—we have as many hours in our day as any other person. We must learn to use those hours intelligently, planning our days with skill. Discipline your time, yourself, and your will to the proper and best use of all of it. Time and talents are too precious treasures to be wasted by lack of purpose.

It involves a discipline of the mind as well. Much of our thinking is quick and jumpy. A first reaction obsesses us, and we do not even attempt to consider a long-range reaction from faulty thinking, nor do we attempt to envision a broader horizon than that of our too quick judgements. Paul put it wisely, "Study to show thyself approved unto God."

So we must consider life importantly by facing it and fashioning our thinking about it in the example of the mind of Christ. Had His mind envisioned only that small and rather obscure corner of the world, He would have been content to carpenter in Nazareth all his days. Had His mind caught only the hours of His age, there surely would not have been the cross with its holy and selfless love laid bare before us. His was the far horizon, His the vision of the eternal day. His the knowledge of love triumphant.

If the buried talents of our minds emerge, it will be because we have through discipline applied ourselves to the tasks and to the thinking before us. Paderewski said, "Before I was master, I was slave."

Success in any art, or in living, means discipline of mind, body, and spirit. Take hold of life—don't be mastered by it—be master of it.

And this involves dedication. It is a strange paradox of our faith that you can best take hold of life as you surrender your life to the Master of Life. Jesus said, "Whosoever shall lose his life, for my sake, shall find it."

Paul only became the master of his life when he surrendered it and became the great missionary to the Gentiles. Livingston became the master of life when he gave his life to God and went to Africa a century ago as a missionary. A hymn you may love puts it:

Make me a captive, Lord,
And then I shall be free;

Force me to render up my sword,
And I shall conqueror be.

I sink in life's alarms
When by myself I stand;
Imprison me in Thy mighty arms,
And strong shall be my hand.
(George Matheson)

What is your life?

Three things you can do with it—you can run from it, but you will never be successful. You can run with it, but you will be defeated ultimately. You can run it, be master of it—this alone is victory!

Roadways to God
Hebrews 11: 1-16

February 28, 1964
First Methodist Church, Sylvania, Ohio

*T*hrough the history of humanity, there runs the account of the human's search. So far as we know from the written records and according to the evidence of mythology, humanity has constantly been searching for something! There are those who go forth to seek for wealth—such was the culture of ancient Babylonia that has its contemporary disciples. The sea-faring peoples—the Phoenicians in the Mediterranean and the Scandinavians to the north set forth to seek out new worlds. The Greeks sought new forms to set forth their culture and their art; the Romans new countries to bring under their sovereign power; the Hebrews searched for God and deeper understanding of God and God's Way.

It is with this search that religious leaders are mainly concerned. It is their fervent prayer that their people seek first a spiritual security—that their first concern be the nourishing of the soul; that their great knowledge in life be an understanding of God. Such religious teaching is our heritage from the Hebrew people—a search for God and a richer fellowship with God.

Someone once said, "A great many people have mistaken something far less than religion for religion, and far less than God for God."

God is not "something"—God is "Someone." God is a person—a person like you and me—with of course a vaster spirit than that of our own. One describes it by saying that God is a person as we are—in the degree that a candle flame is like the sun or as a pebble is like the universe. Jesus describes God, "God is Spirit"— that is, God is a soul—and the writer of Hebrews instructs us that, "He that cometh to God must believe that God is."

Religion—this quest in life with which I am mainly concerned, is a matter of relationship between personalities—between ourselves and that divine Person who is God.

But the world is very full of people who consider themselves religious—and who, speaking from a standpoint of moral character, are fine people and exemplary in daily living. But for them, religion is part of their culture—an appreciation of the beautiful in life—or a moral code under which they live. It is the way—it is truth—but it lacks the third element of wholesomeness. For them it is not life. There is appreciation for beauty and character in living, but for them there is not a relationship between personalities, so that God is left out of the picture. For instance, one fellow said with a measure of boasting to me one day that he lived as best he could up to the Golden Rule—that he conducted himself in his daily life and business as nearly to the high standard of that Golden Rule as he could. This for him—daily conduct—was his religion. However, we cannot adequately describe a moral code as being religion. It lacks the sparkle of communion and the high and noble calling of a greater personality to a lesser being.

There should certainly be no discounting the value of the good life. We surely need souls who live forth unselfishly and with concern for each other. Often these who so live are quick to point out that they lead as good a life as those in the church and feel themselves to be as good or better religious spirits than those others. Good behavior and wholesome attitudes are surely related to religion— goodness in living is required of those who would be Godly. But God is not something we do—God is Someone we know.

"Thou shalt love the Lord thy God" is still the great and holy commandment of the religious life. This is the beginning—in the communion of holy worship between the spark of the divine in humanity that reaches forth in its seeking and finds its help and its satisfaction in that pure Personality whom we can know and understand. For the divine spark within us permits us so to know and understand God. This was the reality that came to Augustine back in the fourth century that led him to finally yield himself to God:

Great art Thou, O Lord, and greatly to be praised;
Great is Thy power, and of Thy wisdom there is no end.
And man, being a part of Thy creation, desires to praise Thee.
Man, who bears about with him his mortality,
The witness of his sin, even the witness that Thou 'resistest the proud,'-
Yet man, this part of Thy creation, desires to praise Thee.
Thou movest us to delight in praising Thee;
For Thou hast formed us for Thyself,

And our hearts are restless till they find rest in Thee.

Some of you are familiar with Somerset Maugham's *The Razor's Edge,* the story of a young man after the First World War who, as some do today, had trouble finding himself. He spent some ten years seeking for something; he didn't know quite what. He went to Paris. There were many experiences. One was with an unfrocked priest who was being pursued, "not by the hangman or the jailer—but by mercy, kindness, forgiveness." He was trying to escape God. So this young man, pursued this "something" that constantly eluded him. Finally, as some of you will recall, his search took him to India and to the top of a mountain there, where he found it—a sense of his oneness with God. He came back so transformed, such a radiant personality, that the people could not help but notice. An awed observer remarked, "There is a man who has discovered a great secret—the greatest power on earth is still goodness." It was the power of a man who had met God—the goodness followed.

Of course, it is not for many of us upon this earth to spend ten years traveling over the world to find this great secret for ourselves. Most of us lack both the funds and the years so to seek. Most of us must find and know our God nearer to our homes and in less dramatic fashion. We must establish such a relationship as this between the Divine Spirit and our own souls in simple ways. And the great truth of our religious quest is that we can so seek and find him.

> *I will arise and to my Father go;*
> *This very hour the journey is begun,*
> *I start to reach the blissful goal, and lo,*
> *My spirit is at one bound, her race has run.*
> *For seeking God and finding Him are one.*
> *He feeds the rillettes that toward him flow.*
> *It is the Father who first seeks the son,*
> *And moves all heavenward movement, swift or slow.*
> *I dare not pride myself on finding Him.*
> *I dare not dream a single step was mine.*
> *His was the vigor in the palsied limb—*
> *His the electric fire along the line—*
> *When drowning, His the untaught power to swim*

Float o'er the surge, and grasp the rock divine.
(John. C. Earle)

There is another pathway down which seekers go, feeling that theirs is a true and adequate religion—such is an aesthetic substitute for religion. It is said that when the musician Rossini first laid eyes on the manuscript of Mozart's *Don Giovanni,* he knelt, kissed the manuscript, and said, "This is God." Now at its very best—it was a sheet of paper bearing upon it notes that may very well have been inspired—but that is NOT God—for God is a real Person.

A certain well-known psychiatrist is reported to have said in an address that man is an idea of God—so we had our beginnings—but more than that, man is a person, too. In the same address then, the psychiatrist added that God is an idea in the mind of man. Psychologically, that may well be correct, but religion goes infinitely further—God is more than a mere idea—that idea in itself results from a divine and creative act of God. If we worshipped only an idea of our minds, how empty and cold and barren would religion be—how coldly intellectual would our presence be before an altar of our faith—how lacking in comfort and in strength and in joy.

Then there is a vast group of our people whose God is nature and the beauty of nature. Many, many times there are those who say to me that they can worship God more readily in the beauty of the out-of-doors than they can confined within the sanctuary. That they find God more easily while tramping down a woodland path or while enjoying life upon a playing field or a golf course. "There," they say, "I can worship God." Whereupon the retort that comes to my mind most quickly is the piercing question, "But do you!"

Very true it is that the beauties of nature still us, and we stand hushed before the brilliance of a sunset or comforted by the presence of a rainbow in the sky, or awed by the color of the autumn hills. And I, for one, thoroughly enjoy and deeply appreciate the wonders and beauties of God's great world of nature. But nature itself is not God—there is no true communion of spiritual personalities between a person and a tree. These things of beauty are evidences of God's goodness, of God's providence for God's children, of God's own love for beauty—but they are not God. God is a Person with whom we can truly commune, so that the best in us is aroused within us when our worship is sincere and completed by fellowship with God.

James Cowden Wallace speaks of this provident presence so adequately:

> *There is an Eye that never sleeps*
> *Beneath the wind of night;*
> *There is an Ear that never shuts*
> *When sink the beams of light.*
>
> *There is an Arm that never tires*
> *When human strength give way;*
> *There is a Love that never fails*
> *When earthly love decay.*
>
> *That Eye unseen o'er watches all;*
> *That Arm upholds the sky;*
> *That Ear doth hear the sparrows call;*
> *That Love is ever nigh.*

There are others who seek to know God through a multitude of things—some who consider churchmanship as religion—some pursuit of knowledge. But a relationship with a "something" cannot adequately satisfy the great thirst of our souls for communion with a "Someone"—the Person whom we call God.

People are turning to religion in our day—many there are who seek after a certain security in life, who yearn for a strength that will abide in every need, who long for a power that will sustain, and who desire a peace in their souls that will stand above and through all the wrecks of time.

Jesus sets the way of the quest. He understood the supreme formula for security—He knew that our greatest nature was our spiritual souls—that the richest satisfaction and the most abundant life must be found in the realm of the spiritual. Again and again He turned to the great divine Person who could fill the needs, grant the peace, and offer the satisfying security of personal and living communion with the seekers after God. Fear of hunger and poverty and violence and death was foreign to Him—fear that the people would lose their vision of God and dwelling places in God's eternal realm was very real and very near to Him. For this cause He wept over the city—mourning the discipleship to the temporary and the material quests and the rejection of the high and holy things of the spirit.

He saw those who thirsted for power and might over the people of the land. He met those day after day who squeezed the pence from the people in unjust taxation. He witnessed the hordes going forth from one idle and frivolous pastime to another. He saw the seekers after God, too. He knew the Pharisees who kept the microscopic commands of the law and missed the real vision of the soul's sincere and spiritual worship. He heard those cry out, no doubt, that they could worship God best through their own feeling for beauty. He knew the many who understood God as the moral way of conduct, and as the beauty of truth, but who missed the communion of personalities with Him that was real and abiding spiritual life.

If we would surely seek to know our God, we may well find God best through this One who understood completely. If, spiritually speaking, we would see our God so that the vision of God fills our lives, we see God best through the simple but powerful life of the Man from Nazareth who so lived historically, that God became more vivid and more personal to the people of the centuries since the first of Christmases. If we would see our God, we see God most clearly through the Lord Jesus who leads daily life into communion with God. All other paths are so trivial and so incomplete—save this one—and this He said to the world, "He that hath seen me hath seen the Father."

And truly we find God clearly in Him-

Nearer, my God to Thee,
Nearer to Thee.
E'en though it be a cross
That raiseth me;
Still all my song shall be,
Nearer my God to Thee,
Nearer my God to Thee,
Nearer to Thee.
(Sarah Flower Adams)

Growing in Faith

(Jim Hartland with son Greg, Ordination Sunday, Pennsylvania)

"And Jesus increased in wisdom and stature, and in favor with God and man." Luke 3: 52

The Marks of Maturity
Luke 19: 1-10

July 11, 1954
Whitaker Community Methodist Church, Whitaker, Pennsylvania

*I*ndeed, one of the most interesting and incisive human nature stories in the New Testament is that of Zacchaeus. It is a story of human tragedy and conflict, of struggle and triumph. The tragedy in the life of Zacchaeus was that he was a small man, both physically and spiritually.

Admittedly, it is no sin to be physically short in stature as that is a condition for which none of us can be responsible. The world is full of little people. However, a rapid survey of our modern churches—as well as society in general—would soon lead to the discovery that the outstanding problems facing us today are not those presented by physical little people, but those which come from our spiritual dwarfs.

A college dean remarked that he had been appointed to supervise a group of freshman students who had aspired to, but had not attained, the stature of men. More profoundly, a man named Overstreet in his book *The Mature Mind* states: "The most dangerous members of our society are those grownups whose powers of influence are adult but whose motives and responses are infantile." One might almost conclude that the problem of our day is that too many big jobs are being filled by little men—it is the dilemma of the three-year-old boy in San Francisco who climbed behind the wheel of his father's automobile as it was parked on the sloping street in front of his home, released the brake, and took off.

The unusual thing about the experiences of Zacchaeus is that in his meeting with Christ, he passed through what we might call a "spiritual adolescence." He grew from midget to manhood. In the light of this unusual occurrence it would be well for us to look into the sequence of events that takes place for Zacchaeus, and from them, to determine those abiding principles which have value for our own lives.

First, Zacchaeus was a small man and knew it! An admirable quality is that which enables a man to evaluate himself properly. To be able to laugh at oneself.

During the last war, [World War II] it was standing practice they tell us for both enemy and Allied Forces to build superstructures of plywood upon the battered structures of old ships—these were used as decoys for battle cruisers. Needless to say, when the camouflage was discovered, these derelicts did not last long. How often our lives are like those battered and beaten hulks attempting to ride out the storm of life.

Zacchaeus was small professionally as well as physically. In the eyes of his fellow Jews, he had a despised job, for taxes were no more popular in his day than they are in ours. In fact, finance was the only thing in which Zacchaeus was big—and that seems to have been the very factor that contributed to his spiritual smallness. Even in our day the size of our aspirations and goals for living determines the size of our spiritual lives.

One of the underlying foundations of spiritual growth requires that we recognize the spiritual smallness of our own lives when we catch a glimpse of the magnitude of the life of Christ. Only as we see clearly our own insufficiencies do we yearn for the fullness of life that Christ can give. If there were nothing else wrong with a sense of pride, it would be sufficient that it forever chokes off within us the desire really to see the Master and know him as Zacchaeus did. It is a rule of spiritual growth that we do not begin to grow until we have seen how small we are.

The second discovery is that Zacchaeus was willing to climb. Zacchaeus may have been short of stature, but he seems in this instance to have been long on insight, for he realized that if he was to see Jesus, he must exercise his God-given capacities to climb. It must have been a torturous experience for him and a humorous one for the spectators.

One sees here a fundamental religious insight, for real religion in any of our lives is never a compulsory process. Unless there is within us a residue of spiritual sensitivity on which we are willing to rise, it is doubtful that we shall ever discover the call of God. We commit the unpardonable sin when we wallow so long in the swamp of unrighteousness that we lose both a consciousness of spiritual need and the faith to look to God. There is a loving Father who waits with anxious arms, but the prodigal must say out of a yearning heart, "I will arise!"

Consider the farm boy who was anxiously awaiting the arrival of a new brood of chicks under the mother hen. When the time was nigh, he was often tempted to reach down and gently crack the tip of the egg to help the unborn chick break its way out of the shell. But with a restraining hand, the farmer would say, "No, son. If he has not the strength to break the shell, he will not have the strength to live!" Salvation, you see, is a process of seeking as well as of finding.

The third discovery is that Zacchaeus came down out of the tree. Recently, our newspapers reported the story of two boys who decided to try out their scanty knowledge of aeronautics. They discovered an unguarded private plane and took off into the "wide blue yonder." Everything seemed to be going along well until they decided to land. Then they realized that they had forgotten to read the landing instructions. Happily, the story ends with the boys getting down alive, by virtue of a lucky pancake landing in a field, with great damage to the plane and not to themselves.

Now this illustrates the yearning of a great number of people who love to sail blissfully in the heavenly heights of religious imagination, but never want to come down to the hard ground of everyday Christian living. Peter voiced this almost universal yearning following his experience on the transfiguration mountain. It is like the yearning of an old man, only recently converted, who prayed, "O Lord, I am willing to do whatever you would have me do, but if possible, Lord, I would like to have something in an advisory capacity!"

Insight and motivation for Christian living may come in the "tree-top" experiences, but redemptive Christian living is wrought on the hard anvil of everyday experiences. Christian brotherhood begins in our block, on our street, today!

Faring Forth—with Open Mind
Mark 8:27-9:1

September 10, 1967
Sidney First Methodist Church, Sidney, Ohio

*I*t is strange, says someone, how prone we are to divorce religion from intelligence. A person, brilliant in his or her work will move over into the realm of religion and accept any strange religious doctrine without a question. Sometimes I think that the more bizarre a religious claim is, the better some people seem to like it.

Whenever a young person—especially from a fairly simple background—makes up his or her mind to study for the Christian ministry by going to college and seminary, many of the home church members fear that the college experiences will destroy that student's faith—as if there was a conflict between religion and education. William Jennings Bryan, whose understanding of the *Bible* was as the literal Word of God, used to bring cheers from his audience when he made this remark:

"It is far more important to know the Rock of Ages than the age of the rocks."

But why the insinuation that the person who knows the age of rocks will not be likely to know the Rock of Ages?

It is often said that Jesus never stressed the use of the mind. His emphasis was on faith. Of course, Jesus placed a great emphasis on faith, but he also challenged the mind with questions which He wanted His followers to face:

"Who do men say that I am?"
"Who do you say that I am?"
"What think ye?"

When Jesus was faced with the question, "Who is my neighbor?" He answered by telling the story of the traveler who was robbed and beaten on the Jericho road. A priest and a Levite passed the traveler by, but the Good Samaritan ministered to his needs. And Jesus asked:

"Which of these three, do you think, proved neighbor to him who fell among the robbers?" (Luke 10: 36)

He told another parable about a certain man who had two sons: *"Go work in my vineyard!' said the father to one son, and the boy answered, 'I will not,' but went. He gave the same command to the other son, and he replied, 'I go, sir,' but went not. Which of the two sons did the will of his father?" (Matthew 21" 28-31)*.

Jesus was continually calling upon people to use their minds, to do some thinking for themselves. The Pharisees came to Him one day saying, "Show us a sign."

He answered them saying, *"Ye hypocrites, ye can discern the face of the sky and of the earth; but how is it that ye do not discern this time? ...why even of yourselves judge ye not what is right?" (Luke 12:56)*.

Jesus was considered a heretic because He dared think for Himself.

"Ye have heard that it hath been said," said He, *"an eye for an eye, and a tooth for a tooth, but I say unto you, love your enemies!" (Matthew 5: 38-39)*.

What a shocking statement that must have been to those religious leaders! Here was Jesus questioning the teaching of their sacred scriptures, and suggesting a better way, His own way. To the Pharisees, Jesus was tampering with divine commands. He was undermining their religious traditions. No wonder they crucified Him! He was using His mind.

We need desperately to use our own intelligence in interpreting the *Bible*. One approach to the *Bible* is the purely devotional. A person thumbs through the books and finds such devotional highlights as the 23rd Psalm, the Beatitudes, the 13th chapter of First Corinthians, etc. and feeds the soul on these passages. This procedure had developed among religious characters. It was the method which Spurgeon, the great English preacher, followed when he said, "I approach the *Bible* as I eat fish. I take the flesh and leave the bones."

But the bones are still there, and we must account for them. I would give every encouragement to the person who finds strength and inspiration in the devotional approach to the *Bible*, but for those who are confused by portions of the Scriptures which raise questions in their minds, another approach must be presented. Ministers in general, and our denominational publishing houses in particular, never refer to the portions of Scripture which raise questions in the mind of the studious reader. It is much easier to treat the highly devotional sections. But I am wondering if we are doing our duty as religious teachers if we ignore the problematical preachments.

Suppose I should say to you who are parents of children, if your child does not obey you, the thing for you to do is to have him put to death. You would be aghast and wonder what's the matter with that preacher—has he finally gone mad as we've been suspecting for some time? Then I could respond by saying—this teaching is in the *Bible*. The *Bible* says:

"If a man have a stubborn and rebellious son, which will not obey the voice of the father, or the voice of his mother, let them bring him to the elders of the city and say to them, this our son is stubborn and rebellious, he will not obey our voice. Then shall all the men of the city stone him to death, so shall ye put evil away from among you." (Deuteronomy 21:18-21).

This idea is correlated in one of the Ten Commandments—which I hear being quoted by many non-church-going as well as by church-going people as their standard of conduct:

"Honor thy father and thy mother that thy days may be long upon the earth which the Lord thy God hath given thee." (Exodus 20: 12).

Is this the reason why we should honor our parents? That we may have a long life on earth? It is evident, according to this commandment, that a person had better obey his father and mother or else he would be put to death.

Or suppose I should say from the pulpit, "Any of you people who do any work whatsoever on the Sabbath, whether you observe the Sabbath of Saturday or Sunday, should be put to death." Again I hear you say, "What a terrible statement for our preacher to make!" But I respond by saying it is Biblical teaching:

"And the Lord said to Moses; ye shall keep the Sabbath…for it is holy; everyone who defiles it, shall surely be put to death; for whosoever doth any work therein, that soul shall be cut off from among his people. Six days may work be done, but in the seventh is the Sabbath of rest, holy to the Lord; whosoever doeth any work in the Sabbath day, he shall surely be put to death (Exodus 31: 14-15).

According to the *Bible*, a person could be put to death for picking up a few sticks on the Sabbath.

"And while the children of Israel were in the wilderness they found a man that gathered sticks on the Sabbath. And the Lord said: 'This man shall surely be put to death.'" (Numbers 15: 32-35).

Once again, think how I would shock you all if I said: "Any of you who feel discouraged and have problems which are difficult to face, why don't you get drunk and forget all your troubles?" You would rise up in righteous wrath and cry, "Unfrock that preacher! He is not fit to be in the pulpit!" But I could answer you by saying that I found this advice in the *Bible*:

"Give strong drink unto him that is ready to perish, and wine unto those that be of heavy heart. Let him drink and forget his poverty and remember his misery no more." (Proverbs 31:6-7).

I could go on giving many other illustrations from scripture to point out the folly of quoting indiscriminately from the *Bible* to buttress a point of view without reference to the context of the verse and the book from which it was taken. Long ago, Shakespeare castigated the proof text method when he wrote, "In religion, what damned error, but some sober brow will bless it and approve it with a text." Witch hunting, snake handling, racial bigotry, polygamy, the liquor traffic, and countless other evils have all been advocated by following this method.

The natural question which comes to mind is; how can one account for these passages which I have just quoted? We account for them when we realize that the *Bible* is not a book, but a library of books of different kinds covering a period of many hundreds of years. It is a record of humanity's search for God and the meaning of life. Through the ages people have sought to know what God was like and what God asked and expected of God's people. The history of that quest can be traced in the *Bible*. Consider that change from the God of Samuel who ordered infants to be slaughtered, to the God of the Psalmists whose tender mercies are over all his works. From the God of the early Hebrews who commanded children be killed for disobeying their parents, to the God of the prophet Micah who loved justice, kindness, and mercy. From the God of *Genesis* who walked in the garden in the cool of the day, to the God who is spirit that no one hath seen or can see. From the God of the book of *Leviticus*, who was so particular about the sacrificial vessels and furnishings of the temple, to the God of the *Book of Acts*, who dwells not in temples made with hands. From the God of *Exodus* who was merciful only to those who loved and obeyed God, to the God of Jesus who sends rain on the just and on the unjust alike.

Think of the changes which have taken place in our thinking during the brief history of our nation; then compare the length of that time period with the span of years between the time of Moses and that of Jesus, and you will not wonder at the tremendous progress recorded in the *Bible*. Once slavery as an institution was accepted in our country as highly ethical. It was defended from the pulpit. "Did not Paul send a runaway slave back to his master?" But common sense and the verdict of history have proven that slavery as an institution is a detriment to society. Dueling as a method of settling quarrels honorably between men was once the order of the day. How childish that procedure appears to us now. War as a system of establishing peace between nations has been accepted through the ages, but we are gradually coming to the conclusion that it must be discarded if civilization is to endure.

There is no problem involved in the quotation about strong drink found in the *Book of Proverbs*. If you will read through the book, you will find other passages condemning the drinking of wine:

"Do not look at wine when it is red, when it sparkles in the cup and goes down smoothly. At the last it bites like a serpent and stings like an adder. (Proverbs 23: 31-32).

How do we account for such opposition in the same book? There is no problem if you realize that the two verses come from a book of proverbs containing statements written by different authors with opposite points of view concerning drink.

Of course, there are contradictions in the *Bible* if you think of it as the infallible word of God with each word equally inspired, but not if you see the *Bible* as the progressive revelation of the nature of God and of the meaning of life. There is a history of the onward march of common sense, enlightened by the spirit of God, clarified by the experience of the human race, and ennobled by new and enlarging concepts of moral and ethical living. The *Bible* is true from this perspective. It is a true record of the dialogue between God and humanity. If a person wants to trace the road on which one's ancestors traveled in search of God and the noblest way of life, one will find that knowledge in the *Bible*.

As we listen to preachers and teachers and radio commentators talk, it is important that we ask ourselves, "Is what they are saying making sense to me? Are the things which they are advocating going to enrich the life of all of us or just a segment of society? Is what they are saying true to the best in life as I understand it? How does what they advocate line up with the spirit of Jesus?"

Think of the religious people who make themselves miserable by believing all kinds of superstition which cannot stand the light of truth! A broken mirror means seven years of bad luck. Walking under a ladder is sure to bring misfortune. Sitting at a table as one of thirteen will certainly result in tragedy. Without intelligence to guide it, religion can become superstition, and one of the major curses of the race. That is why it is so important that we use the brains which God has given us.

O God, I offer thee my heart---
In many a mystic mood, by beauty led,
I give my heart to Thee, but now impart
That sterner grace—to offer Thee my head.
(*Elspeth Campbell Murphy*)

I am aware that all religious beliefs cannot be rationalized. Faith goes beyond reason, but it dare not go against reason and expect to win the allegiance of intelligent people. Let us use our minds fearlessly, remembering the words of Jesus:

"Why of yourselves judge ye not what is right?" (Luke 12: 57).

And then let us act according to our best judgement and our firm convictions!

In closing, I would like to substitute the word "live" for "die" in this verse from S. Hall Young's poem—*Into the Sunset*—with the hope that it may become the prayer of each one of us in our spiritual pilgrimage this year:

> *Let me <u>live</u>, thinking.*
> *Let me fare forth still with an open mind,*
> *Fresh secrets to unfold, new truths to find,*
> *My soul undimmed, alert, no question blinking;*
> *Let me <u>live</u>, thinking!*

A Signpost and a Seed of Faith
Luke 13:10-22

September 29, 1968
First United Methodist Church, Sidney, Ohio

*J*esus came teaching...and the lessons he taught provided and continue to provide a direction to our daily living that fulfills the purposes of God in us and promises sturdy hope for the future for us and for our fellow pilgrims across this earth and beyond this earth.

There are several vignettes running through the gospel accounts concerning Jesus's teaching—there is a certain collected content that we call the Sermon on the Mount which lifts up a summary of that teaching with all its lofty concepts. And, there are the sharper beatitudes that St. Luke records in his gospel—beatitudes that are splendid in their social implications. We read all of these, and we are impressed with their stalwart truth.

But many times a depth of teaching comes forth in an isolated incident or in a travel commentary that also sets our minds to searching out truth and our hearts to soaring into hope. So it is with this story of the woman who had an infirmity plaguing her for eighteen years. Why is it that this particular one stirred Him so—why is it that Jesus healed so few in a land that had so many who suffered? And later on, even those whom He touched died—as will all of us sooner or later.

Yet there is compassion when He encounters the crippled conditions of people's bodies or people's minds—and most of all in the deep concerns he has for those who are sick of soul.

For eighteen years this poor woman had struggled with the burden of her handicap—so bent that she could not straighten herself—so that she could not even see Jesus—which gives insight to our own plight often times when we cannot see Him either. John Bunyan describes it in *Pilgrim's Progress* when he talks about the man with the muck rake who could not see the angel above his head. And how crippled are we when we lack a faith or a reverence for life. Jesus called to the woman—she turned in his direction—He placed his hands upon her—and she was made straight.

Now, let us turn this into the modern day—into all our involved educational processes. We are concerned—and seriously concerned we ought to be with the fostering of knowledge and with the development of skills for using it. But is this all? Do we not have an educational responsibility for developing insights as to what the knowledge and skills are for? Sometimes, though, we are like that man who sets out on a journey who packs a lot of luggage, gets his travelers checks ready for his expenses, takes the taxi to the airport—and then realizes that he has never decided where to go!

In recent years, we have made amazing progress in science and technology—but the direction of the journey and the real reason for going is essential to us, too! And—and this is a big "and"—this progress makes the question of values and ends more insistent than ever. Justice Jackson remarked as he presided over those trials of the Nazi war criminals, "Modern society needs to fear only the educated man!"

Someone else says it, "The only thing worse than a devil is an educated devil."

In this atomic age of ours it suddenly becomes clear that people are not wise enough or good enough to be entrusted with such power as new knowledge has put into their hands.

Now another point for us to consider is that an appreciation of values and goals implies some unifying philosophy of life. An education which does not develop this fails to provide a basic element in the equipment for life. Walter Lippmann calls this an "enormous vacuum at the center" if this unifying philosophy is not pursed. We are confronted then with an array of subjects, or data, or separate compartments of knowledge without an integrating principle or a standard of judgment.

Here is the great burden of teaching—concerning humanity and the kingdom of God. Jesus is consistent at each point and with each personal contact that this unifying factor of life is faith in God. Somehow He arrests this woman from her infirmity—and she turns her thoughts Godward in a great burst of praise. Her cure is complete—and her person becomes whole—with this strong unifying faith to integrate her life and make her truly straight in spirit as well as in spine.

Now the ruler of the synagogue does not comprehend all of this—the form of worship must be maintained—what matter the spirit. But here Jesus points to the purpose of it all: the well-being of humanity is to be served rather than an empty exercise of devotion. The Sabbath and all that it means exists for humanity—to be a source of freedom from routine and a lifting out of the ruts of ordinary life—and to provide a touch of glory to it all. So on this great day of worship, this woman, perhaps alone in all the synagogue, is the one who truly worships God.

Moreover, there is something to be said here about the choices we make in life (these choices become more complicated and more conflicting each year, it seems) and about the responsibility of Christian education to enable us to make intelligent choices and Godly choices. We are called to commitment in the major issues of living if Christian education fulfills its purpose. Facts and analyses which are not seen in relation to responsible action are too sterile for a world of such tumultuous confusion as ours. We must, indeed, know all we can—as I presume this ruler of the synagogue did in his day—but our responsibility in society is not merely for knowing, but for choosing! "Life's business," as Robert Browning puts it, "is just the terrible choice!"

This is the reason for religious education—this is the necessity for religion in education—religion is the great source of motive power. There is no other force as creatively potent as the sense of being related to a divine purpose for our existence.

Modern scholars have poked fun at the kind of education which prevailed in the middle ages. Certainly it was lopsided—religious devotion and the artistic impulse were nurtured—but there was meager attention to empirical studies and factual observation. Today, however, we go off in the other direction. The scientific aspect receives tremendous emphasis while the imaginative and religious side of life is almost ignored!

A single Sunday school lesson may seems a very small thing, Perhaps it is a small thing we are doing in the whole context of religious curriculum, but it is a mustard seed that can grow into a tree—a lovely and beneficial tree through every life that learns these lessons and applies them through faith to life. This seed is God's planting and still carries God's life.

Small beginnings lead to great results...

This is the Lord's doing—
It is marvelous in our eyes.

Creative Thinking
Philippines 4:1-14

September 23, 1979
Tipp City United Methodist Church, Tipp City, Ohio

Many statues have been made to represent humanity. Some have shown the athlete—running, leaping, hurling the discus. Others have portrayed him as the warrior with his armor. Yet others have pictured him as the worker with his hammer, hoe, or shovel. But one of the most remarkable portrayals of all is the famous statue in which a man is shown who is not engaged in any obvious physical activity; not equipped with any kind of armor; not holding any sort of implement. He is just sitting there with his head upon his hand, pondering, wondering, meditating. The name of that statue by the famous French sculptor, Auguste Rodin is *Le Penseur*—The Thinker. Such is a distinctive representation of humanity.

A human is a thinking animal. Oh, this is not to be disrespectful to other animals—a pine squirrel cut green cones, dipped them in spring water and piled them upon a bitterly cold day to freeze, and thus anticipated our deep freeze system of preserving food. A rabbit that was very weary of being chased by a dog plunged into the end of a hollow log and seemed to come out the other end with fresh vigor; he ran a great circle, came back wearily, went into the hollow log, and seemed to come out again renewed and reinvigorated. It turned out that two rabbits had been taking turns letting the dog chase them. When some beavers had three dams wash out at a particularly difficult place in the river, they sent for an old grizzled beaver to come and superintend the building of a dam that stayed. I agree with the editor of the column in which incidents like these are gathered that there are many degrees of knowing, from the primitive instinct of lower animals, to the thoughts of the philosopher, and that in the world of animals, there are amazing episodes which show links between their thinking and ours. Nevertheless, it is humanity in whom the power of thought is most highly and significantly developed, and the human is distinctively the thinker.

Thinking is one of the most important things that we ever do. The book of *Proverbs* advises:

"Keep your heart with all vigilance; for from it flows the springs of life."
(Proverbs 4: 23)

The physiological and psychological conceptions of the ancient Hebrews and of the modern world are different. In comparison with the language of the *Bible* it is customary in the speech of the present day to refer to the various capacities of humans as residing at a higher level. We speak of the heart as the place where the emotions are centered and of the head as the place where we do our thinking. The ancient Hebrews believed that the lower organs were the place where the feelings were concentrated and that the heart was the seat of intelligence. Therefore, when this verse says, *"Keep your heart,"* it means in our language, "Keep your power of thought, keep your way of thinking, with all diligence—for out of it are the issues of life." Marcus Aurelius, the great stoic, emperor, philosopher said, "The happiness of your life depends upon the quality of your thoughts— therefore, guard them accordingly."

Thinking is perhaps the easiest thing and yet the hardest thing that we ever do. It is so easy to think, that sometimes you cannot stop thinking even if you wish to. Yet thinking is very hard work. After work, one requires sleep for rest and repair. A recent study has indicated that as people grow older they generally require less sleep, but a fifty-year-old mathematician may need more sleep than a twenty-five-year-old ditch digger. On the average, the person who works with his brain requires two hours more sleep per night than the person who works with his physical body. This will encourage some of us who are incorrigible sleepyheads—we can at least hope that we are brain workers!

Thinking is something that is invisible, and yet it has visible effects. Nobody can tell whether you are thinking or what you are thinking about. Experiments are being made in recording electrical radiation sent out by the brain and in studying the phenomenon of thought transference; but as yet no one of us can look at another person and discern his thoughts, for the processes of thought are invisible. Nevertheless, they have visible results that are of the utmost importance. In a way, we might say that the thoughts themselves eventually become visible. They become visible in personality and in action. Dean Inge, quoting Marcus Aurelius declares, "The soul is dyed the color of its inner thoughts."

The thoughts eventually show in the person. A false front may be put up for a while, but eventually thoughts will write their lines on the face, be evident in the eye, and recognizable by the slip of the lip. How about your thoughts? Thoughts become visible in action. The Old Testament law spent its emphasis upon regulating outward action. *"Thou shalt not kill. Thou shalt not commit adultery."* Jesus went on back to the root of the action and said it was the thought out of which the outward act emerged that was the crucial point; therefore He forbade hatred, which eventuates in murder; and lust, which eventuates in evil deeds.

Thinking is time conditioned, but it is time transcending. We have to think as people of our day. Yet in our thinking, we have the amazing power of reaching far back into the past and far out into the future. Here, too, there is peril, along with possibility. There is the peril that our thoughts will become attached to something in the past, and remorse, with regret, with reluctance to leave it. There is the peril that our thoughts will become obsessed with something in the future which we view with apprehension, fear, and anxiety. But there is also the possibility that with this time-transcending power of thought, we will gather the riches of the past and project long purposes into the future.

Our thinking is created, and yet it is creative. We think because God, the only ultimate Creator of anything, has given us the power of thought. No doubt we think in an orderly fashion because we live in an orderly universe. Our thinking reflects the patternfulness round about us. Yet our created thinking is also creative. It is creative in the sense that we can put things together and make something new. People put words together and make poems. They put flour and sugar and spice together and make cakes. If I made a cake, it would at any rate be something that never had been seen on earth before! People put levers and wheels together and make machines. They put ideas together and make philosophies. Thought is creative, and again it has both possibility and peril. Thought results in the production of implements of diabolical destructiveness and also of things of beneficent goodness.

Here, then is the thinker. His power of thought is an amazing power. One of the most important things we ever do is to think. *The*

Old Testament does well in advising us to keep our thinking with all vigilance, since from it flows the springs of life.

Since thinking is so important, it is clear that a major problem in a person's life is that of handling ones thinking aright. In the New Testament, we find the great word of the apostle, Paul:

> *Whatever is true, whatever is honorable,*
> *whatever is just, whatever is pure,*
> *whatever is lovely, whatever is gracious,*
> *if there is any excellence,*
> *if there is anything worthy of praise,*
> *think about these things. (Philippians 4:8)*

One who does think about these things will develop an affirmative and positive kind of thought habit which is the best safeguard against the dangers which assail our thinking. One of these dangers is giving an undiscriminating welcome to all thoughts that come crowding into the mind. Nobody can help what thoughts come to the threshold of the mind, but one can determine the ones which will be developed and nourished and encouraged. Here is the poet's picture of the person who lets every kind of thought flood in:

> *Roused by importunate knock*
> *I rose, I turned the key, and let them in,*
> *First one, anon another, and at length*
> *In troops they came, nor looked him in the face,*
> *Show scruples e'er again? So in they came,*
> *A noisy band of revelers—vain hopes,*
> *Wild fancies, fitful joys; and there they sit*
> *In my heart's holy place, and through the night*
> *Carouse, to leave it when the cold gray dawn*
> *Gleams from the east, to tell me that the time*
> *For watching and for thought bestowed is gone.*
> *(Arthur Hugh Clough)*

Another danger is that thoughts may become obsessed with evil. To spend time thinking about the things that are untrue, dishonest, unjust, impure, unlovely, and of bad report, tends to break down the mind. An assistant to Goebbels in the bureau of propaganda of the National Socialist Party in Germany told an American correspondent, "My work is very bad for me. The copy we send out is so depressing that the bureau personnel is always on edge; nervous breakdowns are common, and there have been cases of insanity. Hideous creatures gnaw at our souls continuously, and these, I am sure, are our own fantastic creations."

The mind is not made for such thoughts as these, and it breaks down under them. The mind is made for the kind of thinking of which Paul speaks, and when it concentrates upon the sort of things which he mentions, it finds itself within its own proper homeland.

Is this then an unduly limited area of thought? Is it something like the restrictions once place upon the Empress of Japan who was supposed to think only of six things: her husband, the sun, music, flowers, birds, and perfume? No, Paul's list indicates a great and ample homeland for the mind. *"Whatever is true"*—here is the whole realm of philosophy. *"Whatever is honorable"*—here is the entire area of science, for scientists will not dodge a fact anywhere. *"Whatever is just"*—here we envision the whole realm of law and government. *"Whatever is pure"*—here are all the concerns of ethics. *"Whatever is lovely"*—and this opens to us the wonders of esthetics, art, and music. *"Whatever is gracious"*—here is all that which the common mind of humanity indicates as worthwhile. We are to concentrate our thoughts upon such things, but they constitute that ample field which is the true homeland of the soul.

Does following Paul's advice mean practicing autosuggestion? Yes. Douglas V. Steere points out in *Prayer and Worship,* the opposite of autosuggestion is heterosuggestion. Heterosuggestion is allowing everything outside of us to tell us what to think. You walk down the street, and the billboards tell you what to buy; you listen to the radio, and it tells you what is good. Heterosuggestion is letting your life be pushed in every direction by everything outside. Autosuggestion means selecting for yourself the things that you think are worthwhile and concentrating upon them. In that sense, autosuggestion is recommended by Paul.

Is this meditation? Yes, for meditation means essentially letting something revolve before us. Here is how it is described by Arthur D. Belden of London, England. "To practice concentration of mind in any direction with regularity is inevitably to strengthen it intrinsically. But to do so under the healing, soothing, yet invigorating influence of the thought of God, is to find an altogether new stability entering into the texture of one's inner thoughts. From this there arises, in turn, a new degree of thinking power and a new delight in thought, and there is achieved at last an art of meditation."

This is the kind of thinking Paul is talking about, and in this manner we can control our thinking. There is no greater blessing than to have a clear and calm mind. We can work toward it by thinking about the things that are true, honorable, just, pure, lovely, and gracious. Christians, especially, ought to be great thinkers—Christians worship God, and God is the Thinker who made this universe. As a Christian poet wrote:

Our God is a mathematician,
He ordered the schedule of spheres
And with an unerring precision
They are true to the hours and the years.

Before any metaphysician
He mastered reality's bound;
Before any gifted musician
He created rhythm and sound.

Before any painters or sculptors
He charted all beauty and art;
Before any morals or rulers
He fathomed the unfathomed heart.

And man's most adventurous thinking
Only traces old ways he trod;
Despite all our boasting and blinking
Behind and before us is God.
(Anonymous)

Christians ought to be thinkers, because Jesus Christ Whom they follow, had a keen, clear mind. He commanded the intellectual materials of his time, knew the Scriptures, and told parables of matchless power. His followers ought to use their minds as fully as they can.

Christians belong to the Church, and across the centuries the Church has encouraged learning. In the Dark Ages when the candle almost went out, it was kept alight in the monasteries and in the schools which grew up around them. In America, Christianity pioneered in establishing higher education. It behooves all Christians to encourage and support the institutions of education and to participate with all their power in this great adventure of thought.

God's Loving Call

(Feeding Hill, Massachusetts)

"In the beginning was the Word, and the Word was with God, and the Word was God." John 1:1

Love's Destiny
Ephesians 1: 1-23

September 7, 1952
Concord Methodist Church, Beaver Falls Pennsylvania

One day the poet, Robert Burns, in company with a friend was standing in a shelter watching a storm out at sea. The water moved madly into shore, throwing itself in turbulent heaps against the rocks, riding high in a burst of spray, retreating swiftly again to the open sea. They watched in silent fascination for a time until at last Burns' friend exclaimed, "Is not that a scene to write about?"

"Aye," replied the poet, "but it's more than a word can say."

One always feels something of the vastness of the sea whenever one endeavors to say, "Behold, see what wondrous things God has done." Do we understand that no drama in all history compares with the sweep and majesty of the Christian story? The writer to the Hebrews apologizes for his briefness, but is nonetheless concerned that you and I remember the long history and this heroism of the company in which we stand. He takes a long look back and recalls the faith of Abraham who, when God called him, went out, "not knowing whither he went." You and I stand in the succession of Moses who, when he was grown up, refused to be called the son of Pharaoh's daughter, choosing rather to share ill treatment with the people of God than to enjoy the fleeting pleasures of sin. Your faith and mine is an inheritance from a people who daringly fled Egyptian tyranny, braved exiles, endured a wilderness. Nameless saints—who through faith conquered kingdoms, enforced justice, received promises, won strength out of weakness, put foreign armies to flight. That invincible legion which triumphed over cruelty with courage, over persecution with patience, and over death itself by dying. Is not that a scene to write about? Aye! But it's more than a word can say.

The backdrop, then, of God's amazing grace should be the setting for any contemplation of what we have been called to be; a new creature in Christ. For of God's mighty act, not ours, did such a hope first dawn. By God's act, not ours, shall the dawn become noonday bright. So God dreams high dreams.

Thus, in the first chapter of his letter to the Ephesians, the Apostle Paul give us our central text. Writing to a group of churches concerning the Christian faith he says to them:

Blessed be the God and Father of our Lord Jesus Christ, who has blessed us in Christ with every spiritual blessing in the heavenly places, even as he chose us in him before the foundation of the world, that we should be holy and blameless before him. He destined us in love to be his sons and daughters through Jesus Christ, according to the purpose of his will, to the praise of his glorious grace which he freely bestowed on us in the Beloved. In him we have redemption through his blood, the forgiveness of our trespasses, according to the riches of his grave which he lavished upon us.

All of which is the Apostle Paul's moving and eloquent way of saying that our hope for becoming a new creature involves a dream in the mind of God, a rebellion in the will of humanity, and a reconciliation in the cross of Christ.

Hear again the first words of the apostle, *"God chose us in him— that we should be holy and blameless before him. He destined us in love to be his sons and daughters through Jesus Christ."* That is the dream in the mind of God, that you and I should become sons and daughters of the most High. Unto that end hath God ceaselessly set God's hand. Thus when we come to understand rightly what is meant by the love of God, we shall see how far removed it is from the indulgent, soft, and sentimental thing which we so often make of it. What does it mean to be loved of God? To be loved of God is to be loved of one whose purpose within that love is to make out of creatures such as you and me, sons and daughters like God, holy, righteous, one in whom no darkness dwells. Such love allows suffering, requires discipline, but only because it is holy love aimed at making us children of God. It should always be remembered that He whose life was truly God's, wound up not only with a "peace of mind" but a piece of wood on which He was crucified.

The purpose of God's love for us is not so much to make us happy, as to make us good. C.S. Lewis gives us an analogy:

When we fall in love, do we cease to care whether the one we love is clean or dirty, fair or foul? Do we not rather then first begin to care? Does not any woman regard it as a sign of love in a man that he neither knows nor cares how she is looking? Love may, indeed, love the beloved when her beauty is lost, but not because it is lost. Love may forgive all infirmities and love still in spite of them; but love cannot cease to will their removal. Love is more sensitive than hatred itself to every blemish in the beloved. ...Of all powers, God forgives most, but he condones least; he is pleased with little, but demands all.

To be loved of God, is to be judged of God, and God will take no rest from God's disturbing judgment until we too say, "Yes!" to God's holy dream. Faber in his hymn sets this forth clearly:

Oh how I fear Thee, living God,
With deepest, tenderest fears,
And worship Thee with trembling hope
And penitential tears!

Yet I may love Thee, too, O Lord,
Almighty as Thou art,
For thou hast stooped to ask of me
The love of my poor heart.

It was this truth that overwhelmed the apostle's mind and soul. Time and again he stands absolutely awed by what he speaks of as the grace of God, the faithfulness of God, the love of God. "If God is for us, who is against us?" God who for no reason save that God is that kind of God, destined us in love to be God's children.

Look now at the fact that we have sought to deny God's dream by our rebellion of will. It is only when we understand what we have been called to be that we confess the sin of what we are.

"If we say we have not sinned, we make God a liar, and his word is not in us." John said that.

"I do not understand my own actions...For I do not do the good I want, but the evil I do not want is what I do." Paul said that.

"Whatever we are, we are not what we ought to be." Augustine said that.

Always it is the saint who knows the real ugliness of his or her sin. Modern people have lost their consciousness of sin because they have lost their consciousness of God. Humanity does not understand the idea of a rebellion in the will of humans because they acknowledge no will outside their own. Humanity has, in Hensley's phrase, become the master of its fate, the captain of its soul.

Why has the modern human race come to believe in its own supremacy? Reinhold Nieburh suggest this answer:

> *(Once) man was primitive, living a mean, beastly brutish existence, finding a few fruits from the trees, having skins for his clothes, living precariously. Then he learns to put domestic animals to use; humbly he starts to till the soil; gradually he learns the crafts; he develops commerce and industry; then during the last two hundred years he acquires more and more technical knowledge and power. Man is growing strong. This is man's life and this is history as known to modern culture.*

Then the chorus of the twentieth century rings out in sober parody of the psalmist:

> 'O man, modern man, how excellent is thy name in all the earth! Who hast set thy glory above the heavens. Out of the strength of chemists and statesmen hast thou ordained strength because of thy wisdom. When I consider the heavens which thou has filled with supersonic planes the work of thy hands, the moon and the stars which thou hast weighed, analyzed, and fully comprehend, what is God that thou art mindful of him and the son of God that thou visited him?"

Contrast the two striking thoughts—the high and holy dream of the great creative God who has placed in our hands the freedom of choice among all the wonderful and generous gifts that God has bestowed upon us—and the world that humanity has made out of it all—the lives that mankind is living—selling honorable birthrights as God's children for messes of pottage and the chaffs of sin. Consider the wisdom of God and the folly of humanity, the dream and the rebellion against its fulfillment. Consider it soberly and seriously.

But God still works—and a third scene comes upon us. For the great God—who was and is and e'er shall be—chooses to walk upon earth with rebellious humanity. So great is God's love. Consider this forgiving God who so loves us that God seeks to reconcile us unto God—the work of redemption brings back into the fold these rebellious beings that we are—the work of redemption reconciles us unto the God who dreams great dreams for us. Is this the act of a shallow, uncaring, indifferent love? The holy God can remain holy yet forgiving only by Christ suffering for our sin which is the death of the cross.

Consider too that it is not only in the death of Christ, but in His resurrection and continuing ministry with us that we are redeemed. "Christ in you, the hope of glory," says Paul. Salvation comes not only in that for us Christ died, but in that, in us, Christ lives. Christ, the Bridegroom has eternally wedded Himself to the human race and He will seek no divorce and accept no release from intercession in our behalf until we too love him who first and forever loves us. One, named Dr. Maltby put it memorably:

> *On Calvary, Christ betrothed Himself forever to the human race, for better, for worse, for richer, for poorer, in sickness and in health…It is not simply what God once was, or Christ did, that can save us; but what Christ once did is the sacrament, an indivisible pledge to us of what He is and does forever, and shows to us, each one, if we will, the God with Whom we have to do…We know what it means to wash our hands of a person, but we have no word for this opposite thing.*

It is this opposite thing to which God in Christ has committed Himself—the task of recovering all humanity unto God, however long it might take, however arduous the way, however unrewarding the toil.

The great English pastor, Leslie Weatherhead, illustrates all this as he tells how one night aboard a ship in the Mediterranean they passed quite close to Stromboli, the island volcano which rises sheer out of the sea:

> *It was after dinner and almost dark. Suddenly there was a great burst of flame from the crater at the summit. Huge tongues of flame shot hundreds of feet into the sky, lighting the ocean for miles around. Tons of molten rock*

were thrown up into the air. Through our glasses it was possible to distinguish red hot boulders racing down the mountainside, and gradually a stream of lava forced its way almost to the sea. For many hours—when our vessel had slipped westward toward the last lingering sunset which lay upon the horizon, when the bold outline of Stromboli was lost in the gathering shadows of night—that red hot lava, like some awful open wound, gashed the darkness. What did it mean? It meant that for a few hours there had been revealed the great fires which had been burning in the mountain's heart since the foundation of the world.

The cross itself is the supreme event of all history. But it speaks of something greater still. It speaks of God's everlasting love as revealed in Christ—God's love that will continue to seek and suffer as long as one life remains outside the embrace of God.

If the world says, "If God were good, the sin of the earth would break God's heart."

We answer, pointing to Calvary, "See God's breaking heart!"

If the world says, "If this kind of universe with its griefs and graves is somehow necessary for our growth, then God, if God were good would at least share its pain with us."

We answer, pointing to Him upon the cross, "See God sharing our pain!"

If the world says, "If God is Love, than in compassion God will bear our sins as only God can."

We answer, "Behold God bearing our sins!"

It is a glimpse of God's very heart, you see, just as Weatherhead glimpsed the inner fires of the volcano on a dark night in the Mediterranean. Calvary with its brief instance in history unveils the very depths of God before the eyes of humanity. How can we look upon it and refuse to bow before this God who is greatness and goodness and glory?

Look for this brief instant upon Calvary. Behold there the travail which God bears from the foundation of the world—and will forever bear—until at the name of Jesus every knee shall bow and every tongue confess that Jesus Christ is Lord, to the glory to God the Father.

Not Enough Darkness
John 1: 1-5, Acts 6: 1-6

February 3, 1946
Winona Methodist Church, Winona, Ohio

*T*he other night as one looked from his windows, one could see only a very limited distance. The night skies were filled with snow and the darkness seemed so close about us— except where there were lights in the windows of houses— and these were picked up and reflected with their warm glow by the same snow that filled the skies. Then one with the eye of an artist could work out the patterns created by the darkness and light in those etchings of black and white which gives us one of art's vivid contrasts.

So we might note that the history of the world, the history of life in the world forms a pattern of light and darkness. There have been those periods when darkness seemed to settle about humanity as conquerors strode across the earth and throttled liberties and submerged the multitudes under their iron heels and heavy hands. There have been the centuries when superstition truly "reared its ugly head" and education and learning were suppressed. There have been black moments for Christianity when leaders were more concerned with apparel and trappings and power than they were with the holy truths of God. There have been somber moments when it seemed that hope was near to death—here is Calvary's gloom and it has been echoed in many days since the blackest of all. It comes upon us whenever we gather in the chill air of the early morning at the dock in Boston as another boatload of displaced persons reaches these shores. And in childish eyes there is not the expectant delight of some new game, but the dull and nearly lifeless stare of a poor tired little soul, wondering what fear will next rise before him.

But no matter how thick the encircling gloom may gather about us in our modern periods of transition between light and darkness, there still persists in the Christian heart the one undying light of its high hope. One puts it, "The kingdom of God is like a candle—which when it was lighted seemed but a small thing—hardly worth a person's notice. But, lo, from this small flame others are kindled, and others, till at last it becomes a mighty power, a fierce compelling radiance that shall fill the whole earth."

A newspaper fill-in says, "There is in all the world not enough darkness to put out the light of one small candle."

And a poet theologian puts it:

I do believe the world is swinging toward the light.
So spoke a soul on fire with holy flame.
Amid the dark such faith pierced through the night,
The dreamers wrought, and living fruitage came.
To give of self, and not to count the cost—
To learn, to teach, to labor, and to pray—
To serve like Christ, the least, the last, the lost—
These are the beacon fires that lit the way.
(Anonymous)

And so Jesus came to be the light—so that in His light we might see light—the knowledge of the glory of God as we had not been able to know it before. And to follow in the line of faith to which God calls us is to serve as a beacon fire to the least, the last, and the lost so that amid the "encircling gloom" of their little lives there will shine that "kindly light" that leads us on.

In Him and in His way is the essential connection between the life of God and the life of humanity; this is the great truth of the world.

The wisdom of Solomon sets it forth, "*The spirit of man is the candle of the Lord.*"

Phillips Brooks's description of such a relationship will endure:

An unlighted candle stands in the darkness and someone comes to light it. A blazing bit of paper holds the fire at first, but it is vague and fitful. It flares and wavers and at any moment may go out. But the vague, uncertain, flaring blaze touches the candle, and the candle catches fire and you have a steady flame. It burns straight and clear and constant. The candle is glorified by the fire and the fire is manifested by the candle. The two bear witness that they were made for one another the way in which they fulfil each other's life—the inferior substance renders obedience to its superior—the candle obeys the fire. And the darkness prevails whenever the nature of the candle cannot feel the fire's warmth even close to it—or when the candle refuses to be held where the other nature's flame can reach it—so that candle goes unlighted.

It might be well for all of us to remember these words out of the wisdom of the past, "It is better to light a candle than to curse the darkness." For in that high and exalted moment of mystery when God's presence becomes clear and definite, when divinity breathes upon us, then light shines forth, for the fire of the Lord has found the candle, and the candle is lighted and burns to guide and to cheer and to dispel the darkness about it.

I would ask that we visit this day with such a soul, lighted with the spirit of God, visit with him so that the conviction of his life steadies the light of our own personal candle of the Lord. The clear light of his life shines forth first in a day of difficulty: it was the period of the beginning of the Christian community. Many of the recent converts to this new faith were not allowed to return home and were thus cut off from all financial support. In such a time, charitable men such as Barnabas stepped forth to help in the support of the needy ones, and the funds for this work were placed in the hands of the Apostles for their administration. There were some who felt neglected in the daily serving of the tables, and to remedy the situation, seven men were chosen to care for these business details. So it was that Stephen was chosen for this work, and we get his whole story in just two chapters of the *New Testament*. But we get the effect of his life through twenty centuries of history.

Stephen was a man full of faith—faith in God and faith in humanity. So that in the time of possible breach in the little community, here was a candle of the Lord who shone forth his good will unto men, and men trusted in him. And Stephen was a man full of wisdom—this was one of the qualifications for the job—in these business affairs they needed a leader of sound and worthy judgment. And Stephen was a man full of power—wherever he went, things happened. People arose to argue with Stephen concerning his faith—but his was a faith undimmed—and he used his wisdom and his power to set aside those arguments. And then one day, they brought him before the council and witnessed against him falsely, charging him with blasphemy against the temple and the customs of the Hebrew people. But as they looked upon him, they saw his face, the face of an angel.

And this man, full of wisdom and power, and of the Holy Spirit, spoke forth to them of their ancient faith, the faith of the fathers of Israel, and he spoke to them of their failure to practice with their lives what they preached with their lips. He spoke to them of the truth, of their refusal to heed the prophets, of their persecution of them, and of their betrayal of the great One who had been among them. And the truth hurt; they were furious and gnashed their teeth at him. But Stephen, full of the Holy Spirit, looked up to heaven and saw the glory of God, and Jesus standing at the right hand of God. While they were stoning him, Stephen prayed, "Lord Jesus, receive my spirit." Then he fell on his knees and cried out, "Lord, do not hold this sin against them."

To find the sustaining power in life that Stephen knew and exercised so heroically, we might well look to the words of another courageous soul; Raimon Lull, missionary who was stoned to death by the Mohammedans, "He who would find Thee, O Lord, let him go forth to seek thee in love, loyalty, devotion, faith, hope, justice, mercy, and truth; for in every place where these are, there art Thou."

So in the high and holy moments when the great fire of the spirit of God is upon us, then it is for us to sense the warmth and hold up the candles of our lives in dedication to serve and to glorify God—thus the fire touches the candle, the light shines forth, and the darkness is not enough to put it out.

E. Stanly Jones says in *Choices Before Us:*

> *"Defeated armies succumb more to wounds and sicknesses than do victorious armies. We are sick because we feel no call to a great cause. We are in for changes in the world—and there is nothing absurd in a certain view of the world as the scene of the kingdom of God. Unless we who are Christians can light the way for others, we are not living up to Christ's challenge to follow Him.*

Then there follows his personal decision:
> *"I am shut up to this decision—there can be no other way for me. So I shall choose the kingdom of God, and I shall get as many others as possible to make the same choice. It shall become my magnificent obsession.*

The kingdom of God is like a candle—which when it was lighted seemed but a small thing—hardly worth man's notice. But lo, from this small flame, others are kindled—and others, till at last it becomes a mighty power, a fierce compelling radiance that shall fill the whole earth.

There's No Hidin' Place for Love
Genesis 2:3-7:24

February 14, 1971
Christ United Methodist Church, Columbus, Ohio

Perhaps the best known of several books written after nuclear testing on the Bikini Islands to make plain to humanity the message of the atom bomb is *No Place to Hide* by David J. Bradley. "This message," as the *New York Times* book review remarked, "is done in skywriting, five miles high."

"We have little idea," Bradley writes, "what the long-range effect on our lives would be from an all-out atomic war...We do know that Bikini is not some faraway little atoll pinpointed on an out-of-the-way chart. It is San Francisco Bay, Puget Sound, the East River. It is the Thames, the Adriatic, Hellespont, and Baikal." In the case of such a war, it is suggested, there would be no place to hide.

Some people think that humanity would have to hide again in caves. Here is a cartoon in two parts: In the first part prehistoric man is emerging from his cave and is looking forward to a glow on the horizon that is labeled "Civilization." In the second part, he is looking back at a brief glow on the horizon labeled "Civilization" and is fleeing toward a cave again.

Stanton A. Cobentz wrote:

> *Out of the cave we climbed, through toil and tears*
> *Of half a hundred thousand iron years...*
> *Till Man the Inventor turns to Man the Slave,*
> *And science herds us back into the cave.*

Others think the matter is not yet this serious. R.E. Lapp, a military consultant, has written a book under the title, *Must We Hide?*

The subject we now consider has to do with a matter where there is literally no place to hide. This is suggested in the second and third chapters of the Book of Genesis, in which the story is found about early humanity, personified in the first man and the first woman--Adam and Eve. They lived in a beautiful garden which was somewhere in the Mesopotamian region, as is indicated by the fact that a stream flowed through the garden and separated into four rivers, one of which was the Euphrates. The main point of the story is to explain how sin originated in the world. The origin of sin was in a free act of wrong choice. The choice was on a level that was appropriate to the simple life of the times. At question was whether or not to take a particular fruit from a particular tree against God's command. The act that was done was an act of free choice, and it was an act that was wrong because it was against the command of God. Therefore it was sin. Afterward, Adam and Eve withdrew from among the trees. Then they heard the voice of the Lord God as God walked in the garden, and the Lord God called to them and said, "*Where are you?*"

There is no place to hide from the voice of conscience. Adam and Eve hid in the thickest part of the forest in their lovely garden, and the shades of evening were falling fast, but conscience was there. Humanity's conscience is its intuition of right and wrong; its feeling of praiseworthiness or blameworthiness of what one had done, its sense of inner integrity, either maintained or outraged. There is no place to hide from conscience, for humanity carries it within itself. In the endeavor to improve the safety of airplane travel, one means that was employed was to place in commercial aircraft a sealed set of instruments with graphs to record data. The altitude at which the plane was flown, its speed, its changes of course—all were recorded. After the flight was over, the records were taken out and studied. No matter what the pilot might say, the testimony of the instruments cannot be expunged or denied. This was a "mechanical conscience" as E. Stanley Jones called it, traveling with the plane constantly and recording constantly everything about it. The conscience that one carries within the self is like that. It also goes with the person everywhere, and it is terrifyingly accurate. There is no place to hide from what it records.

Of course people try to hide, but eventually the conscience backs them into a corner anyway. One man came to a doctor's office because he could not sleep and was nervously gone to pieces. Upon examination, the doctor found nothing organically wrong. Finally, the doctor asked the man if he had anything on his conscience. The latter exploded with anger, and declared that he came to get medical treatment, and not to be pried into, and rushed out of the office. The next day, however, he came back and admitted that the doctor was right, and that he did have something on his conscience. When his father died, he was made the executor of the estate. He kept back part of his brother's share, really stealing it. The doctor insisted then and there that he sit down and write a letter to his brother and confess the wrong that he had done. The doctor walked with him to the mailbox, where he dropped the letter in. When the letter was actually in the box, the man turned and shook the doctor's hand saying, "Thank God, that burden is gone." After that he recovered. So there is no way to handle conscience except the way the *Bible* indicates, which is, if we have done something wrong, to confess it to those we have wronged and to God, to make restitution to the extent of our ability, and thence forward to walk as conscience directs.

There is also little place to hide from the verdict of history. At the time, people seem to get away with many evil deeds, but sooner or later they do not "get away" with them. Thousands of years later, we are still talking about Adam and Eve and what they had done wrong. Paul writes, "*In Adam all die.*"

There is something about history that searches out the things done even in hidden places and brings them to light as time goes on. When Charles R. Beard was asked what he had learned from history, he replied with several aphorisms—one of which was this: "The mills of the gods grind slowly, but they grind exceeding fine."

Originally, that was a Greek proverb and is found in the Sibylline Oracles. Then a man named von Logau, about 1650, put it in poetic form like this:

> *Though the mills of God grind slowly,*
> *Yet they grind exceeding small;*
> *Though with patience He stands waiting,*
> *With exactness grinds He all.*

There is something of this in history. A recent book entitled *The Scholar Adventurers*, tells about the research work through which many literary frauds have been at long last uncovered, although their perpetrators were certain that they were foolproof. For example, Thomas J. Wise forged first editions; John Payne Collier fabricated documents, and Sophia Hawthorne inked out passages in her husband's journals. But, as a reviewer of the volume says,

"Wise never dreamed that he would be exposed by microscopic analysis of the paper on which his fakes were printed. Collier never knew that photography would reveal his interpolations as plainly as infrared light has uncovered the passages that Sophia Hawthorne so carefully blotted out."

There is no place to hide from the vision of God. The story in Genesis is told in an anthropomorphic way. The Lord God walks in the garden, and God's voice and vision search out the people trying to hide. In the story of the Tower of Babel, God comes down to see the city and the tower. Later, it was felt that such anthropomorphisms should be avoided, but picturesque reference was made to the eyes of the Lord. *"The eyes of the Lord run to and fro throughout the whole earth."* (II Chronicles 16:9). *"The eyes of the Lord are in every place keeping watch on the evil and the good."* (Proverbs 15:3). Later still, it is said that God is a spirit and that in God we live and move and have our being. The modern philosopher A.C. Garnett writes:

> *God is the only complete person, for He includes all others…A human person is an interrelated set of physical and mental activities of a part of space. The personality of God includes the whole of space and the whole range of physical and mental activities. All knowledge occurs in Him, and He shares the consciousness of all His creatures.*

However you express it, whether in primitive anthropomorphism or in abstract philosophical terminology, there is no place to hide from the vision of God.

But, if there is no place to hide, there is also no place to get lost. Anywhere, conscience can guide us. In his book *The Moral Life and the Ethical Life*, Eliseo Vivas quotes the saying, "In Rome do as the Romans," but he asks the question which we sometimes forget to ask: "Which Romans? The poor, the middle class, the rich, the clergy? The Catholics, the Communists?" Which Romans do you imitate when you are in Rome? That you have to decide for yourself. The conscience then, may be compared not only to a sealed recording instrument, but also to a compass. A compass is that which enables ships to get away from just sailing along the coast line, and even under obscured skies to travel far. In the ship itself is a dependable indicator of direction. By putting our conscience under the tutelage of Jesus Christ, it can become a dependable guide, carried with us everywhere we go. Then there is no place to get lost, because wherever we are, we possess something that shows the direction.

There is no place to get lost from history, if the action of history searches out the humble and speaks the word of truth at last about what has been done. This applies to very simple things. Take a student who works hard and faithfully day after day. Eventually, that student is going to have the mastery which is sought in that field of research. Think of seeking out of history in terms of such a person as Abraham Lincoln. He was defeated again and again, several times in succession, but each time he came back to the battle and aimed a little higher until finally he was elected president of the United States.

There is no place to get lost from God, because God is everywhere. In the depths of the sea and in the heights of the air, people have felt God's presence. There is no place to get lost from God. Sometimes, however, it is not until we try to run away from God and discover that we cannot do it, that we turn around and find our rest in God. I think that was at least part of what the psalmist meant with these words:

> *Whither shall I go from Thy Spirit?*
> *Or whither shall I flee from Thy presence?*
> *If I ascend to heaven, Thou are there!*
> *If I make my bed in Sheol, Thou art there!*
> *If I take the wings of the morning*
> *And dwell in the uttermost parts of the sea,*
> *Even there shall Thy hand lead me,*
> *And Thy right hand shall hold me.*
> *If I say, 'Let only darkness cover me,"*
> *And the light about me is night,*
> *Even the darkness is not dark to Thee,*
> *For the night is bright as the day;*
> *For the darkness is a light with Thee.*
> *(Psalms 139:7-12)*

Francis Thompson had the same experience with the Lord Jesus Christ, and he put it in these words in his poem, *The Hound of Heaven.*

I fled Him, down the nights and down the days;
I fled Him, down the arches of the years;
I fled Him, down the labyrinthine ways
Of my own mind; and in the midst of tears
I hid from Him, and under running laughter.

Fear wist not evade, as Love wist to pursue.

Nigh and nigh draws the chase
With unperturbed pace,
Deliberate speed, majestic instancy;
And past those noised Feet
A voice comes yet more fleet—
"Lo! Naught contents thee who content'st not Me.

Whom wilt thou find to love ignoble thee,
Save Me, save only Me?"
Halts by me that footfall;
Is my gloom after all,
Shade of his hand, outstretched caressingly?
"Ah, fondest, blindest, weakest,
I am He Who thou seekest!
Thou dravest love from thee, who dravest Me."

Palm Sunday

(Tower Sunday School Class, Sylvania, Ohio)

"On the next day many people that were come to the feast, when they heard that Jesus was coming to Jerusalem, took branches of palm trees, and went forth to meet Him, and cried, 'Hosanna: Blessed is the King of Israel that cometh in the name of the Lord.'" John 12: 12-13

We Would See Jesus...Facing Jerusalem
Luke 9:51-62

March 29, 1953
Concord Methodist Church, Beaver Falls, Pennsylvania

I always feel that the Palm Sunday experience begins long before—at that point of great decision in the Man from Nazareth when as we read in our scriptures, "He set His face steadfastly toward Jerusalem."

There followed busy days for Jesus after that decision: days of healing the distresses of minds that were troubled and bodies that were pain-wracked. Days of teaching—tremendous periods of teaching as He tried to use all available time that was fast shortening for Him to have the people at least begin to understand His purpose for the world which He came to redeem. Then there were days of being apart with His little band of close followers—the twelve whom He had called to Him to share in His purpose. Days of desperately trying to prepare these humble men for the tasks and the tumult that were to be theirs to face. But all through the days of busy living and teaching and healing—and through all the withdrawing moments of spiritual communion with His Father, Jesus remained true to His decision to go to Jerusalem. He maintained His loyalty even with full knowledge of the risks which He would face with His entry into the great Jewish city—for there had been spies sent out from the priests there watching His moves and listening to His teaching with an eager hope that one day in a casual moment, He would commit that terrible Hebrew sin of blasphemy and could be tried then by the religious council. And Jesus time and again revealed His wisdom as He did not choose to let them trick Him.

But now His course was run, His revelation as Messiah was near. And on to Jerusalem He must go at this time—along with many other pilgrims who were planning to celebrate the Feast of the Passover there in their Holy City.

And He rode into the city of Jerusalem on that first of Palm Sundays amid the cries of the crowd who were captivated by this man riding into the great city upon a lowly colt: *"Hosanna, blessed is the King who cometh in the name of the Lord! Hosanna!"*

And such was the stir of that day, and so great was the crowd that turned to follow after Him that the Pharisees, those who had sought time after time to trap Him, turned one to the other and said, "Behold, the world is gone after Him!"

Here we have two pictures—look at each searchingly and with all your heart's honesty.

We have through these weeks in Lent been looking closely at the personality of this Man of Nazareth, this Jesus who came to save His people. We have seen Jesus as a youth growing in wisdom and in stature and in favor with God and humanity. We have known Him in that tremendous wilderness experience when He came to the firm decision as the nature and way of the Kingdom of God. We have heard Him as He taught the danger of losing sight of God and spiritual values in life through too much concern over what we shall eat and what we shall wear and all the other material attractions which lure us and leave us empty. We have been held by Him as He preached to us of the Kingdom of God and of our possibility of attaining it. We have, I pray, knelt with Him in those times of spiritual seeking when He, too, turned away from the world of men to the God in whom was strength and courage and comfort and peace. And through it all, we have been convinced of one perfect loyalty in this Man who stands unique in all the world's history for His steadfastness in all things to the will of God.

Some of you may have the custom of reading stories of the life of Jesus during Lenten days. Perhaps some of you this year or in previous years read Lloyd Douglas's novel, *The Big Fisherman*. It was a gripping thing, and the skill of the writer served to make the story very real and vivid. But there is a shortcoming here—very often in this novel Jesus is portrayed as a weak person, One who must lean on others for support because He is tired and weak of body. Somehow, it does not fit this man who was so steadfast, so unflinching in His loyalty to His mission. Indeed, there is great strength in Jesus that led Him forth down through His experiences upon earth and kept Him moving forward with firm determination that would not be shaken on that first of Palm Sundays.

In the face of Jesus Christ
Shining through this world's dark night

There is love and understanding;
There is kindliness and light.

There is patience, there is vigor!
There is penetrating power
Such as all the world is needing
In this dark and tragic hour.
(*Anonymous*)

This is the first picture: Jesus—steadfast.

And the second picture—the crowd. Look here carefully enough and long enough that you see the faces, and a strange thing happens. For there in the crowd standing out from the rest is the reflection of your very self.

Yes, the band of pilgrims who came through Jerusalem's gate that day did gather up the palm branches and did salute this Man and did sing praises: *"Hosanna, blessed is the King who cometh in the name of the Lord! Hosanna!"*

But their loyalty could not face His, for later during that week of world-shattering events, perhaps some of those same voices were raised in that terrible call for condemnation— *"Crucify Him!"*

Oh, I know we don't like to think of ourselves as among them, wavering, changeable, critical, crucifying. But honestly, are we not there? Do we not at times in life join with the joyous throng greeting Him, honoring Him, paying homage to Him? Are there not times in life when we meet the King and bow down before Him? Do we not sing with those of old, *"Blessed is the King who cometh in the name of the Lord!"*

And do we not waver—does not often, too often, the smile of joyous greeting change quickly into a sneer of mockery? Do not our lips change their position from the shout of *"Hosanna!"* to the cry of *"Crucify!"* Are there not times when instead of being helpful, we are downright hindrances to Christ in this world of ours? Are we not destructive in thought, word, and deed rather than being builders of the kingdom? Do our hearts not often burn with jealousy and revenge and hatred rather than with joy and reverence and homage? Do not our petty meannesses and our personal prejudices serve as very adequate crucifixion nails—even we who have broken bread together and drunk the blood of sacrifice?

Oh, I am sure of this—that if we look long enough and carefully enough and honestly enough, we see ourselves in the changing crowd.

How sharp the contrast between the pictures!

The crowd wavers—even Peter, stalwart rocklike Peter denies Him. And through it all, this Jesus stood firm to the end. He could have escaped, you know, up over the brow of the hill, away into the north country, and be heard from nevermore. But he was steadfast and waited there. And they came and took Him and finally crucified Him. And often in life, we must say, "We were there—we helped in it. And now we are sorry!"

> *Whenever there is a silence around me*
> *By day or by night—*
> *I am startled by a cry.*
> *It came down from the cross—*
> *The first time I heard it.*
> *I went out and searched—*
> *And found a Man in the throes of crucifixion,*
> *And I said, 'I will take You down,'*
> *And I tried to take the nails out of His feet.*
> *But He said, "Let them be,*
> *For I cannot be taken down*
> *Until every man, every woman, and every child*
> *Come together to take Me down."*
> *And I said, "But I cannot bear to hear You cry.*
> *What can I do?"*
> *And He said, "Go about the world—*
> *Tell everyone you meet—*
> *There is a Man on the cross."*
> *(Anonymous)*

In John Masefield's book, *The Trial of Jesus*, the wife of Pontius Pilate asks the Roman centurion in charge of the crucifixion, "What do you think of His claim?"

The centurion replies, "If a man believes anything up to the point of dying on as cross for it, he will find others to believe it."

Still curious, she asks, "Do you think He is dead?"

To this he replies, "No lady, I don't."

"Where is He, then?"

And he answers, "Let loose in the world, lady, where neither Roman nor Jew can stop His truth!"

So it is—and we help the onward progress of that truth when we, too, as He did before us, stand steadfast against all the clamors of the world for our loyalty, against all the lesser attractions that try to capture us, against the low and evil forces that tempt us, against our own weaknesses and jealousies, and selfishness.

But it is not enough to stand against—we must also stand for something: for truth, and beauty, and goodness, and love. For Christ Who brings all of these together in Galilee, and Gethsemane, and Golgotha.

We can help when we stand steadfast!

In Germany, all during those war years, when each man and woman and child must raise his arm in salute and cry forth his loyalty to Hitler, there was our Methodist seminary at Frankfort-on-Main that continued to herald forth its motto of action and life—

"We have but one Master!"

How wonderful for us to dedicate ourselves to this: to declare ourselves, to purify ourselves, to witness to others, to bring them to that Man on the Cross—our Master! Not on Sunday with palm branches, but daily with life!

Radiant Heights and Shadows Dim
Luke 19: 28-46

March 22, 1970
First United Methodist Church, Sidney, Ohio

Yesterday, He was at Bethany. Last night they made him a supper there, and Mary anointed His head and feet with the precious ointment—for the day of "My burying," He had said, looking on into the darkness of the week's tragedy. The little village was full of pilgrims on their way to the great Passover feast, and there was much going and coming over the hill which led to Jerusalem. The news that the Prophet of Nazareth was on His way to the feast would be carried speedily into the city.

People were full of expectations. They had been debating one with another as to the likelihood of His coming. Some thought He might be kept away by fear of the priests and the Pharisees.

He had now been going up and down the country for three years. He had preached in city after city. Many had seen His miracles—had heard His teachings. They had heard in Judea, and Samaria, and Galilee that this new Prophet was claiming to be the Messiah. Everybody was interested in Him—it was known also that His claims were being disowned by all the prominent churchmen, and that at last the authorities had publicly proclaimed Him to be a deceiver and a dangerous person. The rumors had mounted into murmurings, and the murmuring into murderous intent.

Now most people, especially in Jerusalem, sided as the world's way is with those who are in authority. Some others were quite indifferent—interested in the day's happenings—ready to join any and every crowd at any time to go in any direction—just wherever there was excitement! Others were there in whose hearts sounded still some word which Jesus had spoken in the streets of their town, in whose eyes was still the sight of Him as He went along one day which was well remembered—blessing little children, healing the sick, comforting the lonely ones.

A terrible thing it seemed to them that He should now be hunted after like a thief by the scribes and the Pharisees. If He came to the Passover feast, He came in peril of His life—they knew that, and they dreaded what might come to pass. And there were His enemies, too, wondering what He would do. Would He come? Would He dare?

Then the messenger came—came running over the hill into the great city—bearing the news that Jesus was in Bethany, and that tomorrow would enter Jerusalem. And there was a stir among the people.

The day dawned—and Jesus neared Jerusalem. Many had gathered about Him. Shouting and singing, they accompanied Him toward the city. Many from Bethany followed along; those from Jerusalem surged forth to meet Him. There He is in the midst of them. Some of them pull off their long cloaks and cast them in the road so that the procession moves along the momentarily softened stones. Others break off branches from the trees—branches green with the freshness of springtime. Palm branches are raised on high; the voices swell into a mighty chorus. God is praised for God's goodness:

"Hosanna," they cry. *"Hosanna, blessed be the King who comes in the name of the Lord! Peace in heaven and glory in the highest!"*

Some of the Pharisees who have come out with the crowd are suddenly alarmed, hearing this name of "king" and witnessing the enthusiastic multitude about the Master Teacher whom they had so often tried to trick and trap. *"Master,"* they cry. *"Rebuke thy disciples."*

To which Jesus answers, *"I tell you that, if these should hold their peace, the very stones would cry out!"*

Oh the enthusiasm was high—there was great joy on that Palm Sunday. Even the indifferent ones joined in the singing.

But across the scene there is sadness, a dark cloud that shutters the joyful sun! For in the midst of the festivity, there are the sad thoughts of the Master of Men. This for Him is no festive parade, no holiday procession. He is indeed a King, and in the Lord's name does He come, but He is to be rejected—He knows that—and at the other end of this road there is a cross!

But on toward Jerusalem the multitude journeys. Now the way descends into a valley; then it rises again and suddenly the Holy City lies outspread across the deep ravine, terrace upon terrace, crowned with the Temple tower, all white with its marble walls and shining roofs. And with the view before Him, and with His thoughts deep within Him, our Lord Jesus beheld the city—and wept over it. He must have loved that city—it was ever the goal of the religious quest to the Hebrew, the center of the nation, and the seat of the culture, the city of the Temple in which alone one could with complete fitness worship the great one God. There Jesus had walked before, and there He had talked and taught—and so few had heeded. And now the memories are deep upon Him, and the weeping breaks forth. Out in the country, out amidst the people of the land, there had been many to listen and to believe. In the Galilean towns there had been many who gave up everything to follow Him. Along the way to the city, great and wonderful things had happened as Jesus met many, and loved and lifted them to new heights. But here in Jerusalem—here in the religious city—where dwelt the priests and the doctors of the law, where the beautiful temple dominated all the buildings of the town, where the church was the central and supreme interest of the people—here they despised and hated Him.

Which gives us cause to pause…

So once again our Lord Jesus is to enter the religious capital. But the city was senseless to Him, deaf and dumb and blind before Him. For this He wept.

"Oh, Jerusalem, if thou hadst known, even thou, at least in this thy day, the things which belong to thy peace! But now they have hid from thine eyes."

And after all the elaborate preparations, after the hosannas, the songs, the flowers, the palm branches; the King who came in the name of the Lord was rejected.

The scene changes; it is evening now. The crowd has gone off to other pursuits. Here and there are the memories of the morning's festivities, a palm branch in the dust of the road, a wilted flower, a disappointed heart that the King was so lowly.

The Palm Sunday crowd vanishes away and is heard from no more. Just a little company of true disciples stand far off watching the end, when darkness falls upon the cross. Then the crowd utters no voice, is not visible, sits trembling at home, or is on the other side, when tragedy falls. When Jesus needs men to stand up for Him in the midst of His enemies and speak for Him, these loud singers of Palm Sunday are not there.

There are two kinds of religion: the religion of the crowd, and the religion of the consecrated heart. Many people who account themselves good Christians are good Christians only in the crowd. It is so easy to go with the multitude! Opposition tests the religion, so that we may see of what sort our religion is. Some unsympathetic and incredulous questioner comes, like the people who looked down from the windows crying, "Who is this?" And if the crowd seems large enough, if the cause seems popular enough, some come out of their houses, and follow along, some going so far as to be the leaders of the procession, the loud shouters on the joyous occasions. So each king, each political leader, each person even in a place of petty power had those accumulate about him who are basking in his wealth, or influence, or prestige—fence-sitters who are ever aware of the turns of tides so they can come to stand on the sidelines, perhaps to join in the popular causes and processions. But their curiosity is easily abated when darkness looms. So the indifferent become interested for a time—until something more attractive looms on their personal horizons.

But the faithful ones—oh, the faithful ones, often those who make the least noise, those who know with what effort the great entries are made into life and into the secrets of living—faithful ones for whom a cause is more than life itself, an ideal nobler than the heart's beating—the faithful ones who follow on to the end—even the end of life's crosses!

So Jesus journeys to Jerusalem—so the little circle grows about Him—so the crowd accumulates only to dwindle away rapidly before His humility, leaving those few with Him at His cross of death, who have left all to follow and who have followed willingly and constantly. The religion of the crowd, or the religion of the consecrated heart—in which group are we?

From Nazareth He comes, the carpenter
Who knows of hammering and blows that break
The worker's hands. From Galilee He comes.
The fisherman who walks upon the lake.

Through fields of harvest, ripe for plucking grain;
Along the dusty roads that go beside
The vineyards. Christ, the noble Carpenter
Goes to the city to be crucified.

Jerusalem's streets are filled with those
Who cry 'Hosanna!' and others, 'Crucify!'
For all of these His hands upon the cross
That lifts itself into the purple sky.

For all of these the Master lived and died.
His lamp is tall and bright: our lamps are dim,
But we can see the way ahead of us
For where the Master goes, we go with Him.
(Anonymous)

Maundy Thursday: Those Who Cross the Kidron

(Western Pennsylvania)

"When Jesus had spoken these words, He went forth with His disciples over the book Kidron, where there was a garden, into which He entered, and His disciples." John 18:1

Neither for These Alone
John 17:20-23

August 24, 1958
First Methodist Church, Rochester, Pennsylvania

On that evening when the humble and holy Jesus went out of the city of Jerusalem, across the Brook Kidron, and into the garden of Gethsemane, He did not kneel and confine His prayers simply to those intimate friends about Him. His mind and heart reached out to everyone who would hear and heed the truth He spoke and lived:

"Neither pray I for these alone, but for them also which shall believe on me through their word." (John 17:20).

As we grow in physical stature and in mental capacity, so, too, should our prayers increase in their depth and in their concern for others. It is quite all right for little Susan to kneel beside her bed and pray:
"God bless Daddy and Mother, and little Brother Johnny and Cousin Betty—and me."

But for the mature thinker and believer, prayer must contain a concern that is not limited by family ties alone—for we cannot both be Christian and be selfish.

There is a common curse that often lays hold upon us in which we see ourselves as something of the world's choicest plum and our own little circle as being the best fruit tree in the orchard of the world. And this curse does not only beset us individuals beings, but as nations and as races as well. Cecil Rhodes once spoke that he thought, "The British were the greatest people the world had ever seen." Voltaire believed that the culture of the French would be the mark to which people would refer in the future times. Professor Lasson of Berlin thought the Germans to be without peers both morally and intellectually, and one of our American diplomats felt convinced that God, "has yet made nothing or nobody equal to the American people—and I don't think He ever will or can."

And this curse penetrates into the life of our modern churches as we go about convinced that our particular little denomination has all the Christian outlook, the true view of religion, and the reserved seats on the train into heaven.

In the face of such narrowness, comes the words of Jesus's prayer:

"Neither pray I for these alone, but for them also which shall believe on me through their word."

And surely this Christly character who could not confine Himself to the rules of one little Jewish group of people, would be ill content to step into the scenes of modern life and see the tremendous barriers which we place between the classes—even in democratic America—even in our Christian churches—through which we catalogue people economically, socially, and racially or nationally.

To be sure, the known world in Jesus's day was small—but there were those who felt themselves politically, economically, or religiously superior, and so He knew these barriers as they existed. There were even then the conflicts between the favored race and the less-favored races. And yet that night in the garden, He could not limit Himself in prayer for the Jewish people alone, nor for His followers alone, nor for those of His age alone—but he prayed:

"for them also which shall believe on Me through their word."

From childhood days in Sunday school, I still remember a certain painting of Jesus, *The Hope of the World*, by Harold Copping. And in this painting there is the little Negro boy who sits looking so intently up at Jesus, there is the little Indian girl sitting there contentedly upon His knee, and there is the little Chinese fellow looking up, and the little brown girl, and the little white girl. And truly the title is good—for it is in such a love that all men and women of all races can come together before the personality of the stainless Jesus. In such love as this, truly there is the "Hope of the World."

And there is such hope—and the answer comes when we realize that those who were bitter enemies—American soldiers and Japanese youth—could at Christmas time lift their voices together in singing the great music that proclaims for humanity each year that Jesus is born. There is such hope for the world whenever amazing personalities can step forth out of hardship and overcome barriers because the fire of Christian love burns so deeply within them that they must speak it forth for all people to hear.

Such a personality lives today in the man, Roland Hayes, who so sings forth his spiritual belief, that people come close to Christ and His way. This is an amazing story of overcoming hate and of being bigger than the narrowness which too often besets and hampers our Christian progress, for Roland Hayes is the descendant of southern slaves. His great-grandfather, a majestic appearing man, was brought to America as a slave on a southern plantation. There he gathered the Negroes together for secret meetings—and one night, this leader was beaten to death in the swamps. Peter, his son, later married Mandy, the daughter of a Negro and his Cherokee wife. Then the Civil War broke out over the land, and the owners fled, and their slaves with them. But Peter would not flee, and he—as his father—was beaten to death. Mandy, left alone with five children, went off to Chattanooga. Roland Hayes writes of their struggles, "Grandma Mandy and her daughter, my mother, ate abundantly of the bread of suffering."

There a Negro, also with Native American strain in his blood, met Fanny, the daughter, and they were married. There they had a comfortable home and happy family life. Father William was a great huntsman and musician. Roland speaks of him with great devotion, "When my father called a deer, he was a buck himself."

But this father died, and the mother and her family went off to Chattanooga where the boys took turns going to school and working. The deep religious nature of the mother filled their lives—and Fanny's religious faith was to become the deep obsession in her son's life—for he, too is a deeply religious man. As his mother says, "Son, yo' is the continuation of me."

Then when Roland Hayes was seventeen, a white man invited him to his home. There Roland heard on a record Caruso's voice. "That night," he said, "I was born again. It was as if a bell had been struck that rang in my heart, and it has never ceased to ring there."

To Boston he came to study, his mother helping him as much as she could. His teacher suggested him for a solo in the church at Milford. However, there the good people did not want a Negro singing in their church—such was their narrowness. Whereupon, that famous teacher lost his patience with the church committee and shouted at them, "You may be followers of the meek and lowly Jesus, but a long way off!"

This awakened them to sense, and Roland Hayes was off to sing on Easter Day at Milford where he has returned time and again. Through his career, there have been insults hurled at him, denials of concert halls, and slurs against his personality. Yet he has never wavered, his larger vision never dimmed, and he has never fallen into the narrow rut of those who would refuse to hear him. In Berlin in 1924, he was to sing before a great audience, which began a tremendous uproar when the Negro singer came upon the stage. There he held his ground and began to sing that wonderful piece by Shubert, "Thou Art My Peace," and the audience was his.

He sings in Spanish, Russian, Italian, German, French, and English, but it is in the work of the Negro spiritual that I like him best. For to me the spiritual contains the pathos of human suffering and the simplicity of the Christian Gospel all sung with the depth of feeling that the singer feels for his Jesus. And as one hears this great singer of our day pour forth his warm soul into the deeply moving spirituals of his people, we are not conscious of racial color and characteristic, nor do we feel within ourselves any smug superiority— for he sings of Jesus with such sincerity that we in that high moment are one people. Through his singing he preaches a thousand sermons in one concert, but you aren't aware of the text—you simply feel that you have been in the healing presence of a great spirit who has lifted you above your petty selfishness and narrow prejudices; who has made you feel clean inside; who has thrilled you in every part of your being; who through the universal language of music has spoken the language of God for everyone in his audience. When the concert moves to that place where he sings of the Crucifixion, we think of Jesus there in the garden praying for all humanity—and then going forth to a cross of death—but then, as this soulful singer puts it:

> *"Not a mumblin' word He spoke—*
> *No, not a mumblin' word.*
> *(American Spiritual)*

We will all pray together, and as One People, face the rising sun.

Life's Wider Vistas
John 17: 24-26

August 6, 1950
Circleville/Miller Methodist Churches, Irwin, Pennsylvania

At the heart of Christianity is the irresistible power of genuine devotion. That is why Jesus prayed that his disciples should experience the same love which God had bestowed upon Him. His petition is in thorough harmony with this idea— *"I in them, and thou in me."*

These words are more than poetry or sentimentality, for our religion is both romantic and reasonable. While some of the world's religious beliefs leave us tasteless, Christianity is as alluring as a powerful magnet to pieces of steel. It constantly appeals to people's hearts as they catch the vision of the sinless Jesus and arise to follow after Him.

Christianity can never be dull, for it is so inspiring, and those who catch its vigorous attraction find themselves lifted as did Paul, the Apostle, who cried forth with full heart— *"Christ liveth in me!"*

The religion of Jesus begins with love—as we know Him more intimately we are more surely convinced of this love for the Will of the Father and for the welfare of humanity. So He attracted wayward women, the little children, the fishermen, and all those who stopped to hear His words and to look into His eyes. And it was this tremendous love that comes forth that critical hour when He knelt to pray and arose to sacrifice Himself for his beloved humanity. It is this tremendous love which becomes very clear to each of us who in some tremendous moment of discovery find Jesus and know that from henceforth we must follow His way. It is this experience of the Christ Love that sets humans forth on a quest to know Him, and knowing Him, to follow after him—even across that Brook Kidron—into a deeper fellowship with God the Father so that we, too, are led to submit our lesser wills to that greater will, and to arise humbly to serve—even if that service leads to a cross. But we often ask:

"Have not the long years passed—have not all those early devoted followers long since perished? Does not the miracle of this marvelous attraction belong to the previous centuries? Surely Jesus does not in this modern and complicated culture in which we live and move and have our being possess the dynamic attraction for humanity, so that He inspires in them the great leadership that He wrought in Peter and in Paul and in the early Saints."

These are the questions asked by the skeptics—and these are the thoughts running through the minds of the doubters of our modern times.

And the answer comes forth in an amazing personality who, in my opinion, is among the greatest of men: Albert Schweitzer, born in the year of 1875 in that contested land of Alsace which lies between France and Germany. His home life was a happy one as he grew up in an atmosphere of gentle but serious religious piety. One of the great problems of Europe early broke upon him as he noticed the scorn and the mockery of the neighborhood boys for the Jewish peddler who came through the town. But he, Albert, was deeply impressed by the "kindly eyes" of the peddler so that he himself could not be scornful.

In the academy during his boyhood, he developed rigorous habits of study. Here, too, he heard the strong and sturdy music of Richard Wagner and the deeply sacred and moving music of Bach.

As a young man at the University of Strasburg, he saw Bartholdi's statue "Emancipation." This depicts an African arising from slavery, and this work impressed upon the mind of the student this curse that had been upon the land before his day.

He was a brilliant student in both philosophy and in theology. As he wrote it, "Preaching became a necessity of my being," for he had to tell others of the way of Christ as he knew it in his own life.

Then, on one spring morning when he was nineteen, he came to a momentous decision concerning his life—he mentally divided his life into thirds. The first third he would spend in serious study as he prepared himself for the world's need. The middle third, he pledged to give his time and ability to the neediest place he could find in the world, and the closing third he hoped to return to his home in Alsace. Now at the age of seventy-five, Schweitzer has not yet reached that final third part of retirement.

Albert Schweitzer has more gifts in one person than has any other living person today. He is a gifted musician, not only an organist, but a writer of music, and a builder and repairer of organs. He is a master of philosophy which is an amazing feat for anyone, and is learned in theology—which also is alone a sufficient field for any one person. But this even was not enough. He determined to study medicine, and by working at his studies twenty hours daily, he completed this preparation as well and looked about for the neediest spot in the world for one with his abilities.

That spot was in Africa, and in 1913, Albert Schweitzer sailed for his work there. War broke out in Europe and he was taken prisoner by the French, for he was in one of the German Colonies of Africa. A serious illness came upon him during his military imprisonment, and he was later released as an exchange prisoner.

During the score of years between the wars, he was alternately in Europe and at his work in Africa. He would hasten off to Europe for a concert tour during which he would perform with great artistry on the organs of European cities, and then with the profits from the concerts, he would go back to his work at a medical station deep in Africa. Thus, he supported his own work there by his concerts. During the second war, he remained in Africa while his wife and children were in Europe. During this past summer, he made a quick trip to America to speak in Denver, Colorado, but here he could not stop long for his work in Africa constantly demands his presence. Thus does one man, in his daily living, shine forth as a world-renowned example of what following the Christ can mean.

Early he was convinced of the ethical love of Jesus, and in his life this fire of Jesus's love burns undimmed. His entire life is not one of denial, but rather an expression of affirmation of the reality of Jesus as a man of history and as a way of life. He has channeled all his great gifts of philosophy, theology, and medicine into the gentle hands of Christian charity through his own conviction of "Reverence for Life."

He lives on the heights.

There are wide vistas for the soul
Where manuscripts of space unroll,
Where God's great goals and peaks of snow
His majesty and beauty show;
Great vistas where His prophesies,

His dawns and springs and mysteries
In one swift flash of vision sweep
To wake the listless soul from sleep.

There are wide windows of the soul
Through which we glimpse a far off goal;
Through which all humble spirits see
The meaning of eternity.
The secret of both part and whole
Will in one far-flung reach unroll
Like tablets of immortal light
Let down from Sinai's regnant height.

There are great singing wonder hours
Where Truth's eternal peaks and towers
Rise up in grandeur and our eyes
Are looking into paradise;
One unrelenting flash of light;
One great, majestic moment, white
As the dawn when man was born,
White as creation's sunlit morn.
(Anonymous)

Good Friday

(Mountain Cross, Jumonville, Pennsylvania)

"For God so loved the world that He gave His only begotten Son, that whosoever believeth in Him should not perish, but have everlasting life."
John 3:16

Love So Amazing
1 Peter 1:19

April 9, 1976
Tipp City United Methodist Church, Tipp City, Ohio

In the midst of the joys or sorrows of life, in the web of our days filled with things that are useful, exacting, or bothersome, we are at times seized by a strange anxiety. It is as though a hand were suddenly placed upon our shoulder, stopping us. It may happen when death comes to a very close friend, or when we are informed that we are suffering from a very serious ailment, or it may be when some friend causes great sorrow to another. It may come also, simply when a thought arises out of the very depth of self. We are confronted, irritatingly, exasperatingly, with the sudden question, "What's the use? What use am I?"

Our very existence is questioned: our presence among those who surround us, our relationship to those who have gone before and to those who come after.

Quite instinctively we answer, "I'm not useless, rather I'm needed by those who are dependent upon me. I am certainly useful to those causes to which I have given myself."

Then what happens? When trials suddenly come, those who seemed to depend upon us forget our usefulness. We are deeply grieved and upset about it. Or it may happen that these causes for which we were working and were willing to give our enthusiasm collapse, and we are again seized by this sense of uselessness. If, on the other hand, that particular endeavor meets with success, there is really little difference, for we discover that success in its brevity is just as disheartening as failure. And together with *Ecclesiastes* we say, "Vanity, all is vanity."

Why so? Because death is inescapable. All mortals are, as their name implies, mortal. And death makes all things useless. At least that is what people think and say. Some put it bluntly in everyday speech, "I've caught on! I've caught on to one thing and that is that life is useless."

Are we the only ones who claim that life is not worth living? Have not all pastors, standing by open graves repeated Paul's statement, *"If Christ, be not raised, your faith is vain, if in this life only we have hope...we are of all men most miserable! Let us eat and drink for tomorrow we die! All that dies is vain."* (I Corinthians 15:17, 19, 32)

All is vanity. God says so, too. Yet, at the same time, God says more. Paul proclaims, *"God has ransomed your life from the futile ways inherited from your fathers. God has ransomed your life from its futility."*

God has ransomed it. The word has become trite in Christian speech; it is used in season and out of season. If to some the word is not trite, it is either revolting or mysterious and there are those who ask, "To whom could God pay the ransom about which Jesus spoke in that memorable phrase, *The Son of man came to give His life a ransom?'"* (Matthew 20:28)

When Paul is using the word, he is thinking of the ransoming of a slave. God is like somebody walking past a slave camp—today we could think of a concentration camp, or even upon those affairs and habits that make prisoners (and sometimes willing prisoners) of us. As God looks, God sees people living futile, worthless lives. To this God will not consent. It may well be that these slaves are guilty—not merely born in slavery. They may have been reduced to slavery because of theft, like the slave Paul mentions in his letter to Philemon. Or perhaps they are innocent slaves, prisoners of war...or perhaps they are slaves because of habits to which they've become addicted or through patterns of living that circumscribe them and keep them from being as free as they ought to be. One thing is certain. God does not consent to people living their lives in the slavery of a concentration camp or imprisoned by degrading habit or custom—so God pays. God must pay. As God, God wants people to be free.

So God pays—but what price?

The Apostle says that God pays a price which is above human calculation. God could, of course, have paid with silver or gold. God is Master of all—Treasurer of the world. The treasures of the world, however, cannot pay the ransom for a person living in the concentration camp that is his own life and death. All the treasures of the world eventually end up being devalued by death. God paid with God, with that which is priceless, both to God to humanity.

That is the ransom paid for our life—and the lives of all caught in some circumstance of imprisonment.

And the fact that this has happened is the reason for us gathering in this sanctuary this afternoon. For over a hundred years people have come in through these doors and gone out again because of this. On a certain Friday in history the ransom price was paid with the life and blood of one man, the Son of God Himself. This has happened—and it has happened to us. Before we knew about it, without our knowing it, perhaps even without our realizing that we were in a slavery condition, it has happened—and this is the Good News, the Gospel.

All else that is not related to this event is vanity, chasing after wind. Henceforth, your whole existence is wrapped up in this event. The Lord Jesus Christ Himself, the precious Victim; more precious than our church offerings, more precious than anything in heaven or on earth. As a matter of fact, it was heaven itself; the very Heart of God that ransomed our lost life.

If that has happened—and it has—what are we to do about it? What does God expect us to do with our ransomed lives? The answer is simple—through this redemption, God wants to make us useful. Useful to others, so that we will no longer be men and women living next to each other, but for each other.

When we come to understand what has happened, we will no longer, like the *Ecclesiastes*, see the lives of our neighbors in an unending circle of worlds moving toward an all-embracing nothingness. We will see them as beings bearing names who need our presence and whose presence we need; they will have really become neighbors, *near* to us. That is the new usefulness for which our lives have been ransomed by the death of Jesus Christ.

God, however, does not only tell us that we are to be a neighbor to someone. That is secondary in a life ransomed by Jesus Christ. God speaks about another usefulness. We are to be useful to God. God has paid such a high price because God wants our life for God.

True, God did not need our life in order to be God. God was not unhappy when we were not in existence. And yet, mysteriously somehow, God desired the need for our love. For God loves us. And now, God expects of us that we give God this ransomed life, ransomed from all slavery and futility. God wants our life, our person. God is longingly waiting for us, giving us a rendezvous. God wants to meet us in our offerings, in our prayers, in the things we undertake. And so we become useful to God! "Pleasing God." What a wonderful expression! To be able to give pleasure to God, to give to God the joy of our repentance. The kind of joy about which Jesus spoke when He said, "The angels of heaven rejoice when one poor little earthling, guilty and rebellious, repents and comes to God with a cry for pardon." (Luke 15:7)

Not only is there the joy which comes to God from our repentance, there is also the joy that comes from the simple existence of our love for God, and our prayers to God.

There is also the joy of our daily worship, and the joy which may be caused tomorrow when, called to choose, we choose that which will be pleasing to God. There are the joys about which our confession of sins speaks when it refers to fruits of justice and saintliness. There is the joy of being present at God's holy table where God invites and welcomes us.

To know that our ransomed life can be put to such great usefulness thrills us and gives us hope, even when we may be moving toward the grave. Our hope is in the *living* God. Yes, but our hope is not in the living God as long as we do not agree to be ransomed by God, and made useful.

May our hearts respond to God's love:

> *Love so amazing, so divine,*
> *Demands my soul, my life, my all!*
> *(Isaac Watts)*

It Is Finished
John 19:30-37

April 13, 1979
Ecumenical Stations of the Cross Service, Final Station
Tipp City United Methodist Church, Tipp City, Ohio

"*It is finished!*"

Death came to claim the prince of life—Jesus was dead! The world had fallen into darkness. All hopes were lost. Jesus hung alone upon the cross. Righteousness had been defeated—God denied. It was a terrible fate.

It was about midday, but darkness came over the whole countryside until three in the afternoon, for there was an eclipse of the sun. The veil in the Temple sanctuary was split in two. Then Jesus gave a great cry and said,

"Father, into your hands I commend my spirit."

Yet Christ died with the shout of a conqueror; still undismayed, still valiant, still full of fate. Though everything seemed down—and not much had come of His life's investment of energy and time, He died still trusting God.

Out of the darkness, out of the despair, out of the shattered world on the first of Good Fridays, through the great God—so that the tables were turned—a cross that had heretofore conquered life and snuffed it out grimly and cruelly, now became a symbol of life to the world.

See from His head, His hand and feet.
Sorrow and love flow mingled down.
Did e'er such love and sorrow meet,
Or thorns compose so rich a crown.
(Isaac Watts)

John Ruskin writes in *Modern Painters*:

"Our best finishing is but coarse and blundering work after all. We may smooth, and soften, and sharpen till we are sick at heart; but take a good magnifying glass to our miracle of skill, and the invisible edge is a jagged saw, and the silky thread a rugged cable, and the soft surface a granite desert...God alone can finish; the more intelligent the human mind becomes, the more the infiniteness of interval is felt between human and divine work in this respect."

His friends then came—those of the Sanhedrin—Joseph of Arimathea and Nicodemus who had come by night—to follow Christ when it is hard...

"It is finished."

The Daring One

*I would my soul were like the bird
That dares the vastness on the bough
Breaks into rapture even now!*

*He sings, tip-top, the tossing elm
As tho he would a world o'erwhelm.
Indifferent the void he rides
Upon the wind's eternal tides.*

*He tosses gladly on the gale
For well he knows he can not fail—
Knows if the bough breaks, still his wings
Will bear him upward while he sings!*
(Edwin Markham)

"Father, into your hands I commend my spirit."

Easter

(Easter Sunday, Christ United Methodist Church, Columbus, Ohio)

"Early on the first day..." John 20: 1

Love-Bearer to Mankind
John 20: 19-31

April 6, 1980
Tipp City United Methodist Church, Tipp City, Ohio

*T*he doors were shut—literally and spiritually, too, I suppose it was for those early disciples following the crucifixion. They were a little band of threatened and badly frightened men, huddled together, feeling far from secure. So they had shut and probably bolted the door—and felt they must keep it shut and bolted—for Calvary was so horribly near and crucifixion was horribly near in all its grim reality. Crucifixion was so grim a death—and this had happened—the best of all, noblest of all was crucified.

But to these men Christ appeared—so evidently and obviously and undeniably that their doubt was gone and their unbelieving minds convinced once and for all that this impossible thing was true. When He comes among them He shows them His hands and His side—the marks of His suffering and the death that God Himself would undergo in this mission as Love-bearer to mankind.

And He offers them peace! That was, of course, the customary greeting—Shalom—but the fact that Christ repeats it shows that He had more in His mind by far than simply that. What He meant was peace in their own hearts and consciences—and indeed they had grievous need of it. No more dispirited and unhappy people could be found the whole world over than this discomfited and frightened little group of broken men. For on the one side, they had failed Christ, sadly and inexcusably. And their consciences must have been clamorous and sore, their self-respect wounded and raw. And on the other side, far worse than even that, was the incredible fact, yet fact it was, that Christ, their Christ had failed them no less tragically. That His confident promises had proved to be only cheating words, with no body or substance in them. That the Master to whom they had pinned their faith, and for whom they had risked everything had proved if not an imposter, at least woefully and miserably self-deceived. That the wonderful dream He had awakened in them was out, had come to absolutely nothing, was only a mocking memory that would jeer at them down the years.

And then suddenly their Lord broke in upon them in that darkness of disillusionment and despair. "I, on my side," he said, "am proving that your doubts of Me are ungenerous and wrong. And I want you to know that whatever you have done and whatever you have been, I still trust you, and still believe in you; want you to take it in that God's love is big enough to cover your case, your need, your sin; and God's power is strong enough to lift you up above all that; want you to accept and to walk in the sunshine of God's forgiving grace."

As Paul put it to the Romans, if we really believe in the immeasurable, generous loving-kindness of God toward us in spite of our unworthiness, let us have peace with God through our Lord Jesus Christ. Do not let your past get you down. But shake it off, rise up above it, humbly accepting God's unthinkable grace.

Christ startles the disciples out of their downheartedness and the belittling of themselves as proved failures by throwing Himself frankly on their help and asking for it. Again He reminds them of the fundamental fact:

"You have not chosen Me. But I have chosen you. I did it deliberately, believing you the likeliest to be of service to God and to Me in our vast plans for the saving of the world. And knowing all there is to know, the very worst, remembering how you failed Me in the last few hours, I stand by my choice. I look to you with confidence. I lean my cause against your loyalty. I leave my hopes unafraid in your hands. The dream has not faded away. The adventure has not broken down in a ridiculous fiasco. For with Me you are going to make it all come true. As the Father has sent Me, even so I send you. And greater works than Mine shall you do."

So Christ said to men who had abjectly failed Him.

In World War I, a fine lad in a battalion failed through illness in the face of the enemy and was court-martialed and punished. All that the colonel said to the chaplain was, "We must show him that we still trust him or the lad will go to pieces." And not once did the colonel allude to the unhappy incident, but treated the boy with the old friendliness, and a few weeks later, put him in a tight corner in command of the very company with whom he had been when he made his slip. In a few days of grim fighting, the boy won honor after honor, and promotion for gallantry in the field. "What else could I do?" he said to the chaplain, "I failed him, and he trusted me!"

We, too, have failed Christ often and wretchedly and without excuse. Yet He too somehow still dares to trust us. Are we big enough to respond to that call on our gratitude and adulthood?

But how? The poet says it:

> *Unless above himself he can*
> *Erect himself, how poor a thing is man!*
> *(Samuel Daniel)*

How does one "erect himself above himself?" Experience has proved disheartening, has shown us how unstable are our sturdiest and most vehement resolutions, how frail and undependable these fickle hearts of ours. How?

The answer is that by ourselves the thing just cannot be done at all. But then, Christ does not ask impossibilities from His people. He gives what makes it possible. So here. He breathed on them, and said to them, *"Receive the Holy Spirit."* He gave them something of His own ways and mind, and nature—His own spirit. God's own spirit. And with something of Christ within them, all things spiritual came within their reach. Alone you cannot do it. But Christ and you together can confront anything and see it through with honor.

It is no use to push this aside impatiently as mere words which mean really nothing at all. For the facts are there, plain, obvious, undeniable; facts that prove that ordinary people, once Christ's spirit has touched and inspired and quickened them, can live and do live, can serve God and the cause and do serve God and the cause, as they could not do before. Look at these very men. How abjectly they failed! And yet once this Spirit entered into them, how valiant, daring, unbreakable they became! These things are hard and solid facts that must be faced and of which account must be taken. Robert Burns put it:

> *Not ev'n the Apostles, in the days*
> *They walked with Christ, loved Him so well*

As we may now, who ken His praise
Reading the story that they tell.
Writ by them when their vision grew
And he, who fled and thrice denied
Christ to His face, was proven true
And gladly for Him his memory died;
So strong the vision, there was none
O'er whom the Fisher's net was cast,
Ev'n of the fearfullest no one
Who would have left Him at the last.

The fact that He breathed on them seems to imply that He felt that He could now communicate to them something of His own nature as hitherto He had not been able to do. Why? Perhaps because heretofore, in spite of all that He could say to them in warning, they had been too self-assured, too confident. But now, taught by their own tragic experiences, humbled and made aware of their shocking instability and insufficiency, they were at last willing and ready to receive what Christ could give them. So William Temple says it:

He *imparts to them His own life-breath; the outward sigh, helped by the play on words, suggests that henceforth His own spiritual energy will be within them. Receive holy spirit. The gift is freely offered, but it can be refused; there is a definite act of reception. The lord now fulfills the promise of the Baptist concerning Him. He baptizes His disciples not in water which washes away stains, but in holy spirit—the energy of a holy life in obedience to God. Receive holy spirit—not the Holy Spirit. What is bestowed is not the Divine Person Himself but the power and energy of which He is the source. Earlier it had been said not yet was there spirit because Jesus was not yet glorified. But now that glorification is complete, and it is possible for the new divine energy, which operates through man's response to the manifested love of God, to begin its activity.*

There is a lesson for all days, and not the least for our day. Of ourselves we can do nothing. To attempt in our own strength the life we feel we ought to live is to be dogged by failure. Anatole France quotes Prevost, "How difficult it is to pick up a little strength when one has made a habit of one's weakness, and how much it costs us to fight for victory when for long past one has found it sweet to yield!"

We must live in Christ and draw from Him what in ourselves we have not got, if we are to be fit for what He asks of us. In particular, so Christ promises, it is a spirit of discernment that they are receiving, enabling them to know what kind of life a person should live; to recognize what things are wrong and evil, and what are worthy and right; to determine when repentance is genuine and when it is only an empty sham. *"If you forgive the sins of any, they are forgiven; if you retain the sins of any they are retained."* Confessedly the church has stumbled disastrously in these matters, mistaking prejudice for principle and mere human whims and preferences for the eternal Will of God. All that—often and scandalously. Yet are we not justified in agreeing that as we look back, subsequent ages watch with amazement and awe how the church has found its way through difficulties that seemed inescapable and problems that could not apparently be solved? In very truth, a pillar of fire had led Christ's blundering people through the darkness of the night.

That night that Christ came, Thomas had not been present. We do not know why. But is there not here a warning for us not to forsake the assembling of ourselves together? How much many must miss who make only an occasional, spasmodic irregular appearance at the worship of God in God's house! *"For where two or three are gathered together in My name, there am I in the midst of them."* So Christ promises. And sometimes surely had they been there, to them, too, He would have appeared.

When the other disciples told him of what had happened, Thomas was flatly and openly incredulous, pushing the whole thing aside as on the face of it ridiculously impossible. As to the first reports, it had been dark, or nearly so; the women were strained and overwrought by all they had been through; their eyes were full of tears and did not see clearly; they had imagined what was not there and could not have been there, for Christ was dead, and dead men do not rise. And as for this alleged appearance to the ten, self-evidently the thing could be nothing more than sheer hallucination born of frayed nerves or of longing for what could never be. It was wishful thinking that had seemed to come true.

Nearly everybody is severe with Thomas—but had we been there we should likely have argued as he argued, and said what he said. His tests sound crude, almost repulsively so. But were they? His was a doggedly honest mind, almost stolidly so. For he had not much poetry in him, one thinks; was a matter-of-fact person, with his feet planted firmly on the solid ground; not one to be rushed into believing what he wanted to believe, but sincere enough to face the facts and to accept them, however grim and dark. Essentially he was a valiant soul, loyal to Christ even when in his own mind the last hope was out. Certain that if the little band made for Jerusalem, it meant the inevitable end, yet he leaped to his feet. *"Let us also go,"* he said, *"that we might die with Him."* He did not stand to it, alas! But there spoke the real man. So here. With no such hope as the others had to encourage him, Thomas stood fast by the lost cause, for so it seemed to him; waited to go down with the sinking ship. For days on end nothing further happened and with that, no doubt, the man grew more and more confirmed in his rejection of the wild rumors. Till suddenly Christ again appeared and accepted His disciple's challenge.

"Put your finger here and see my hands; and put out your hand and place it in my side; do not be faithless but believing."

Often Christ acts so to people, blowing their truculent doubts into thin air; shutting them up into belief by the facts of their own experiences; facts there, unanswerable and indisputable. In one real sense only thus does a person believe at all. Only when the Gospel of Christ is for us no carried story, no rumor heard, but first-hand evidence, what we have seen, and what we have looked upon with our own eyes, what we have handled with our own hands, what we have proved in our own experiences, not simply an unthinking agreement in what others say, which may be all very well as a beginning, but something that has happened to us—only then does our belief grow vital.

Yet Christ tells us here that there is a bigger faith than that, a faith that can dispense with tangible proofs and visible evidence, which believes heroically even when there is no obvious and immediate confirmation building unafraid and confident on God's naked Word.

No prayer is so real a prayer as that which seems to ourselves no prayer at all, so cold and dry and lifeless are our hearts, so full and wingless our words. And the saints are sure that the most heroic of believers are not those who are swept on happily and without effort by a gale of the spirit in their souls, visibly making progress, but one who like Christ Himself on the cross can believe on undauntedly in the utter darkness, and when all seems lost. It is easy to be faithful when set in a sphere where there is much to encourage one—crowded pews, and a buzzing of pleased excitement, and souls being saved. But consider the one in loneliness, the one who labors with so little results—consider Christ Himself who died without one soul that really and completely understood—consider how He looks understandingly at such tried folk and smiles encouragement to them, *"Blessed are those who have not seen and yet believe."*

Thomas may have been slow in starting, but at a bound he leaped ahead of all the rest and reached full truth. *"My Lord and my God!"* a saying which as this Gospel was originally planned, was its apex and climax and culmination and end. Here was a man who had seen Jesus as He really was—the Christ, the Son of God. Through Him, he had learned to know God as God is, arguing from the Christ to him, sure that if Christ's life was one uninterrupted unselfishness, and His character a purity and grace which spent itself ungrudgingly for others, so must God live, so must God be. And seeing that, life grew another thing for Thomas. New standards for it thrust themselves upon him. New possibilities leaped into view and offered themselves to him. With such a Savior representing such a God, the old way of things would no longer do. Thomas was being fashioned into a new type of being, was henceforth a new creature, living in a new world, endowed in Christ with quite new possibilities and powers.

And that, says the Evangelist as he lays down his pen—is what I have written my book to prove that Christ can do for anyone who will accept it from Him.

Then something sacred whispers from the skies
Then something deathless looks from dying eyes

Give thanks, O heart, for the high souls
That point us to the deathless goals.
(*Anonymous*)

From Tomb to Triumph
Isaiah 53:1-12 Luke 23-24

April 9, 1950
Lay Memorial Methodist Church
Feeding Hills, Massachusetts

*O*ne of the deepest experiences that comes to a man and woman is that moment of committing one's beloved dead— committing the bodily remains of a dear one to the gentle arms of Mother Earth and commending the soul to the encompassing care of God. And about the world, this experience is another token of the sameness of humanity apart from color and cultural background; for wherever we travel in the shrinking planet, we come upon the tombs wherein man has laid his dead so that in days to come the hallowed place is marked, and time and again, one can stand at the spot of commitment.

Tombs stand forth as earth's most famous pilgrimage. We travel to Washington, but our visit there is not complete until we take the delightful river ride down the broad Potomac to Mount Vernon. And there are the relics and the possessions of him who guided the nation in its first unsteady days of walking upon newly-found legs. There we stand before the tomb and know that therein is all that earth now holds of the great Father of his country.

Beyond the Rio Grande in the multi-colored mesas of New Mexico, the weathered ruins of ancient Puye stand where a thousand years ago the cliff-dwellers abandoned the great cliff but left behind the dead of many generations there on the crest overlooking the river.

In the heart of the mountains of Peru, are the great stones which remain from the mighty terraces and giant stairways that climb up the mountain side to the summit where the Sun-temple was and behind the temple the burial place of the Sun-worshipers. And all that remains of this dead culture is there.

In the land of lakes and lotus, the Emperor of Japan would yearly make the pilgrimage to Nara, the most ancient capital—and there the emperor, his ministers and councilors would worship at the graves of their imperial ancestors, for there they lie buried.

And in Delhi in the hills of India stands the Taj Mahal, the most beautiful tomb humanity's hand has ever reared. And there in that shrine which stands forth as one of the most memorable buildings of earth are the remains of the beloved dead in whose memory the tomb was wrought.

And the millions of Buddhists turn to their most sacred spot, the great bell-shaped temple of Ceylon where they believe rests the dust of the heart of The Buddha.

In the land of the great river, after these thousands of years of change, still stand the majestic pyramids—reminders of the ancient Thebes of the Hundred Gates that once ruled the world. The pyramids stand as the gigantic tombs of the mighty men of Egypt, the tombs of the dead.

Over to Rome, along the Appian Way stand the crumbling remains of marble memorials that tell us that along the broad avenue leading out of the gate of Rome were placed the bodies of the generals and the Caesars of the long-time ruler of the world.

Venerable Westminster Abbey stands in England, shrine of all travelers. For there they touch upon the greatness of the past. There the warriors, benefactors, painters, singers, poets, statesmen, and missionaries of Britain lie buried.

So around the world we go, mindful that along our steps there lingers the memory of those who have lived and left the living, those who are our honored dead.

And we turn on this Easter Day to the tomb wherein was laid the Hope of the World, the tomb in a private garden of a leading Jewish citizen who secretly followed Jesus and who openly asked for His body after the cruel work of the crucifixion was wrought upon it severely so as to kill the precious spark of life. And there Joseph took the body of Jesus and entombed it. But the Sabbath drew near, and the good Jewish people left the body there to keep the religious day that was upon the land, the day of rest through which the Lord Jesus lay dead in His borrowed tomb. Over that tomb there was not an inscription, only the seal of mighty Rome to assure that no one would break in and steal this body and spread abroad the gossip that He had risen as He said.

But the new dawn broke over the land, a dawn fresh with the sweet glory of spring. The birds were singing, and the lilies were fragrant—and the women came to the tomb upon which was no inscription—only the proclamation, but a proclamation of a word that no one had before heard:

"He is not here! He is risen!"

Not here! And yet in every land across the earth are the tombs of the dead; but in this tomb in Joseph's garden there is life, a new and vast conception of life that stands unconquerable over the wastes of time—an eternal life that has become the imperishable hope of humanity! For over the tomb, over its finality, there had come a higher law than nature's death, a law of life proclaimed by the Father God for His beloved humanity. For in the tomb, there was not death, but triumph!

Wherein arises this triumph of Jesus of Nazareth; wherein does He conquer humanity's last enemy? There is the triumph of the Garden of Gethsemane where He knelt alone to pray; and through the lonely hours He prayed in agony.

> *Into the woods my Master went*
> *Clean forspent, forspent*
> *Into the woods my Master came*
> *Forspent with love and shame*
> *But the olvies they were not blind to Him*
> *The little gray leaves were kind to Him*
> *The thorn-tree had a mind to Him,*
> *When into the woods He came.*

And there in the Garden of Prayer, I believe our Lord Jesus faced a severe decision. He knew that danger was all around, and He could choose to give up this profession of His, to throw it aside, to steal out of the garden, back into the north country home. Or He could stay, He could face the humiliation, the torture, death itself, and by facing it maintain His loyalty to His vocation which made it imperative for Him to constantly proclaim the Kingdom of God. It was a hard decision for a man to face; to choose between life and disloyalty or death and abiding faith for His work. There in the garden, through the lonely hours He faced the choice; and He triumphed!

Out of the woods My Master went,
And He was well content;
Out of the woods my Master came,
Content with death and shame.
When death and shame would woo Him last,
From under the trees they drew Him last,
'Twas on as tree they slew Him last,
When out of the woods He came.
("Into the Woods" by Sidney Lanier-this verse and above)

Then there was the triumph of the Cross—there came the historic necessity for Jesus of Nazareth to die; but as His vocation for life lay in the proclaiming of God's kingdom, so through this death upon a cruel cross, He continues to proclaim that message. So the message has reached around the earth in space and down through the long centuries of time.

Upon the cross, we do not witness a conquered Christ: His greatness emerges as He looks at His executioners and forgives them for their trespasses. His greatness emerges as He loses hold of the Body's breath and commits the Soul unto God, the glory from whence it came. His greatness is witnessed in the very word of the centurion who was there in charge of the grim proceedings, "Truly this was the Son of God."

And there comes of triumph of the Tomb—a miracle beyond the understanding of humanity; for it is not given to us to know all things. We do know this; that from an ugly bulb, a bulb that has all the cold appearance of death, there can come forth the beauty and the fragrance of the Easter lily. We do know that from the crawling caterpillar there emerges the gorgeous butterfly. We do know that out of death, there came everlasting life. This is the witness to all the centuries of humanity from those who went first to the tomb and from those who felt the spirit of Christ Jesus upon them on that memorable day.

And the message of the Triumph—what does it hold for us on this Easter Day? And there comes the promise: the victory of the true, the beautiful, the good, over the false and ugly and evil; the victory of light over darkness, of life over death, of love over the world's hatred.

"I am the light of the world," He said; and He lives to prove that *"the light shineth in the darkness and the darkness has not overcome it."*

How do you know that Christ is risen? Someone one day asked an old fisherman whose faith in Jesus seemed very simple and sure. "Do you see those cottages near the cliff?" he replied. "Well, sometimes when I am far out at sea, I know that the sun is risen by the reflection in those windows. How do I know that Christ is risen? Because I see His light reflected from the faces of my fellowmen every day, and because I feel the light of His glory in my own life."

"I am the Resurrection and the Life," He said. *"I am come that ye might have life and that ye might have it more abundantly."*

And He lives to reveal the way of that life, a spiritual life that shall endure in its unhampered glory when this body of time and space dimensions shall fall away.

> *All that is, at all.*
> *Last ever, past recall.*
> *Earth changes, but thy soul and God stand sure.*
> *What entered into thee,*
> *That was, is, and shall be.*
> *Time's wheel runs back of stops;*
> *Potter and clay endure.*
> *(Rabbi Ben Ezra)*

A child riding on a train was mesmerized by the journey. He exclaimed, "Someone just put bridges for us all the way!"

> *Lives again our glorious King: Alleluia!*
> *Where, O death, is now thy sting?*
> *(Charles Wesley)*

"God so loved the world that He gave His only begotten Son that whosoever believeth in Him should not perish but have everlasting life." This is the heart of the gospel of Christianity. And the Son so loved: *"Greater love hath no man than this, that a man lay down his life for his friends. Ye are my friends."*

And He went to His cross of death, and He was laid in His tomb tenderly by those who loved Him, but who were helpless to save Him, and He rose again from the dead to proclaim to all the world the victory of God the Father over the powers of death and darkness, the victory of love over hate.

Edwin Markham stood on the shores of Maine talking to a native fisherman who told the poet of his love for the changing sea, how he looked upon the sea as his earlier hero; but then he pointed to the huge black rocks that jutted out into the wild seas. "These," he said, "are my real heroes. See how strong they are and how fearless. No matter how mightily the waves pound them, those rocks stand firm! I used to favor the sea, it was my first love. But now I favor these rocks. Water can all evaporate, but these rocks will stand forever!"

And the poet stood thoughtful for a moment before he replied, "But the rocks, too will crumble away in time. However, there is something that will stand for all time,"

"What is that, Mr. Poet?" asked the fisherman.

"Love!" Edwin Markham replied.

Forget it not till the crowns are crumbled
And the swords of the Kings are rent with rust
Forget it not till the hills lie humbled
And the springs of the seas run dust.
(Edwin Markham)

And so abideth light and life, and love. And our Lord Jesus stands forth as triumphant witness to their victory.

O Saul, it shall be
A Face like my face that receives thee;
A Man like to me,
Thou shalt love and be loved forever;
A Hand like this hand
Shall throw open the gates of new life to thee!
See the Christ stand!
(Robert Browning)

So do we see Him who is our Lord stand triumphant on Easter Day. Our hearts and voices can do no other than join in the mighty chorus of the ages of Christendom:

> *Hallelujah! For the Lord God omnipotent reigneth*
> *King of King, and Lord of Lords!*
> *(Hallelujah Chorus from Handel's Messiah)*

Earth's Darkness Turns to Day!
John 20:1-18

April 6, 1958
First Methodist Church, Rochester, Pennsylvania

"Lead me," says an undaunted thinker in the *Upanishads*, "to the other side of darkness," and with that fearlessly plunges into it, sure that there is another side where light is shining, and sure too that it can be reached. There has been darkness in plenty in the telling of the life and passion of our Lord. But in these final chapters we have left all that behind and have emerged into the clear shining beyond. For here begins the wonderful story of the triumph of Jesus Christ, the Son of God. Not even the Old Testament has tales at once more simple in their telling and more vivid and moving and heart gripping than the records of the appearances of the risen Lord. And what is more, these stories are the climax of the gospel—without them, indeed, there would have been small gospel; no shout of good news but only the setting forth of a gallant enterprise that had failed; the story of a heroic soul, who, risking everything for humanity, went down and perished. And of God, throwing in all God had—all God's all—against the powers of sin and evil, but in vain. It was Christ's resurrection that made the Christian church, that transformed a huddle of dispirited and frightened people into that valiant band ready to dare anything and doing it; that brought into being and set in motion this mighty force which has been told to nearly the whole world and changed the face of humanity.

The Eastern Church is accustomed to gather about the manger, feeling the Incarnation to be central; and the Western Church lingers upon Calvary, taking the Cross as its symbol and finding in God's sacrifice for us in Christ its chief inspiration and compulsion. But the New Testament keeps exulting first of all, most of all, last of all, in the empty grave, finding in that the proof of Jesus's victory, that God is really over all, and that evil and sin, impregnable and ineradicable though they seem, are beaten and doomed. If we do not press on there, that is at best to believe a gallant tale that may indeed shame us somewhat out of what we are, and even be able to constrain us toward better things, but it is not the gospel of our Lord and Savior Jesus Christ.

It is a memorable fact that the first person to see the risen Christ was a woman who, so our tradition has it, He had plucked back from a life of open, ugly shame. Of her He had said that she loved much because she had been forgiven much. And she gave love and reverence to the Christ Who had saved her with her whole soul and being. It was like her to be at the garden while it was still dark. Apparently, she was not alone, but had some other women with her—though not, it would seem, Christ's mother. The foretold sword had pierced her heart, and she, poor soul, was too stricken, it seems to be there—but her sister was there, and certain other women.

It was a gracious office on which they were bent—for of necessity our Lord's burial had been hurried and in some ways makeshift. Joseph of Arimathea and Nicodemus had done all that time had permitted. But the women now purposed to do what was customary, and to do it in a more thorough and seemly fashion.

John in this gospel mentions only Mary Magdalene as being at the tomb—but he lets slip that others had been with her, in the cry of dismay which the panting woman gasped out, *"They have taken the Lord out of the tomb, and we do not know where they had laid Him."*

These kindly hearts had risen early and gone out to the garden while it was still dark, discussing as they went what they would do about the great boulder that lay at the mouth of the sepulcher. Arriving before day had broken, they discovered that the stone had been moved aside, saw with dismay that the tomb was open and that Christ's body was gone! Their fears confirmed, Salome, it would seem, went home, possibly to break the news of this fresh calamity to her sister Mary, the mother of Jesus, while Mary Magdalene ran in haste to tell the leaders of the little band of broken men who had been Christ's disciples of this new outrage committed against their friend.

Apparently Peter had rallied, had found his nerve again, and unlike unhappy Judas, would not allow himself to be exiled from Christ and Christ's friends by his own failure, but had pushed back among them, declaring that in spite of the dreadful failure of that night, he was still Christ's man and would prove it. There is a lesson for us all in that—and we had better take it. The past is past, sadly mishandled by us. And it will not come again. But we have still the present and the future, and can use them for Christ's glory!

At a crisis, people fall naturally into their proper places. There are some who take the lead and some who follow. Characteristically, it was Peter who took the initiative. The moment he heard the news, he was up and running hard. The other disciple followed suit and being probably a younger man, outpaced him, and arriving first, stooped and stood gazing in. But Peter, when he came, at once entered, and looking about him saw what suggested surely the most majestic scene in human history.

There are those who are incredulous of the resurrection of our Lord. The whole idea simply bounces off their minds. For them, it just cannot be true. But to those who can and do believe in it, there is something indescribably impressive in the very simplicity of these verses:

He saw the linen cloths lying, and the napkin, which had been about His head, not lying with the linen cloths but rolled up in a place by itself.

Isaac Watts in his mighty hymn goes some way to put into words part of the feeling which that awakens in us:

Wrapt in the silence of the tomb
The great Redeemer lay;
Till the revolving skies had brought
The third, the appointed day.

Hell and grave combined their force
To hold our Lord, in vain.
Sudden the Conqueror arose,
And burst their feeble chain.

But there was nothing sudden in what followed. Unhurriedly He discarded the useless grave clothes, folded the napkin that had been about His head and laid it by itself apart. There is something that grips at the mind in that; in the orderly simplicity of it by such a one at such an hour. He had died for a world of sinful humans. He had faced and overcome the powers of hell that could not hold him. Yet this is the first action of the risen Lord! May He help us to bring our religion also into touch with the little nothings which make up our lives, that we may learn to carry them through with something of His quietness and orderliness and thoroughness, devoting them also, not less than the great sacrifices which are asked of us, to the glory of God. So Dora Greenwell writes,

> *The Christian ideal alone meets the habitual., the practical, meets it while immeasurably transcending it—embraces it, and walks hand in hand. The Christian must be friends with every day, with its narrow details, its homely atmosphere; its loving correction must make him great. Is there not the very life-core of Christianity in this picture—the broken tomb and the risen Christ, the angles in their shining garments, the linen clothes folded and laid in a place by themselves?*

Mary Magdalene had returned to the garden. She could not stay away from it; kept searching here and there, not knowing where to search, yet unable to desist from it. And by and by, she came back to the tomb and peeped in once again, with some idea in her mind no doubt that the whole thing was impossible, must be only a hideous dream. And it was then that she had her vision. Sensing that someone was behind her—she turned, and perhaps without looking closely, simply assuming it was the gardener, broke out,

> *"Sir, if you have carried Him away, tell me where you have laid Him, and I will take Him away."*
> *Jesus said to her, "Mary."*
> *She turned and said to Him, "Rabboni,"which means Teacher.*

We must realize this in our own searching. First, because Mary was seeking for a dead Christ, she could not find Him. For He was not dead, but alive. And many keep making that same mistake. The Christ they know lived in Palestine 2000 years ago. The record of what He did and taught and suffered moves and impresses them. In thought they often take their stand on Calvary with a very real emotion in their hearts and a new inspiration surging up in them. But they have no experience of the risen Lord, do not walk with Him day by day. And that means that their faith, genuine enough and really effective so far as it goes, is something greatly less than Christianity.

R.W. Dale of Birmingham, England, was well on in life and a distinguished leader in the church when one day, writing an Easter sermon, the thought of the risen Lord broke in upon him as it had never done before.

> *"Christ is alive," I said to myself; alive! and then I paused—"alive!" and then I paused again. Alive! Can that really be true? Living as "really as I myself am? I got up and walked about repeating, "Christ is living! Christ is living!"It was to me a new discovery. I thought all along that I had believed it; but not until that moment did I feel sure about it. I then said, "My people shall know it; I shall preach about it again and again until they believe it as I do now." Then began the custom of singing in Carr's Lane on every Sunday morning an Easter Hymn.*

Then too, for all her searching, it was not Mary Magdalene who came on Christ, but Christ Who found her. That is the usual experience. So Paul pulls himself up to correct himself, and to state things more accurately. That is the whole point of the gospel—that God is seeking us, not only when we have lost Him and cannot come on the way home to Him again, search how we may, but even when we are alienated from Him and do not miss Him, when we are impudently and deliberately rebellious and set upon our unworthy ways. Even the wonderful story of the prodigal son is much less than the whole gospel. For after all, the wayward boy bethought himself and repented, and came home hesitantly, and by no means sure of his reception; still he turned home and reached it. After all, the sheep caught in the thicket bleated out and let them know its whereabouts, though the shepherd did all the rest and effected its rescue. But the little piece of silver dropped and could do nothing for itself at all. Yet groping hands were seeking for it, drawing nearer and still nearer till they fell on it at last. If you have lost Christ, if your spiritual life has dimmed, and become thin and drab and meager, you can be sure that He is searching for you—for He will not lightly let you go—has missed you, wants you back with Him again. And, says the scripture confidently, *"He seeks until He finds."*

Although she was seeking Him with her whole being, Mary did not recognize Christ when she saw Him. That was not altogether her fault. For apparently the risen Christ was different in some ways from the Jesus she had known. Nor were the accounts of Him given by those who had talked with Him always consistent. He appeared to them in another form, we read. Mary, face to face with Christ, failed to recognize Him. Supposing Him to be the gardener...So it often is in life—with all of us. Sometimes sullenly, sometimes bravely, we accept some wounding providence—yet God is in it and has come quite close to us, is calling us to do some service for God; and with God's own hands is fashioning us into the instrument God needs for some lofty end. But our eyes are blinded and we do not see God. Francis of Assisi was terrified of leprosy. One day, full in the narrow path that he was traveling, he saw horribly white in the sunshine, a leper. Instinctively his heart shrank back, recoiling shudderingly from the contamination of that loathsome disease. But then he rallied; and ashamed of himself, ran and cast his arms about the sufferer's neck and kissed him and passed on. A moment later, he looked back and there was no one there, only the empty road in the hot sunlight. All his days thereafter he was sure is was no leper but Christ Himself whom he had met. So often all that we see is some needy and perhaps not attractive soul; someone who does not appeal to us, but who lacks friendship, claims assistance. *"Did you not recognize Me?"* says the Master. *"That was I. And inasmuch as you do it to the very least of these my brethren, you do it to me."* Supposing Him to be the gardener—how very blind we are!

So this is Christ's message to his followers after their sorry flight and ugly failure! Here there is no word of condemnation nor reproach. But stepping across the wide gulf of their shame that had opened between Him and them, our Lord begins again on the old friendly and trustful terms, even draws nearer to them than ever. In the upper room He had told them, *"Henceforth I call you not servants—I have called you friends."* But here He takes a further step and speaks to them and to them as, *"my brethren."* Now that indeed was not altogether new. Once when a man interrupted Him to tell Him that His mother and brothers were out on the edge of the crowd asking for Him, He stretched out His hand to His disciples and said, *"Here are My mother and My brothers! For whoever does the will of My Father in heaven is My brother, and sister, and mother."*

But these men of whom He was thinking now had not done the will of God, but had lamentably failed. Yet He will not lose faith in them, nor His affection for them. So true is it as the writer to the Hebrews tells us, that He is not ashamed to call us brothers, as He well might be. For as John Tillotson put it long ago, "We have no cause to be ashamed of the gospel of Christ, but the gospel of Christ may justly be ashamed of us."

Nonetheless, Christ is not. Such is His loyalty even to the most undeserving of us as we limp back out of the sad mess we have made of things, unkempt and ragged creatures, with no case, and not a shadow of excuse. The Lord never disowns us, does not look the other way from us, but comes out eagerly to meet us, letting us see the difference our coming makes to Him. It is all very wonderful and sounds impossible. And yet, experience proves it true. For says Paul in Romans, *"God never goes back upon His gifts and call."*

So Christ says, *"Go to my brethren and say to them, I am ascending to My Father and your Father, to My God and your God."*

What Christ tells us about God is true not only of God's attitude toward Him, but of God's attitude toward us. It is not surprising that God should be loving and gracious to Him Who is loveable and pure and like God. But how can God be all that to us who are none of these things; who indeed must surely be repulsive to the clean Eyes of the holy God? That was a real perplexity to Paul. He knew that is was so. He walked with gladness in the sunshine of it. But how could it be? God being what God is, we being what we are, was a moral enigma to him; and he could find an explanation of it only in the one direction where an explanation can be found. As the prophet told us long ago, *"God's ways are not as our ways, not His thoughts as our thoughts, but rather as the heaven is high above the earth, so great is His mercy toward them that fear Him"*—even if and when they make a sorry mess of their blundering endeavors.

All of which Mary Magdalene reported to the disciples, and was met, as was natural so Luke tells us, with the blankest incredulity and open disbelief. But these words seemed to them an idle tale, and they did not believe them... Though some ancient authorities declare that Peter, and he apparently alone, thought or half thought there might just possibly be something in it, thought it at least worth testing, and ran to the tomb to see. *That* moves one. For if Christ were alive,

Peter must tell Him how much he repented of his cowardice and treason.

And so, he ran…

Eastertide

(Parsonage lilacs, Urbana, Ohio)

"And He said unto them, 'It is not for you to know the times of the seasons, which the Father hath put in His own power. But ye shall receive power after that the Holy Ghost is come upon you: and ye shall be witnesses unto Me both in Jerusalem, and in all Judea, and in Samaria, and unto the uttermost part of the earth.'"
Acts: 1:7-8

More than Memory
Job 10: 1, 23-24; 1st Corinthians 15: 12-22

April 2, 1967
First Methodist Church, Sidney, Ohio

*T*wo men walked despondently along a lonely road. They had been to the city to celebrate an important holiday, which they had hoped would be marked by an important announcement about the future of their nation. Instead, the Leader whom they had trusted would declare Himself, had been arrested, tried, sentenced, and put to death. He was immediately buried and His grave guarded by soldiers lest His friends spirit away the body and use it in some way as a rallying point for revolution.

They were dejected men who trudged toward home that evening. They discussed their false hopes. Had not their leader talked about the kingdom of God being at hand? Had He not urged them and others to seek the kingdom, to be ready for it, to enter it? Why did He fail them? Why did He not accept the offers of those willing to back Him up with arms? Why did He not call upon God for help? Why did He let them crucify Him—Why, why, why?

On they walked. Their feet and faces soiled with dust; their spirits soiled with disappointment. As they walked, a stranger fell into step with them. "What is this you are talking about so sadly?" He inquired.

"You don't know what has happened in Jerusalem?" one asked. "Then you must be the only visitor to the city who hasn't heard."

Straightaway they explained to Him that Jesus of Nazareth, Who in the eyes of God and many people was a great prophet, and Who they hoped was the promised restorer of Israel, had been put to death as a common criminal three days before. And now His body had been reported missing from the tomb.

Then the stranger conversed with them about the scriptures and their hopes—would that we knew in some detail what He said! Perhaps He explained that Israel could not be delivered by force or even by miracle; that the only deliverance which really matters is deliverance from false ideas, aims, and hopes; that a change of mind and heart is more important than a change of government and rulers.

Maybe He explained to them that the leader who could bring that kind of deliverance is not an earthly king, but a servant of God who would obey God and stand by God's ideals and God's friends, even if it meant death on a cross. And no doubt He tried to impress upon them that such a leader, one who obeys God rather than humans, cannot really be put to death on a cross—or in any other way.

They reached their destination. The Stranger was intent upon going on, but with true Oriental hospitality they urged Him to remain with them. So it happened that, when they asked their guest to break bread and bless the food, they recognized Him by the familiar way in which He held the loaf and thanked God. The Stranger Who had walked by their side on the road, Who sat at meal with them in their home was Jesus.

He had kept His promise. After a little while, they had seen Him again. He was no longer confined to a physical body so that He could be in just one place at a time, limited by the same factors which limit humans. He was more than a memory.

He was a Living Presence!

Christianity centers in the faith that *"God raised Jesus Christ from the dead,"* and gave Him back to the Church as a Living Lord. There is no reason to doubt the fact of His resurrection. Without it, there would have been no Christian Church. When Christ was crucified, faith fled from the disciples and they were all as despondent as the two who walked along the road that afternoon. Then something happened; they emerged with a faith that was great enough to enable them to meet persecution and death. They built a Church which endured persecution and which has grown to encircle the earth. They started a movement which had largely changed— and is further changing—the moral climate of the world.

The early Christians knew that God did not allow Jesus—the perfectly obedient Servant and Son—to be defeated by a few spikes driven into His hands and feet. As a broken bottle allows the fragrance of the perfume it contains to fill the room, so His broken body released His real personality as a spiritual presence in the world. Within a few days of the crucifixion, His followers were sure that He was with them, directing them, comforting them, adding meaning to their lives. His followers in ages since have shared in this experience.

So Easter gives to us Christ as an eternal presence as so much more and richer in meaning for us than memory. The spiritually aware see Him and are glad He is with us always, even unto the end.

That gives meaning to human life. An Oriental king once asked his wise men to prepare for him the history of the world so that, knowing what had been, he might better rule in the future. After twenty years, they returned with many scrolls. In these scrolls they had recorded the rise and fall of nations, the inventions and discoveries of humanity, the history of the world. "But I can never read all of that," said the king. "Go back to your libraries and reduce it to one book."

After another score of years they returned, bearing one large scroll. But the king was old, his hands too feeble to hold the scroll, his eyes too dim to read it.

"Must I die then," he asked, "without knowing the history of the world?"

One scholar said, "Sir, I will summarize it for you. This is the history of mankind: they were born, they suffered, they died."

Of course, that historian was wrong. There is more to human life than suffering. There is joy aplenty for those who earn it and know where it is to be found. The Eternal Presence of Christ reveals that joy comes in service when we are engaged in creative helpful activity.

Joy is the wine that God is ever pouring
Into the hearts of those who strive with Him.
(Oswald Chambers)

But even suffering has meaning when we meet it not alone, but with the Eternal Presence of Christ. *The Book of Wisdom* in the *Apocrypha* asserts that the souls of the righteous are in the hand of God...and while in the sight of humans they seem to suffer, yet is their hope full of immortality, for God proved them and found them worthy of God. Jesus put it in even clearer words, *"Whom the Lord loveth, He chasteneth."* He pointed out that as a farmer prunes and trims his vines that they might bear much fruit, so God prunes us to make us better persons.

Suffering is meaningless—as is joy and every other experience of life—if we are unaware of the Presence of Christ. But Christ walks with us through life, Christ is with us always.

What is the meaning of the world's history? Is the human enterprise just one great spinning flywheel on which we just go along for the ride? A few years ago we believed in the inevitable progress of history toward a better society. All we had to do was wait. Then came two world wars, depression, inflation, revolution, godless persecution. Demonic forces were unleashed upon the world, the last of which was the atomic bomb. Will history now come out only as destruction—the earth a rubble of ashes? Now it is all so futile; all we can do it wait for the end. But is it?

The clue to history is in Christ crucified and resurrected. In His resurrection we have the pledge of final victory over all evil. It has already been won, that victory, in His conquest of the powers of evil. The empty tomb is God's promise that *"though the wrong be oft so strong, God is the ruler yet." (Malthie D. Babcock)*

John S. Whale tells the story of a musician who, on hearing "one perfectly convincing phrase" in one of Beethoven's symphonies said, "Of course, if that is so there is no occasion for worry." We Christians have the same confidence when we hear the perfectly convincing chord of Christ crucified and resurrected. There is no need to worry. Everything will come out right.

The Eternal Christ gives meaning to our life on earth. Christ still walks on earth with all who are aware of Him. Christ lays upon us responsibility in bringing to completion the conquest of evil.

A contemporary author points out two events that took place in Rochester, New York in the middle of the 19th century. One night in 1844, a group of people were sitting on Cobb's Hill near Rochester, arrayed in white robes and little else. The night was cool and damp and many of them caught cold and some of them contracted pneumonia. Why were they here? A leader, named William Miller, had promised that Christ would come to earth for the second time that night, and his followers were there waiting. At about that same time there were other people in Rochester who believed in Christ and in the future. But instead of going out to Cobb's Hill, they founded a university on Christian principles. That university continues to be a force for good. Which of the two interpreted the will of God?

The Eternal Presence of Christ in history makes us feel personally responsible for the future. The politically minded person says, "There ought to be a law." The Christian says, "I ought to be a better person." It is easy to ask, "Why doesn't God do something?

132

Why doesn't the government do something?" It is the Christian to say, "I must do something!" Changed people are more important than a change of politics or of leadership.

The little we can do may seem small. But it will not be futile, since the Eternal Christ is with us, and He has already secured the outcome of the struggle with evil.

The last thing about the Eternal Presence is that the Presence gives meaning to the experience of death. Our assurance is that Christ brought life and immortality to light through the gospel. What people believed dimly, He showed clearly. Once people thought of the afterlife in terms of a shadowy existence, drab continuation, half-life. By His resurrection He brought to light the fact that immortality is a bright experience in the nature and love of God. Some people have believed that after death the soul merges with all other souls in a vast ocean of forgetfulness. The Greeks thought of the immortality of the soul. By His resurrection Jesus brought to light the individual continuation of each person. In Christianity the key word is not immortality but resurrection—the re-establishment of personal life on the farther side of the grave, the conviction that the total personality, invested by God with an appropriate body, lives on in the presence of the Father.

Our understanding of the resurrection of the body must not be in coarse, materialistic terms. We do not mean by it the renewal of this same body of flesh and blood. Let us admit that it is but a tool to serve us for a few years here, a house given us for occupation between birth and the birth into eternity. It is subject to ills, to decay, and to death. But as the body is part of our personality here, so we must think of some kind of organism to be used by our spirits in the life to come. St. Paul said that the body is buried as a physical body and raised as a spiritual body. In an even finer passage he asserts that *"if this earthly house our body—is dissolved, we have a dwelling of God, a house not made with hands, eternal in the heavens." (2nd Corinthians 5: 1).*

Strangely enough, it is the new science which enables us to begin to grasp the meaning of these assertions made so long ago. If it is true that material substance is in reality an arrangement of electrical energy in certain patterns, and if energy cannot be destroyed but only transmuted into other forms, then why can we not believe in the experience we call resurrection? If Christ is raised from the dead and is an Eternal Presence walking with us along life's road, why need we fear anything that is beyond?

So the story comes to the beginning again: Two men are walking along the road. They are overtaken by a third—the Eternal Presence—Who walks with them. Suppose you are standing by the roadside. You see them approaching. They pass you. They walk on until they get to a bend in the road. Then you see them no more. Does that mean they are no more? Of course not; the two travelers are going on, the Eternal Presence of Christ still by their side. They are just out of sight.

I think of a line from one of the most beautiful of prayer, written by James Martineau:

> *Death is only a horizon, and a horizon is nothing save the limit of our sight. Beyond the horizon as here, we are in the Eternal Presence of Christ.*

Do you know the name of Lord Robert Baden-Powell, the founder of the world scout movement? They tell us that the grave marker on Baden-Powell's last resting place is a small stone with his name, the dates of his birth and death, and a scout sign—a circle with a dot in the center, which means, "Gone home." That is an authentic Christian insight about those who are around the bend in the road.

"Lo, I am with you always, even unto the end."

> *So I go on not knowing,*
> *I would not if I could,*
> *I'd rather walk with Christ in the dark,*
> *Than walk alone in the light.*
> *Phillip B. Bliss*

Ah, but when you walk with Christ, it is light!

Of Spring—and Life—and God!
Psalm 65

April 13, 1946
Winona Methodist Church, Winona, Ohio

I like April!

I like April because it is the time of unfolding spring, the time of the bursting forth of life in the natural world about us, the time when Easter's revelation of eternity becomes realistic in the new life of nature.

The Psalmist agrees and cries forth his gratitude:

> *Praise waiteth for Thee, O God, in Zion,*
> *Thou visitest the earth and waterest it;*
> *Thou greatly enrichedst it with the river of God which is full of water.*
> *Thou waterest the ridges thereof abundantly;*
> *Thou settlest the furrows thereof;*
> *Thou makest it soft with showers;*
> *Thou blesses the springing thereof.*
> *(Psalm 65)*

And Chaucer, in his *Canterbury Tales,* chooses the setting of this month:

> *When April with its blossom-scented rain has vanquished March and*
> *quickened earth again...*
> *Till every blod is bursting with the power that kindles life...*

Then he sets his little party of assorted people off on their pilgrimage to Canterbury—on a religious journey to the shrine of Thomas A. Becket.

His refrain runs through April's reality of new life:

> *Every blod is bursting with the power that kindles life...*

Spring is a time of crusading, a time of the up-surging of emotions, a time of a world reborn! A time when God's love is revealed in full flower!

A man named John wrote words that to me become significant in springtime:

> *"Behold, the tabernacle of God is with men and He will dwell with them, and they shall be His people, and God himself shall be with them and be their God."*
> *(Revelation 21: 3)*

Humanity in this age, as in every age, is crying out, "If there is a God," and April comes each year with one answer—for the goodness and the glory of God are revealed in the unfolding of natural life about us—so much for our benefit here—so much of beauty, too. Not Hindu nor pantheistic—behind it all is a force of order and unity—a power that kindles life—

And we call that God.

April is a time when really we can know God. Moreover, April is a time for singing!

Prayer in April

God grant that I may never be
A scoffer at eternity—
As long as April brings
The sweet rebirth of growing things;
As long as grass is green anew,
I shall believe that God looks down
Upon His wide earth, cold and brown,
To bless His unborn mystery
Of leaf and bud and flower to be;
To smile on it from tender skies—
How could I think otherwise?
Had I been dust for many a year
I still would know when spring was near,
For the good earth that pillowed me
Would whisper immortality,

And I, in part, would rise and sing
Amid the grasses murmuring.
(Sarah Henderson Hay)

So it is that in April the earth is quickened and bursts forth in new life that sings its praises to God the Creator. And as nature sings its praises, we too, a part of nature, ought to sing—to be human clods bursting with the power that kindles life—to sing with lips so that our hearts are made light; to sing with lives so that the world is made right.

For as the unfolding life about us truly reveals the power and the goodness of God, with that revelation there comes a clear call to our own living—to make a genuine contribution through our time and our abilities to the ongoing work of God's world. Spring is a time of crusading—a call to renewed activity—and the opportunities of our activity are about us as we walk down the roadway of humanity. As nature is shared with us, and the beauties and love of God are made known to us through this natural world all about, so, we, too, must be sharing people if we be worthy of our creation. Life's gratitude unto God deepens with our service and sharing with our brethren as we brush shoulders with them and love them. And as nature shares so richly with us, for our benefit and beauty and thus reveals God unto us—so in our human sharing with others, we share the goodness and the love of God. Truly God is our God and we are God's people, and in sharing, others come to know God, too. It's the way of nature when nature is attuned to God—and it's the way of Christ-like living. Perhaps the little story of the flowers told by Gabriela Mistral intensifies this truth for us:

Once upon a time, it was that a lily in a rich man's garden was asking the other flowers about Christ. The lily's master had named Christ while praising a newly opened flower.

A rose of Sharon of vivid purple answered, "Well, I do not know Him, He is perhaps a rustic for I know all prominent men."

"I have never seen Him, either—and no delicate spirit fails to breathe the perfume of my flowers," boasted the jasmine.

"Nor I," said the camellia. "He must be some clownish fellow; I have been worn on the breasts of handsome men and beautiful women."

"But if He were, He would not be like me; and my master was reminded of Him when he looked at me this morning," persisted the lily.

"Then," said the violet, "there is one of us who has certainly seen Him, and that is our poor brother, the thistle. He lives by the roadside and knows everybody who goes by, and salutes them all with his head covered with ashes. Although he is humiliated by the dust, he is sweet since he bears a flower of my color."

"You have said one true thing," answered the lily. "The thistle certainly knows Christ—but you make a mistake when you call him our brother. He has prickles and he is ugly like an evil-doer."

"Brother Thistle, do you know Christ?"

"Yes, He has passed along this road, and I have touched Him—I, a sorry thistle."

"And is it true that He is like me?" asked the lily.

"Only a little, and that is when the moon gives you an air of sadness—you carry your head too high, He carried His a little bent."

"Tell us, Thistle, what are His eyes like?"

The Thistle opened a blue flower.

"What is His breast like?"

The Thistle answered, "He goes with his breast like this," opening a red flower.

"And what does He wear on His head for a wreath in the spring of the year?"

And by way of answering, the thistle held up his thorns.

"And does Christ love? What is His love like?"

"The love of Christ is like this," said the thistle, casting the tiny flowers of his crown to fly upon all the winds.

"I should like to know Him—how could that be, Brother Thistle?"

"'o see him pass, to get a glance of Him, become a wayward flower. He goes continually along the paths without rest. When He passed me, he said, 'Blessed be you because you blossom amid the dust and cheer the fevered glances of the wayfarer.' And He would not tarry in the rich man's garden even for the sake of your fragrance—because as He goes, He scents in the wind another odor—the odor of the wounds of men."

But neither the lily, nor the rose of Sharon, nor the other of the flowers wished to become wayside flowers, and like so many prominent men and women who refused to follow Jesus over the scorching plains of self-sacrifice and service, they remained without knowing Christ. So it often is that one's own little garden of self is far from the dust of the ways of humanity, is comfortable and casual—and people hesitate to leave it to serve Christ—

But as they miss the arduous work of serving Christ, so they miss the glory of knowing Christ, too.

April comes—newness of natural life—eternity of truth, and joy and love.

Just as the song in Jerome Kern's musical *Showboat,* Nature is like "Old man River that jus' keeps rolling along"—and we are a part of it all. But as there are the changes in the flow and level of the water in the river, so there are the highlights in nature—spring stands forth as a time that permits us to glimpse the greatness and the goodness of the Eternal God. For as in spring, it seems that all nature stands with happy and hearty praise before God, when earth unfolds in new life, so we, too, should sing our praises with our very lives. Often a sadness touches us as we ply our way along the dusty roads of the ways of humanity, but as the little thistle who could help even in so small a measure, so we sing our deepest thanksgiving as we give ourselves to a ministry of love toward humankind—a ministry that is worthy of followers of Christ who loved so deeply that He gave His all.

We should take full advantage of the days that life affords unto us, to cherish the hours, not waste them idly but to expend them in the praise of our sincere service unto God and God's way.

> *Sunup and sundown*
> *And between them the high blue arc of the sky.*
> *And the hours that must be lived*
> *And I the one that must live them*
> *Oh, my heart*
> *Let us do splendidly our part*
> *God has done His...*
> *(Anonymous)*

Missionary Theophane Venard, imprisoned and sentenced to execution for spreading his faith in Vietnam in the nineteenth century, wrote tranquilly to his father from his prison in Hanoi:

> *It is nearly midnight. Around my wooden cell are lancers and long sabers. In one corner of the room, a group of solders is playing cards,*

another group is playing at dice. From time to time sentinels beat on the tom-tom and drum the night watches. Two meters from me, the electric light bulb projects its wavering light toward my sheet of Chinese paper and allows me to scratch these lines. From day to day, I await my sentence. Tomorrow, perhaps, I shall be led to my death. A happy death, is it not? Death which is desired, for it leads to life. An easy sabre blow will remove my head, like a spring flower which the gardener picks for his own pleasure. We are all flowers planted on the earth, flowers which God picks as He wills, some a little sooner, some a little later. One is the purple-stained rose, another the virgin lily, another the humble violet. Let us all, each according to the perfume or brilliance which is given us, seek to find favor with our sovereign Lord and Master.

Eighteen centuries ago, Apollonius responded to the prefect who was questioning him, "I love life, Perennis, but have no fear of death through my love of life. Nothing is more precious than life, except Eternal Life, which assures the immortality of that soul which has lived rightly in the present life."

"Lo, I am with you always!"

Christian Family Life

(Marilee Hartland Lake, Rochester, Pennsylvania)

"Children's children are a crown to the aged,
And parents are the pride of their children."
Proverbs 17: 6

This Business of Happy Living
John 2: 1-13

May 12, 1956
Community Methodist Church, Whitaker, Pennsylvania

Soon we shall be again to June—that proverbial month of marriages. All over this country, and perhaps here in our church, young couples will stand before the altar in hushed silence making the most solemn pledges of their lives. We call it Christian marriage.

There has been a tradition in fairy tales and very often in our modern motion pictures that romance culminates in marriage and that necessarily from that moment on the couple lives happily ever after. Quite often it seems that marriage becomes the end of romance rather than the beginning of it. Yet, if our ideal for marriage is mature and understanding, it may well become the beginning of the most satisfying form of fulfillment that is possible in life.

You will always find those who criticize marriage. Every age has had its critics of marriage, but there is something so basic about it that no one has come up with a better idea.

There have been utopian communities that have tried to abolish marriage. One, in northern New England about a hundred years ago worked out a system where everyone would be brothers and sisters. No one would be married to anyone else, and everyone would be able to live without any of the problems of marriage. When they wanted children in the community, they adopted them, and the children were everyone's children. Yet that community has faded away because it fell short of the ideal that is so important to fulfillment in marriage. It failed to satisfy the basic social, biological, psychological, physical, and spiritual needs of the persons in the community.

In our day there is quite a general agreement that all is not well with marriage. Two million couples walk to the altar or appear before a justice of the peace, and in the same year eight hundred thousand persons are separated by divorce in our courts. They give up and say, "This is not for me." Probably as many more again would like to be separated but are unable to do so because of religious, financial, or other considerations.

There is a book entitled *For Better or Worse* written by a man named Morris Ernst that points out that our legal system is not particularly interested in making marriages work. People with problems and troubles that might well be resolved, doom themselves by becoming involved in irresponsible legal machinery.

Marriage is an adventure with its ups and downs. It requires growth in personality and adjustment. All too often "growing pains" are mistaken for "going pains." Staying power, imagination and belief that problems may be solved, can go a long way toward resolving them. Certainly, dissolution is not the only or the best solution.

Once I read a little book that told what was wrong with the American husband. Of course, it was written by a woman who evidently knew. She claimed that the shortcomings of the American husband can be summed up in one sentence: He fails to give his wife an important place in his life. Then she told why. The average American man has grown up in a country with a pioneer tradition. He likes to think of himself as a he-man who can be at his best when associated with other men. He is embarrassed by the presence of women. His ideas, though not too clearly defined, center about the more masculine traits of producing, controlling, making money, of being efficient and successful. Profits are the important yardstick of his life, and woman are usually not profitable. Too often money and business are first place in importance, and his heart is there rather than in his home. The woman feels excluded, less than a partner, and frankly resentful of the place she is obliged to take in the man's scheme of things.

The book pointed out further that very often men cannot understand women and so feel threatened by them. Though they may surmise that women are more inherently intelligent, they do not dare admit it, and so often turn a deaf ear to their words. One of the most common sentences in American life today, the author said is, "You are not listening to me; you are not paying attention to a thing I have said."

Now all of this undoubtedly grows out of some lack of understanding of the basic nature of marriage. That is probably the reason many women are restless and unhappy. The average man does not know what he is asking when he proposes marriage to a woman. Equally true it is that the average woman does not understand that nature of the life she accepts when she agrees to a marriage.

A survey made by Bryn Mawr College points out that the average farm woman works 68 hours a week in household tasks. The average woman in a small town works 77 hours a week at similar tasks, and her sister in an urban home spends over 80 hours a week at duties about the home.

Probably no man has been honest or realistic enough to get down on his knees and say to a charming young woman, "Would you be willing to work 80 hours a week for me for nothing?" You have heard young women talk about marriage and say something like this, "After you are married, are you just going to keep house or are you going to do something???" Seldom in our talk of careers do we recognize that marriage and homemaking can be an exalted and full-time occupation with its clearly defined tasks and its own rich rewards.

Do some arithmetic, figure out the magnitude of this important career we call homemaking. One husband asked his wife how many times a day she goes up and down stairs. After some figuring it came out like this: Would a young man ask his bride-to-be if she is willing to climb to the top of the Washington Monument 12,000 times? That is about what it would amount to. Would he propose that she wash 150,000 cubic feet of soiled dishes for him? Taken a few at a time they might not be so bad—but at best it is an assignment—as many of you parents know when you try to get the children to do the dishes.

Would our young man ask on his knees, "Are you willing to wash and iron the clothes on a clothes line 47 miles long with two extra miles of specialty items added for each baby?" That's quite a long hike down the clothes line—but it's all a part of the process that is involved in the routine of building a successful home life.

Now and then a husband comes home with a gadget to ease his wife's burdens, but you have to take care of the gadgets, too. You buy a dishwasher to abolish that chore—and wind up having to clean the dishwasher. Oh, a woman these days has to be a genius, an engineer, a pilot, and a mechanic.

One of our sociologists has tried to picture the workday of a wife and mother:

One pair of hands to cook the meals, pack the lunches, bathe the children, lock the door, walk the dog, put out the cat, order the food or shop for it, set the washing machine in motion, send flowers to the sick, bake the birthday cakes, keep the accounts, defrost the refrigerator—and we call this simplified living.

Only one woman's hands to feed the baby, answer the telephone, turn off the gas under the pot that is boiling over, soothe the older child who has had a squabble, and open both doors at once. She is a nutritionist, a child psychologist, an engineer, a production manager, and an expert buyer all in one. Her husband sees her as free to plan her own time and envies her. And she see him as having regular hours and envies him.

So some women are dissatisfied at their position in life. They are not valued for their important careers as homemakers. The man who is absorbed outside of the home thinks the home should support him in his activity away from home. He rather expects his wife to be bright and fresh and cheerful after her 80-hour work week so that she will have plenty of leisure to comfort and soothe her over-worked husband when he comes home from his 40-hour work week in the shop or office.

Perhaps this is an overdrawn picture. I am inclined to think it is in most cases, but there is enough truth there to give us pause. The home at one time found stability in the fact that mother and father worked together to sustain the social unit that satisfied their deepest needs. The father's preoccupation with things outside of the home has subtly changed the function of the home. Now he expects it to support him emotionally while he supports it economically. This places strains on the wife and mother whose emotional resources are limited.

That, of course, gives us the sequel in the attitude of so many women who are persistently dissatisfied with their lot. Their complaints about a multitude of petty concerns may well be a bid for more consideration, but the corrosive effect upon the husband and father destroys his satisfaction, and more and more he is driven to look elsewhere for the things that may satisfy his deeper needs.

The fact remains that there is a failure on the part of many of us to understand the personality needs in this basic cooperative adventure of humans that we call marriage. Within the framework of the home we alone find the conditions that can lead to the satisfaction of our deepest social and spiritual needs. When we record the failures that exist, we must keep the record straight by recognizing the glorious heights of satisfaction and achievement that are attained by many couples. Though they may not be as well publicized, they are the type of success that proves the value of the home and becomes the yardstick by which all others should be measured.

A basic principle is involved. Scientists are always trying to work from the variety to the particular and specific idea that can give unity to their observations. In the world of business, efforts are made to simplify and unify so that more unity may be gained in production and distribution. In marriage one not only tries to understand unity and discover its principles, but also significantly, one tries in the actual process of life to create that unity that can become the deepest source of satisfaction for human souls.

We know very well that true love makes people vulnerable. As the life of the person who is truly in love reaches out beyond him or herself, so he or she can be injured more easily and deeply. This is part of the high adventure. The capacity to do this only accentuates the glory of this capacity for fulfillment through love. A person who never gambles, never loses. The person who has never compromised his or her own individuality through the adventure of love cannot begin to understand the daring faith that the venture involves.

The persons who stand before the altar making sacred vows—for better or worse—should understand that they are pioneering on the frontiers of human experience. Through their commitment to each other they struggle to achieve the maturity of their own souls. When they pledge themselves for "richer or poorer," they admit that their commitment to each other is deeper than economic consideration. Some of the most unhappy people I have known have had the most money, and some of the happiest couples I have known have had little more than each other. Marriage is so much more than money or convenience. When they pledge themselves in sickness and in health, they recognize the physical variables in human experience, and look beyond them to the spiritual factors of this unity they would create.

Sometimes marriage is spoken of as a contract. It is so much more than that. It is a commitment with deep spiritual implications. Even persons who are not religious recognize that. They want to stand before an altar when they make these solemn pledges because they sense that there are places in life where you cannot take your paganism straight. They recognize that marriage, if it is to be sustained, must be built on something much deeper than material values.

Many of the problems that develop in the early years of marriage might be relieved if a plan for simplicity could be developed during the early years of life. If young couples would develop the high art of learning to know and truly possess each other, they would be able to grow into the possession of other things with understanding. But to measure the success of their venture by the number and quality of things they possess creates false standards at the beginning. It is quite generally admitted that the first fifteen years of marriage will be involved in economic and financial strain.

This is the period when people need the resources of a religious faith that can help them to grow into a richer acceptance of themselves and others. Here they can find the fellowship that enriches life without the false standards that so often injure human insights, to help them move beyond selfishness to understanding. Then they can begin to understand that their happiness is not dependent upon the number of things they possess, but upon their ability to truly possess each other.

A sociological survey made in a typical American city of all the cases that came into marriage courts during a given period indicated that, when husband and wife went together to the same church and took their religious life seriously, there was a 600 percent better chance of them keeping out of the marriage courts. That seems like good marriage insurance. This indicates quite clearly that the spiritual undergirding of marriage is important for the achieving of its goals.

The church has a function. If the church can make clear the central place of the home in life, if it can make homemaking the most significant career in our society, persons will enter into it with more understanding and insight. If the church through its ministry can counsel with young couples so that they will be aware of their common goals, they may work toward them more diligently. If in times of stress persons go to their minister rather than to the law courts, they may find the counsel and redefining of goals that can lead to readjustment and reconciliation. Doors may be opened to the understanding of each other's needs that can mean a new and valuable life for their home. Religious faith can help people to have faith in each other.

This idea of living happily ever after does not happen automatically. It is an achievement of the mature self, and between mature selves who build together in loyalty and with deep moral sensitivity, a common life. Through such a life together, they may find the meaning of the nature of God who is love. Through their faith they may grow to heights of religious acceptance where, because of real "at home-ness" in the family circle, they may build a sense of "at home-ness" in the universe. Then they have found not only the key to marriage but also to life.

> *Help us, Our Father, to sense the spiritual obligations that are at the root of the richest human experiences; and to give ourselves deeply to the fulfilling of them. By living beyond the trivial and the unreal, may we find that which can satisfy the needs of body, mind, and spirit, for we would understand that love is always a matter of giving self in order to find the meaning of self, giving to others that we may find the meaning of others, and living together with that ideal so that we may find the true meaning of Thy nature as eternal love. These things we would seek through the revelation of Jesus the Christ in whose name we pray. Amen.*

To Have and to Hold
Psalm 90 John 2: 1-12

May 3, 1963
First Methodist Church, Sylvania, Ohio

"*I* John, take thee Mary, to be my wedded wife, to have and to hold from this day forth…"

It takes a lot of living and a lot of loving to understand thoroughly these magic words which we recite in the marriage ceremony. It is not until the years pass by and our love and our faith in each other has grown firm and deep and has taken upon itself a well-worn, well-experienced, enriched color that our married life together as husband and wife begins to accomplish and to fulfill that which we vowed as we stood before the altar of God. It is not until you and I discover the meaning of those words, "as long as we both shall live, in sickness and health, in plenty and in poverty, in joy and in sorrow," it is not until, as husbands and wives, we've tried it out through the years and found, on the anvil of life, that it really works, that love pays its rich reward in the depth of real happiness.

Perhaps it is this that the psalmist had in mind as he wrote the psalm we have read today. Particularly as he wrote those words of our text: "So teach us to number our days that we might gain a heart of wisdom."

We spend our years together so freely and so causally. Life is so busy and so intense that it is not long after the marriage vows that we begin to assume our home and our marriage and to take for granted our love. All too seldom do we, who are young, stop to consider the fleeting years of joy and of happiness. Each day piles one upon another and are quickly spent and vanish into the pages of the past. How quickly today becomes only a picture upon the walls of our memory. How seldom we stop to realize that this life of ours together, this love, this home, this family circle—is here but for so brief a time.

We ought to face each day, each moment, each thrill, each affection, each experience, like the eater of a delicious fruit, slowly, with real satisfaction. As a marriage continues through life, it grows in its maturity, in its depth, in its understanding, and in its confidence.

The beauty of a Christian marriage or a Christian home is most completely seen in the mature years of life, as the husband and wife reveal in their love and in their confidence, and in their serenity, the promises of Christian marriage and of Christian love.

Old age is a state of mind. If someone should ask you how old you are, you should never answer them in terms of chronology. Perhaps that is why ladies prefer not to give that information. Actually, you are only as old as the state of your mind at the time you are asked your age. There are days when I feel like I'm a hundred and ten and not sure I'll last until evening. Then, at other times, I have energy to burn and seem to be young and youthful again. After all, calendar age is a relative thing—you've heard the saying, "You're as old as you admit, or you're as old as your arteries."

We are told that a man is old for the hundred-yard dash at 25, he's old for professional boxing at 35, and he's old for professional baseball at 45. There are some men and women who come into the very fullness of their lives, into the very prime of their faculties, after they have reached the age of 60. Basically, age is simply a matter of your personal evaluation of yourself. More popularly, old age is the slowing down of interest in life. It is the loss of something in us which, when we accept it, marks senility.

Dr. Barker writes it this way:

It should not be forgotten that Sophocles wrote his Oedipus at 90 years of age; Pope Leo XIII inaugurated most of his enlightened policy after he was 70; Titian, who lived to be over 99, painted his masterpiece, the bronze doors of the sacristy of St. Mark's, at the age of 85. Benjamin Franklin was born in 1706 and lived to be 84. By the time he was 70, he was one of the most talked about men in the world. At the age of 72, he was appointed sole plenipotentiary to the French court, and at the age of 75 was appointed a member of a commission to make peace with Great Britain. After his return to America at the age of 75, he became chief executive officer of Pennsylvania until he was 82 years old. Elihu Root died in 1937 at over 92 years of age; one of the greatest statesmen of our country. Or think of Oliver Wendell Holmes, John Dewey, Bernard Baruch, Henry Ford, Arturo Toscanini, John Foster Dulles,

Dwight Eisenhower, who did or are doing their most significant work after passing 60.

It is only as you and I, through the years, take upon ourselves, not the breakdown of life, but the fulfillment of life, the maturity, the growth in understanding, and the wisdom of time, that the love which we pledged at the altar becomes rich and deep and full. Then life takes on the completeness of its being, and we rejoice with those who have also shared and say, "See, it is true. As long as we both shall live." The years, rather than marking the necessity of decay and senility, can equally mark a growing maturity and understanding, a wisdom which can come only with time.

Paul, the great apostle who wrote the letters, the epistles to the various churches in Asia Minor, wrote the letter to the church at Philippi at the age of 62 while chained in a prison in Rome, awaiting death. He gives to us the wisdom of maturity as he writes these words to the church at Philippi. He says, first of all, that the wisdom of maturity is the ability to be content with whatever life may bring. It is in the maturity of the years, in the love of husband and wife, as we overcome the impatience of youth, that we learn to discover the riches of every experience. We find that God gives us the power to rise above or to live beyond, any experience that life may bring. Instead of life crushing us down through sickness or health, through joy or sorrow, through poverty or plenty, we discover the power through the years to live in terms of the riches of whatever life may bring. Life takes on a maturity which is not subject to the whims and moods of periodic changes of mind.

Paul writes that the wisdom of maturity is to learn to abound in any and all circumstances, to learn to live lives that are bigger than the trivia with which we clutter the days and the hours of our youth. To learn that the most basic things of life, in the final analysis, cannot be measured in terms of the annual economic accounting or in terms of the storehouses filled to overflowing, or in terms of power and position, is a lesson which the years can teach best. Rather, real happiness is measured in terms of the dedication of one life to another in love, and in confidence, and in faith, and in the maturity of our joy and of our understanding. Paul says this is the key to it all.

This is the key which gives you the ability to live together in marriage as "long as we both shall live."

"I can do all things through Christ who strengtheneth me," says Paul. I can live with confidence, and with faith as long as "we both shall live" when I live in the strength of One who lives within me. I place my hopes, my faith, my dreams, my longings, and my goals in the hands of One who is the center of my home, who is the heart of my heart, who is the light of my life. As I build tomorrow upon the foundations of my God, I can do all things through Him who is my strength and my Redeemer.

This is the wisdom of maturity. This is the goal, this is the witness, the ministry of mature men and women. The ministry of mature couples is so to live and so to reveal in their relationship of husband and wife that warmth of love and affection that younger couples, watching them and sensing the beauty of that relationship, take heart and say to each other, "See, it can be done."

Life can be rich and full, and our love, regardless of what life brings, can be strong and permanent. It is the task of Christian husbands and wives, in the mature years of life, to be witnesses in their married life, in their love for each other, in the marriage experiences, to those about them. For some young people who may be having trouble, going through the necessary adjustments of early marriage, or whose hearts may be sick through misunderstanding, your witness to that power by which we can live and build may be the difference of continuing marriage or of divorce.

And when God breaks up the home, this is not the end of love, In a Christian marriage, it is only God that ultimately breaks up that home. Seldom are a husband and wife privileged to live to the very end of life together. There comes a time in our marriage experience when suddenly we wake up with a start to see the end of life beginning to heave over the horizon, and we begin to realize that the days are numbered when we shall be together in holy marriage. Perhaps the greatest price of happy, full, rich love is the price that we must pay, in aching heart, in sense of loss, in half-lives which are lived, when our husband or wife has gone on, and we must for a time walk alone. We cannot put in words nor share that heartache that comes when we listen for that familiar step and those familiar sounds that have become so dear which shall not sound again. That is the greatest price of the fullness of love.

Dr. Arthur Gossip of Glasgow, in a volume of sermons tells about a friend, presumably beyond middle age, "the first acuteness of whose agony of parting lay more than twenty years before. Whenever he spoke of it, his face went ashy gray with the pain of it still. 'It was the mornings,' he said almost to himself, 'the terrible mornings, when one cried out: not yet, O God, not yet. Have I another whole long day of it to face alone so soon.'"

There comes a time when one or the other must go on alone. But such a person can find in God the sort of peace that the world cannot give, cannot take away. Such a person can find, when his life is rested on these foundations, that his love can go on and that only love in reality can bridge the span of time and eternity.

Jesus was asked the question one day by the Pharisee about marriage in heaven. Does death end it all? Is it finished when life moves on into its eternity? And Jesus said to them in reply to their question that in heaven there is no physical union, there is no need for that, there. Jesus said the basis of marriage is not physical, it is spiritual. Marriage is love. Marriage is faith. Marriage is confidence. And Jesus said that this is part of the Kingdom of Heaven. Heaven is love. Heaven is faith. Heaven is confidence. It is the union of spirit with spirit. And the promise of God is that, instead of death ending love as long as we both shall live, rather God has promised that there comes a time again when we shall see each other, and we shall be together, and we shall love as we are loved, where there is no pain and where there is no heartache. For all eternity, there shall only be love one with another.

The riches of the promises of God are so complete that you and I, as we stand before the altar and pledge our love one for the other, pledge that love for all eternity. As we live in that love, and as we build our lives and our home in the faith of God, to make that love true and pure and real, we can live in confidence and in security that God will be with us and will bind us forever.

"*Love never ends,*" wrote Paul in the 13th chapter of First Corinthians. Love is so deep, so much a part of the very makeup of life, that there is no end to a real love. "*When I was a child,*" Paul said,

"I spoke as a child, and I thought as a child, and I reasoned like a child, but when I became a man I gave up childish ways. For now we see in a mirror dimly, but then face to face." And to change one word: *"Now I love,"* said Paul, *"in part; now I love in the limitations of my emotional experience, or my intellectual insight, of the time that is allowed me in this life, but then I shall love fully as I have been loved. So faith, hope, love, these three abide; but the greatest of these is love."*

Grow old along with me!
The best is yet to be,
The last of life, for which the first was made:
Our times are in His hand
Who saith A whole I planned,
Youth shows but half; trust God: see all, nor be afraid!
(Robert Browning)

See all, trust God, nor be afraid!

On Making Houses Homes
Proverbs 31: 10-29 John 2: 1-12

May 5, 1986
Urbana United Methodist Church, Urbana, Ohio

We have new housing developments all around us. Each development is carefully planned; each new home has the ultimate in latest technology and design. When we think of our homes, we have a very human and warm tendency to attempt to make them fine places. We want to feel a sense of pride when we view our houses.

Many years ago, when Strickman Gilliam was traveling through an African American section of a southern city, he was astonished at the neat way most of the residents of poor, run-down shacks kept their gardens. One particular garden attracted him—morning glories twisted up the side of the shack, roses grew along a wooden frame, sunflowers loomed up to bloom brightly; and sitting in an old rocking chair was an ancient woman—mistress of all she surveyed. He paused and said, "What a beautiful garden, ma'am."

"What you say, sir?"

"A beautiful garden!" he shouted back.

"Sholy, it ought to be fine! I live here!"

But there is in this process of making fine, a very present danger—that we become so involved with the appearances all about that fine new house, that we leave out the thing needful to make it a real home—a spiritual thing, the heart of it—an indescribable something that composes itself out of many things, and all of them we speak of together as living. It takes a more highly skilled architect to make a home.

If these shells of our houses are to become the warm and friendly and sheltering homes that we'd like them to be, there must be an interchange of ideas, and experiences, and emotions in theme. In the farming homes of the past century there was the planning and the sharing in the many chores and activities of the farm; there was the participation of each member of the family in a common enterprise—and the success or failure of the whole enterprise was in some measure dependent upon the activities of each one. Too often in our modern homes, we each go our separate ways—a common bond of interest and activity does not encircle us as it did them, and we lose one vital factor in the strength of a family's life. There should be the sharing with each other, the serving of each other, so that in the home circle each senses the others' needs and uses him or herself to meet and to satisfy those needs.

Then too, the members of the family should grow together as do the giant redwoods so that the strength of all is united. Those great trees of the west reach down into the earth and then have the unusual habit in nature of running their roots forth until they find the roots of other redwood trees—and then these roots have the peculiar habit of winding about each other so that in each tree there is the strength of the roots of many trees, and each stands up tall and strong because each is united with all.

In the circle of the home there must not only be this feeling of cooperation and togetherness, but also a concern for the individual being, for one's personality, temperament, and desires. There should be some measure of privacy so that each may grow as a unique being needs to grow for itself. There are many examples of parents attempting to mold their children's lives, to set their ways into certain grooves, and to become frustrated in their attempts or deeply dissatisfied with the results—for they have thwarted possibilities of personality development which are for each alone.

Susannah Wesley had nineteen children, but had a special set-aside time for each one. There should be this respect for each as a separate creation of God, for each as unique among the beings of the earth, an understanding of the value of each one as a human being, and not as a fulfillment of dreams of what a mother or a father yearned to be and failed to attain for her or himself.

And there should be as the warm hearth fire in winter and the fragrant breath of spring, a constant and continual presence of love.

> *There is beauty all around*
> *When there's love at home.*
> *There is joy in every sound,*
> *When there's love at home.*
> *Sweeter sings the booklet by*
> *Brighter beams the azure sky;*
> *O there's One who smiles on high,*

When there's love at home.
(John Hugh McNaughton)

This is not just the light and frivolous and beribboned love that our pulp magazines describe so vividly, but a strong and encircling and powerfully undergirding love for each other that lifts life out of the humdrum into a genuine joy.

Our own Lincoln, president during a day that was in its age fully as critical as our own, must have had this deep feeling of a bond of love that existed between his mother and himself. And such is not a dictating imperative, but rather an influencing example that challenges the lives of children.

There are quite vivid examples on every hand in these days of heightened standards of living when parents have a false sense of love—they are anxious to provide for their children many little luxuries that they themselves in a less prospering age lacked. But so sadly often, they pile about their children an accumulation of so many articles, playthings, and such that the children lack a sense of appreciation and are but confused with the number of things set before them—or become so spoiled that they want everything upon which their eyes feast for even a fleeting moment—and in later years determine to follow their childhood's shaping by taking that which they want regardless of the rights or needs of others. We cannot make up for our failure to love our families by piling about them the trivialities of earth that soon fade away. On the other hand, there are many wise parents who know that life has its limitations, and that training their children in selectivity helps them in later years to make the right choices. Possessions are no fit expressions nor an adequate excuse for a lack of love in the family circle.

Then, too, the home should be a place for growth—for expansion of interests in life, for deepening appreciation of those all about us, for enlarging concerns, a place of character-building. Many times there are the desires to make things easier for our children; and at times we make them so easy that their characters are blemished with our mistaken attempts at assistance. A certain amateur naturalist tells us his experience in watching an emperor moth slowly making its difficult way from the chrysalis stage. Day by day it squirmed its way, trying to emerge. The opening of the cocoon was so narrow that the naturalist decided to give that emperor moth some help from the outside, so he took his penknife and cut into the narrow end of the cocoon, slightly enlarging the opening so that it would be easier for the moth to emerge. He wanted this harsh struggle for life to be over as quickly as possible. So we often treat our children, trying to save them from all hard experiences, difficult problems, from hurt and bewilderment of thought, and we step in and help them—and hurt them deeply. For we too, cut a hole in the cocoon to lighten the struggle with the same result that the naturalist found—the conflict was over and the moth emerged, but its wings were imperfect. It can flutter feebly, but cannot fly. So, the strength that comes through struggle was not in the moth's makeup and its life was henceforth blighted. Likewise, some children never get to fly—for they have not developed their own strength of character to lift them high and let them go forth ably through life.

Then, too, in our contorted vision of love for children, we often spare them from any discipline. We were caught up a few years ago—largely through the misguidance of some dabbling amateurs in the developing field of psychology, in the theory of complete freedom for children. Some schools were organized around that idea for the fears of frustrating our children were great among us. Now, from present indications, we are swinging somewhat back to the common sense of a previous generation to know that in love frequently there comes chastening as well. God is a great and loving God—but there are two arms of God's activity—with one God restrains God's children—holds them back from God, disappointed because of their waywardness, and with the other draws them to God—hating their misdeeds but always loving their souls. The Native American's version of a portion of the Twenty-third Psalm gives us this thought memorably:

The Great Father above is a Shepherd Chief. I am His and with Him I want not. He throws out to me a rope, and the name of the rope is Love. He draws me, and He draws me, and He draws me to where the grass is green and the water is not dangerous; and I eat and lie down satisfied. Sometimes my heart is very weak and falls down, but He lifts it up again and draws me into a good road. His name is Wonderful. Sometime, it may be very soon, it may be longer, it may be a long, long time, He will draw me into a place between mountains. It is dark there, but I will not draw back. I will not be afraid, for it is there between these

mountains that the Shepherd Chief will meet me, and the hunger I have
felt in my heart all through this life shall be satisfied.
Sometimes He makes the love rope into a whip, but afterwards He gives
me a staff to lean on. What I tell you is true, I lie not.
(*Anonymous*)

So we see that so many godly qualities are needed to make the house a home—not just a place to go when there's nowhere else—not just a hat hook—but a real and joyful fellowship of living together. And crowning the Christian home, there is a sense of holiness prevailing. There is the feeling of devotion unto God and faith in God. And the psalm of our scripture reading recalls for us the pleasure of home life under the blessing of God. It is one of the priceless pictures of family life in the entire Old Testament. There is the wife bearing the children, standing with her husband in creating a family and upholding him in his household. And the father worships the Lord and fears Him, and the Lord's blessing is upon that house.

In home life there can be strength that holds us together as the redwood roots, a place for each to stand forth individually and beneficially, and underneath the encircling roots of love that enable each to stand tall, sturdy, and strong. As we lift our eyes above the earth, there is this glimpse into the vastness that makes us grow heavenward. The strength of love about us so that life moves on in its complete circle, and the trust of God over us so that we live in bright and wholesome hope.

Mother's Day

(Helen Jane Hartland, Greg Hartland, Jim Hartland, Joel Hartland, and Marilee Hartland Lake, Sylvania, Ohio)

"Woman, behold thy son."
John 19:26

A Smile and a Dream
Luke 1: 46-55

May 11, 1952
Circleville Methodist Church, Miller Methodist Church, Irwin, Pennsylvania

In all the world's literature, one of the great gems is Mary's song of joy at learning of her destiny in history—to bring forth the world's redeemer.

> *My soul doth magnify the Lord,*
> *And my spirit hath rejoiced in God my Savior*
> *For He hath regarded the low estate of His handmaiden;*
> *For behold, from henceforth all generations shall call me blessed.*
> *For He that is mighty hath done to me great things,*
> *And Holy is His name.*
> *And His mercy is on them that fear Him from generation to generation.*
> *He hath shewed strength with His arm;*
> *He hath scattered the proud in the imagination of their hearts,*
> *He hath put down the mighty from their seats,*
> *And exalted them of low degree.*
> *He hath filled the hungry with good things;*
> *And the rich He hath sent empty away.*
> *He hath holpen His servant Israel in remembrance of His mercy;*
> *As He spake to our fathers, to Abraham, and to his seed forever.*
> *(Luke 1: 46-55)*

And I do believe that motherhood everywhere shares something of the joy of Mary's song at knowing that they are to share something of their own life with the world. It's a smile of joy that comes upon them from time to time wondering at the mystery of this good thing that has come to pass. So motherhood shares with the world's universal feeling of joy.

Then, too, I believe that accompanying the smile of joy, there comes with the expectancy a dream of hope—a high hope that this tiny one cherished tenderly, protected and guided, might one day come to a place not necessarily of fame and fortune—but a place of accomplishment in living the good life upon earth. I do believe that the great God on high in those majestic acts of creation dreamed holy dreams for the future of this high creature, man. And I do believe that motherhood shares in this high and holy dream in that it cherishes the hope that some little good might be brought to pass by this child of its bosom.

Alfred Noyes catches something of what I want to say:

Dreams, dreams; ah, the memory blinding us,
Blinding our eyes to the way that we go;
Till the new sorrow comes once more reminding us
Blindly of kind hearts, ours long ago;
'Mother-mine,' whisper we, 'yours was the love for me!
Still though our paths lie lone and apart,
Yours is the true love, shining above for me,
Yours are the kind eyes, hurting my heart.'

Dreams, dreams; ah, how shall we sing of them.
Dreams that we loved with our head on her breast;
Dreams, dreams; and the cradle-sweet swing of them;
Ay, for her voice was the sound we loved best;
Can we remember at all, or forgetting it,
Can we recall for a moment the gleam
Of our childhood's delight and the wonder begetting it,
Wonder awakened in dreams of a dream?

Then we saw that the tunes of the world were one;
And the meter that guided the rhythmic sun
Was at one, like the ebb and the flow of the sea,
With the tunes that we learned at our mother's knee.

But often is it not sadly true that in the honest moments of reflection upon the days of our own living that we know we have fallen far short of the dreams of our mothers? Frequently through our own failures at fulfillment, does not the smile of joy become an anguished sorrow?

We are caught up in a world of busy living—often we are a people cumbered with much serving of lesser causes so that we have little time or energy left for the really good and rich abundance of living that our Savior—the world's perfect Child of His mother—set forth. Frequently in the clamor of living, we become a people lacking in appreciation—oh, we usually thank those who are more or less strangers to us, but wherein we fall short in gratitude is to express our thanksgiving to those who help and lift and lead us through the ways of daily living. Many times is it not true that we forget to say, "Thank you," to those right at home—our family and friends—for all the good and kindly things they have done for us? So it was that Anna Jarvis, schoolteacher of Grafton, West Virginia, launched her campaign to express her own appreciation to her mother.

Ann Reeves Jarvis came to live in Grafton in 1865. She was the wife of a merchant and a teacher in Sunday school. After the Civil War days, in an effort to reunite the family ties that had been broken during this period, she organized the mothers of the community and announced a "Mother's Friendship Day" to be held at Pruntytown, county seat of Taylor County. A special invitation was given to every Union and Confederate soldier and their families—and a historian of the region recounted that it was an inspiring sight to see the men in gray and blue meet, shake hands, and to hear them say, "God bless you neighbor; let us be friends again." For more than twenty years, Mrs. Jarvis taught in the primary department of the Sunday School of Andrews Church, and during those years, she often spoke of the appropriateness of a day to honor the mothers of our country, both the living and the memory of those at rest. It was this mother who inspired her daughter to promote the idea of a Mother's Day. Upon the death of the father, mother and daughter moved to Philadelphia to live with a son and brother. There it was in 1905 that Mrs. Jarvis died. Two years later, Miss Jarvis invited several friends to her Philadelphia home to spend the second Sunday in May to commemorate the anniversary of her good mother's death. On that day, she announced her plans for a national observance of Mother's Day. She acquainted John Wanamaker with her plan, and he helped to encourage the movement. She also wrote to the superintendent of the Sunday school in Andrew's Church suggesting a Mother's Day. So there it was on May 10, 1908 that the first official Mother's Day service was held. Both the Sunday school and the morning worship times were given to this theme, and the pastor preached on the word from the cross, "*Woman behold thy son, Behold thy mother.*" So it was that old Andrews Church became the Mother's Church of Mother's Day.

So it is that the traveler coming into Grafton reads on the highway marker, "Grafton, home of Anna Jarvis, founder of Mother's Day."

Anna Jarvis sent 500 white carnations, chosen as an emblem of purity—these were presented to each mother and to each son and daughter at the service. In the year of 1910, the governor of West Virginia signed this proclamation:

> *The beautiful custom of setting apart one day in each year to pay just tribute to our mothers should not be abandoned or forgotten. Our days of youth may be over, and the closer ties that bound us to our mothers may have been loosened, but not a link in the chain of affection that bound her heart to ours has been broken, and we think of Mother today as we always did, the noblest, sweetest, and best of all God's creation,*

The Methodist Episcopal Church was convened in 1912 in its general conference, and there it was that a resolution was introduced to set aside the second Sunday in May as Mother's Day in the church. In 1914, upon approval of President Woodrow Wilson and proclamation of William Jennings Bryan, secretary of state, the nation joined in official recognition of the movement, with the request that the flag be displayed on all government buildings upon that day. Representative Heflin of Alabama, co-author of the resolution to Congress said, "The flag was never used in a more beautiful and sacred cause than when flying above that tender, gentle Army, the mothers of America."

So it was that a tender endeavor to pay fitting tribute to a mother by her daughter grew into a national observance, and in some measure to a universal tribute to Motherhood. So it is, that in its annual keeping, we are stirred out of our unappreciative attitude and remember much that has been good. So it is that we often resolve for ourselves that the smile must not fade, nor the dream perish because of us. So it is that the keeping of the day may well serve as an inspiration to higher living that in us the joy may be realized and in us the dream fulfilled.

Mother's Day when it comes around each year is a forget-me-not of a day that warms our hearts with rich and wonderful memories, that quickens our lives with a very real and personal consciousness of a deep love, that lifts our thoughts and our aspirations to a more serious endeavor to live more worthy of this good gift of our mothers to us.

A story is told of a great German poet named Uhland. He was a very learned but modest man, and when the King of Prussia offered to give him the badge of an order that many famous people were glad to receive, he declined to accept it. When the poet was explaining to his wife the reason that moved him to refuse the honor, there was a knock at the door. A small peasant girl from the neighborhood entered and presented Mr. Uhland a bunch of little forget-me-nots.

"This is a gift from my mother," she said.

"Your mother, child," said the poet. "I thought she died last autumn."

"That is true, Herr Uhland," said the little girl, "and I begged you at that time to make a little verse for her grave, and you kindly gave me a beautiful poem. These are the first forget-me-nots which have bloomed on Mother's grave. I have plucked them, and I like to think she sends them to you with her greetings."

The poet's eyes moistened as he took the flowers, and putting them into his buttonhole, he said to his wife, "There, dear woman, is that not something more valuable than any king can give?"

So Mother's Day comes upon us, and may we be truly appreciative people, remembering her who did so many kindly deeds each day. One who pointed out to us a beautiful poem, or a sunset, or a blossom or mountain peak. Those who in moments of trouble and suffering, bewilderment and sorrow, stood with us, those who sacrificed for us without stint. Those who did battle for us and helped us to keep faith in ourselves because they had faith in us—our mothers.

God, thank You for our mothers.

The Madonna of the Tear
Luke 2: 40-52

May 10, 1964
First Methodist Church, Sylvania, Ohio

We have often heard it said that while Rome conquered the world, it was Greek culture that prevailed. To each we are debtors: to one for philosophy and architecture, for drama and poetry; and to the other for government and for the disciplines of law. But while that which attracts the minds of humans is influential, and while that which controls the actions of humans is significant, yet it is that which grips the heart of humanity that is of eternal value.

So true are the words of the poet:

> *Thou hast conquered, O Pale Galilean*
> *The world has grown gray from Thy breath.*
> *(Algernon Charles Swinburne)*

For it has been the leavening of influence of the Christ, the Christ-mind, and the Christ-love that has touched the hearts of humanity in all the centuries since Bethlehem to change, and to inspire, and to commit us to life's loftiest ethic and love's undying loyalties.

So the travelers to our fabulous World's Fair [1964 World's Fair held in New York, City] tell us that among the exhibits and the displays and the extravaganza of it all, it is the presence of the religious that touches the heart.

We have read the story of the examination and the crafting and the insuring and the traveling of *La Pieta*—Michelangelo's famous statue of the Madonna holding the broken body of the Christ—and this has proven to be the most popular visit of all at the fair. This noble work of art established upon a homely relationship with all the deep joys and all the human pathos that that relationship involves. As I stood in Rome last summer and looked upon it, I remembered the story of Bethlehem and of Golgotha—of Nazareth and Cana in Galilee, and of Jerusalem in Judea—and I realized how present Mary was in the moving experiences of Jesus and in the miracle of His life.

Now frequently, we of the Protestant profession are inclined to ignore or be indifferent or to neglect these stories and this influence because of our aversion to Mary's high regard that touches upon divinity in the Catholic practice. Yet, can we refuse to admit that these lessons—about a candle in a home, about oil in a lamp, about leaven in a lump had other than origin in a humble home where there were tender affections, and brooding anxieties, and a humble and holy regard on for another.

It takes a heap o' livin'
In a house t' make it home—
(Edgar Albert Guest)

And it takes a lot of planning and of patience and of persistence to keep a house a home.

So let us look at Mary, Mother of Jesus, housewife of Nazareth who mingled with the daily grinding and baking and washing, the affection that brought her to high anticipation in the magnificent, to wonder in the days of His Nazareth youth, to deep concern in the ministries in Capernaum, and to tragic loss in the last experiences in Jerusalem.

I would like to suggest to you that there is a Madonna quality in all mothers, and on this day of high regard I should like us to hold this forth before us and to respect it with our own daily loyalties and deeper desires to live taller because of it.

In the House of Art in New York City, there hangs a painting by a German artist, Hermann Kaulbach, *The Madonna of the Tear.* This artist was born in Munich in 1946 and studied his art both in Germany and in Italy. The painting is one that reveals not an ethereal quality in a brocaded robe as do so many of the Madonna paintings, but a dark-eyed girl with dark hair held back by a black cloak that looks to be of the simple homespun material of the mothers of Nazareth. She is holding her sleeping child, and thinking the thoughts that must touch the minds of all mothers, wondering, apprehensive—and on her cheek, a tear.

The artist catches a brooding mystery in the Madonna's mind and heart that touched everything about this infant. The annunciation of the heavenly messenger at the time of His conception filled the maid of Nazareth with alarm and confusion as well as with joy over the honor bestowed upon her. This confusion and alarm must have grown as the months of her travail went on, and especially when it looked for a time as though Joseph, her betrothed, would misunderstand and put her away from him. Mary was young—the authorities agree she was still a teenager—when these responsibilities fell upon her. Her trip to Bethlehem must have been a frightening experience—robbers along the way, rocky roads and hills to jog up and down on an uncomfortable donkey. And then the disappointment of this place—Bethlehem—town of David, but so full of people that there was no room for this quiet, brooding, anxious mother-to-be, no kin-folk to wait upon her. How fearful a time! Perhaps the tear was one of fear.

And then all that happened—shepherds, wise men from the east, the village people, a star in the sky, gifts, a midnight warning to Joseph, and the weary journey across the wilderness to Egypt. Strange land and strange tongues of the people of Egypt—loneliness. Perhaps the tear was one of apprehension.

So the artist catches up this personality—deep-set eyes and tragic face in one so young, as she leans above her sleeping child—pressing His baby fingers against her mother-lips. He is secure, trusting, as He sleeps—she is weary and worn with travel, and wondering of the future. Yet here they are in Egypt at the end of the journey. She rests now. Perhaps the tear is one of relief—even as her far-away look makes her ponder over the will of her Heavenly Father.

Motherhood is never without its anxieties, its heartaches, its cares. Perhaps it is just this that gives to mothers everywhere their unusual sympathy, insight, and understanding. Certain it is that the circumstances attending the infancy of the Christ Child were such as might strike terror to the stoutest heart. But always the Madonna Mother when she could not understand, prayed and kept buried deep in her own heart the anxieties and fears that beset her path in rearing this Child of prophecy.

Even during that last cruel week of expectation, despair, and agonizing grief, His faithful mother followed Him in loving sympathy, unspoiled by reproach, to the fateful end.

So the artists of the ages combine their talents—Kaulbach of Germany in catching the apprehensive hope and fear of the days in Egypt in his painting of the *Madonna of the Tear*, and Michelangelo in

Italy brooding upon the feelings and emotions of the mother clutching a body broken by a cross.

From Syria comes the poet Gibran to speak of it:

> *"My Son, who is not my Son, if this be of God, may God*
> *give us patience and the knowledge thereof.*
> *And if it be of man may God forgive him forevermore."*

> *And then turning to John and the other women who were with her, she said:*

> *"Now, behold He is gone. The battle is over. The star has shown forth.*
> *The ship has reached the harbor. He who once lay against my heart*
> *is throbbing in space—"*

> *And Mary returned to Jerusalem, leaning upon John the youngest*
> *disciple. And she was a woman fulfilled.*

As we look into the tear-stained face and eyes of this young Madonna Mother, we know that God's way of making great women out of inexperienced girlhood is in the process, and in our own hearts we thank God for all the Madonna mothers of the centuries.

Cupboards and Clasped Hands
Luke 2: 1-7. 22-40

May 9, 1971
Christ United Methodist Church, Columbus, Ohio

*T*here is a song that tells us how boys and girls are made—and when I was young, we sang it as I suppose many of you did:

> *Girls are made of sugar and spice*
> *And everything nice—*
> *Boys are made of snips and snails*
> *And puppy dogs' tails—*

But what are mothers made of? This is a more involved matter—for it touches on the practical, the evolutionary, the ethereal. There is a quality about motherhood that brings earth and heaven into radiant personality.

Think of it as a scientific progress: in the physical order a flames lights a flame, a torch lights a torch. In lower forms of life, such as the amoeba, there is a fission or splitting, as the young life breaks off from the parent cell. Motherhood is still a long way off, for there could never be a mother without an intimate close and vital relationship between the body of the mother and the body of the young offspring.

This took centuries of evolution—some land crabs come down from the mountains to the sea, push their eggs into the water, and then abandon them—there is no real motherhood there, for the young never see their mothers, nor do the mothers care for their young. This universe of ours is full of orphans, the young that are begotten are completely forgotten. Almost all fruit is orphaned in as much as it lives an independent life from the tree. Butterflies are thoughtful to some extent, inasmuch as eggs are often hatched under a leaf, where they are least exposed. Maybe nature is kind to certain butterflies, for how shocked mothers would be to see a fuzzy-wuzzy ugly caterpillar—the kind that only a mother could love. Hens are much kinder to their young—our Lord Jesus used them as an example of His concern for humans:

How often would I have gathered my children together,
As a hen gathers her chickens under her wings;
And thou didst refuse it! (Matthew 23:37b)

No boy—or girl for that matter—who ever gathered eggs from the barnyard or crib, as some of you have done, will ever forget the wrath of a cackling, setting hen.

As we see nature unfold, there is an increasing unity of mother and offspring, until finally many mothers carry the young within them. Despite all this cosmic evolution, however, there could never be a human mother until love came into the world. What a different quality this adds to generation. In addition to sex, which is common to the animals, there must also be love, in order that there be no ravishing or stealing away of the worth of a person. If a mother is to be made, then what is begotten must come from a free set of the will, in which a woman freely submits to the love of a man. Such surrender would not be a passive one, like the earth to the seed, but rather an active one in which two humans who are freely united in soul freely unite in body. One might almost say that the generation begins in the mind and in the soul with love and completes itself in the body.

All love tends to be an incarnation—even God's. Generation, then, is not a push from below, but a gift from above; it is a reflection of the eternal generation in the bosom of the Father, who in the agelessness of eternity says, *"Thou art my Son. This day have I begotten Thee."* The roots of it are hidden in heaven, for in the great Hebrew tradition we read a line wherein God speaks and says, *"Shall I who give generation to others, myself be barren?"* The offspring now is seen as the incarnation of the mutual love of a husband and a wife. When a mother carries the young life within her through a free act of love, she has a different kind of love from that which any person has for a neighbor. Most of us love a non-self, or something extrinsic and apart from our inner life; but a mother's love during the time of her pregnancy is not for a non-self, but for one that is her very self, a perfect example of charity and love which hardly perceives a separation.

Mothers in the animal kingdom care only for a body—this is the cupboard quality. Food to eat, protection from enemies, some shelter for periods away from the hazards of the environment. And our mothers are concerned for these matters as well—washing and ironing and mending clothing, cooling of fevers, food to nourish, teeth to repair, hair to manage—all of these time and energy consuming matters of physical sustenance.

But there is something more: mothers in the spiritual kingdom must care also for a soul, a mind, and a heart. You know it does not take long in the animal order to generate and develop the brain of a monkey, because the monkey brain does not have very much to do. Do you remember that delightful story of Bambi, the little deer? Very early Bambi set off to forage for himself. But consider that little deer in my home—or in your home. It takes years before we feel they can manage decisions, more years before we consider a maturity to vote, to marry, to live away from us. It takes a long, long time to inculcate ideals of purity, honesty, patriotism, and piety.

Animals can quickly leave their parents because they have no eternal destiny—but humanity is under a compulsory educational act, and to fulfill this, there must be domesticity. The home is the schoolhouse for affection wherein a mother completes the work that was begun when the child was born. Motherhood then turns into mother-craft, as biology hands the work over to ethics. The canoe can quickly launch out on the waters when it is made, but the big ship has to wait for engines because it has a better port. A tiny ball of unconsciousness needs much mother care to become all that God destined it to be. Maybe that is why mothers are against war; they realize better than anyone else how long it takes to make a person.

Mother love requires greater attention to the individuals of the species. A mother must love each child as if it were the only one in all the world. This means recognizing that human beings are not just individuals, but persons. In the animal world there are individuals; in the human order, there are persons. The difference between an individual and a person is this; individuals are replaceable, and persons are not. For example, you go to buy oranges in a store and say, "No this one is bad." This is one of the mysteries of life for me—I never could judge a watermelon, or a grapefruit, or any of these objects by looking and lifting and touching as do some people. At any rate, some can, and return that orange and say, "Give me another." But you cannot say that about children—a child is a person, unique, the incommunicable, irreplaceable. That is why there is so much sorrow for a mother when one is lost. It is a person and an immortal soul that has departed. The other side of the coin, too, is that there is faith and trust—for while a body is gone, a soul lives on—this we believe and there is joy even in our sorrow in that!

Every mother gives the child a name which implies dignity, uniqueness, and apartness. There is not greater refutation of communism in the world than a mother. Because communism denies the value of persons, it affirms that we are like grapes who have no other destiny than to have our life ground out of us for the sake of the collective wine of the state. Every mother arises to protest and to proclaim, "This child of mine is a person and may not be subjected to any totality of a class or a state or a race. She is unique; he has a name, she is my child!"

That is how mothers are made. Nature had to prepare for them through millions of years by begetting a love that would freely desire children, a love that would educate them, and a love that would sacrifice for them because of their sovereign worth as persons endowed with immortal souls. Such love could not come from the breast, for that kind of love is a gift of God.

Now for the clasped hands—it takes a lot of prayer—prayer arising out of concern, out of compassion, out of hope—to be a mother! Motherhood is too noble to be without an ideal.

Whistler was complimented for the beautiful painting of his mother. Some of you saw this painting this year when it was displayed in our art museum. His answer was, "You know how it is. One tries to make one's Mommy as nice as one can."

So with Jesus. She, the ideal mother conceived and brought into the world the Guest who became the Host of the world. This mother gave further example to all mothers by caring for both the body and the soul of her Son. She cared for his body, for she wrapped Him in swaddling clothes and laid Him in a manger. She cared for His soul and His mind, for He was subject to her. What a lesson for children to learn! This child who was subject to His mother was also the Creator of the world. Every mother, when she picks up the young life that has been born to her, looks up to heaven to thank God for the gift which made the world young again.

Finally, Mary gave the example of the worth of personality to all mothers, for like every mother, she gave her Child a name. Since this Child was unique, it was fitting that He be given a name that would describe His mission. This Child came not to save people from insecurity, or to make them rich and powerful, but to save them from their sins. Hence He was given the name Jesus—which means Savior. It was an irreplaceable name before which the heavens and the earth trembled, and before which our knees bow.

If anyone of us could have made our own mother, we would have made her the most beautiful woman in the world. The mother is both the physical preserver of life and the moral provider of truth; she is nature's constant challenge to earth, the bearer of life, the herald of eternal realities, God's greatest cooperator.

One of our Methodist ministers of another generation put it so well:

> *Blessed are the mothers of earth, for they have combined the practical and the spiritual into one workable way of life. They have darned little stockings, mended little dresses, washed little faces, and have pointed little eyes to the stars, and little souls to eternal things.*

Phillip Brooks sums it up for us:

> *God make us worthy of our mothers!*

Pentecost

("Drive-in Church Service Pennsylvania)

"And when the day of Pentecost was fully come, they were all with one accord in one place. And suddenly there came a sound from heaven as of a rushing mighty wind, and it filled all the house where they were sitting. And there appeared unto them cloven tongues like as of fire, and it sat upon each of them."
Acts 2: 1-3

181

"...And Pentecost"
Acts 2: 1-21

June 10, 1984
Urbana United Methodist Church, Urbana, Ohio

Pentecost—which comes upon us fifty days after Easter—(the word Pente in Greek means fifty) was once observed along with Christmas and Easter as the third great festival of the Christian Church. For a number of years, for various reasons, it fell into disuse. Our *Christian Advocate* editor described it as something of a lost holy day. But recently, it is becoming restored to its onetime prominence in the church calendar.

The growing interest in church unity has brought about this revival of concern, the occasion when the disciples came together "of one accord." They had a common devotion, a common experience, and a common life in which they knew that all they had come from God, still belonged to God, and that God expected them to share it with all the members of God's family. So it is that in these past few years, we have seen churches come together in the World Council of Churches.

Pentecost is the birthday of the Christian Church. The story is told there in the first two chapters of the Acts of the Apostles—and might prove very good and interesting reading for you sometime today. One man says that the story has four scenes:

> Scene One: The risen Christ was gathered together with His disciples and warned them not to leave Jerusalem. "Something is going to happen to you," He said. "In a few days you will be baptized with the Holy Spirit." One of them asked Him, "Are you going to establish the kingdom soon?" Jesus answered, "That is not for you to know—when. But it will be established and God will use you to be establishers." Knowing their own lack of power, they swallowed hard at that; but Jesus added, "You shall receive power when the Holy Spirit is come upon you." Then he left them.

Scene Two: The disciples were now alone. They had lost their leader. They were helpless. But they continued in prayer. They waited for that something which Jesus had promised, to happen. They put themselves in the way of God…and they waited.

Scene Three: The day of Pentecost arrived. The disciples were in an upper room. Suddenly, there was the sound of as a mighty wind, and tongues like as of fire descended upon them. They began to speak in languages which could be understood by everyone. *"And they were filled with the Holy Spirit."*

Scene Four: They were reborn into men of amazing power. They went to work. Peter made a speech. That same day, three thousand people were converted to Christ. The Christian Church was born!

So often we worry ourselves with the physical circumstances concerning this and other Biblical stories—worry so much that we miss the deeper meanings and the great truths. Here was an experience which happened in these men—the coming of God's spirit—which defied description in ordinary terms. We would have said, "Thunderstruck." They said, "A sound from heaven as of a rushing wind." We would say it, "They were on fire." They said it was as if tongues of fire descended on them. We would have said, "They spoke a universal language." They said, "They began to speak in other tongues—so that every man heard them speak in his own tongue." It is the inner miracle that matters; the Holy Spirit came upon them, and with that they received power. That was what Jesus had promised, "Ye shall receive power when the Holy Spirit is come upon you."

What is meant by the Holy Spirit? This is always a difficult term to describe in our preparatory classes—or in our youth discussion groups. Correctly, we should ask, "Who is meant by the Holy Spirit," for the Holy Spirit is one of the three Persons of the Trinity—the Father, the Son, and the Holy Spirit.

Holy, holy, holy, merciful and mighty!

"God in three persons, blessed Trinity.
(*Reginald Heber*)

No man hath seen the Father. How, then, can we know God? The answer comes—through Christ. He is the Christ-like God. But Christ had left them! Yes, but on the day of Pentecost they were sure that though He was gone in the flesh, He was with them in the Spirit. His Spirit had descended upon them and within them. Then this spirit was Christ. If Christ, then God. This was the Holy Spirit, always with them. As E. Stanley Jones expresses it, "Christ was no longer the Christ of the Galilean Road, or of the road to Emmaus; He was the Christ of every road. Christ was no longer there—He was here—in the Spirit. And where Christ is, there God is. 'The Holy Spirit,' they said, 'is with us forever. Now nothing is impossible.'"

Suppose, in order to make this clearer, we skip doctrine for a moment and just consider the word, "spirit." This is a familiar word to us. It is a part of personality. A man was describing a young man. "He has his father's brains and drive—but unfortunately, he did not inherit his father's spirit." We know what this means. Next fall, thousands of new freshmen will be entering colleges in America. These colleges will do all things possible in those first college days and weeks to help the new students catch the spirit of the school. All the traditions will be brought out and explained, the Alma Mater will be sung and re-sung until it is familiar; there will be assemblies, and rallies, and chapel talks. And as someone puts it, "Then within six months the freshmen will be ready to do or die for dear old Siwash." They will have caught the spirit of the school.

And so the spirit manifests itself; it generates enthusiasm for one thing. Some of you have been to baseball games and to football and basketball games—and know that there is no neutrality at such events. There is enthusiasm that lets itself be known in cheers and in jeers, in shouts and groans. I was at a baseball game in Boston a number of years ago. All of a sudden, there was a stir that ran through the stands, and I wondered what was happening. It was Ted Williams coming up to bat. We were enthusiastic, there was no doubt about it!

Then, too, when one catches the spirit of a thing, it generates "undiscourageableness". A certain naval officer tells how after a particularly grueling fight, it looked as if the ship would close in combat a second time, without much chance for recovery. He went

185

below. "The spirit of the men was high," he said. "I was proud of them." When one has caught to spirit of a thing, one is not easily discouraged.

One more thing—spirit generates power. The world is quick to now give credit to the Royal Air Force of Britain for holding off Germany in those early and hectic days of war when Britain faced its darkest hour and was all but lost. It was the defense of London by a relative handful of fliers that drew from Churchill the memorable words, "Never in the field of human conflict was so much owed by so many to so few." They demonstrated an incredible courage, and unbelievable endurance—in short, an unconquerable spirit—power!

Now let us consider all of this religiously—let us see how the Spirit of God or the Holy Spirit can be thought of as working among us here and now. That Spirit has enthusiasm and fosters support. A person who has that Spirit touch upon his or her life takes sides for holiness, for righteousness, for Godliness. Some people seem to have no opinion in life—take no sides for goodness and righteousness and love—and surely these people have never been touched by the Holy Spirit. Someone has said, "If a person is a socialist, I'll know it in 24 hours; if he is a member of a social fraternity, I'll know it in a couple of days; but if he is a church member, I may go years and never learn of it." The Holy Spirit goes beyond mere membership. The Holy Spirit generates an enthusiasm for the high and holy things of life—for Godliness!

Again, the Holy Spirit generates "undiscourageableness". There is enough all about us in these days to discourage even the most stouthearted—when we read spine-chilling headlines, or catch blood-curdling newscasts—but those who have caught the Spirit of God cannot be discouraged. They are sure of their ground. "Crisis," as the Chinese characters indicate it, "means only opportunity." When Titus went to Crete, he was shaken by what he saw there—the Cretans were liars, gluttons, terrible creatures—*"For this cause I left thee in Crete, that thou shouldest set in order the things that are wanting." (Titus 1: 5)*. When a person has caught the Holy Spirit, he or she is impossible to discourage. There is a story about a young minister who was sent from the country to an industrial city in England. One day, he was standing on a bridge, looking out over the grime and smoke of the factories, his heart heavy. He felt a hand on his shoulder and turned to see the gentle face of the famous preacher, Dr. Thomas Chalmers—and Dr. Chalmers said to him "Grand field for operations, that!" Where others saw only hopelessness, Dr. Chalmers saw opportunity.

Finally, the Holy Spirit generates power—power for holy things. The Lord knows we have power as such—enough of it and more than we know how to use aright—we ought to pray daily that we use power rightly in these days. Probably our deepest fear just now is that we have too much power—too much material power unmatched by moral power. We have turned to education, and for a few years it was confidently expected that education would save the world and usher in Utopia. When all were educated, there would no longer be error, or sin, or strife. It is far from my thought to underestimate the value of education, but it alone can never be the means of salvation. Indeed, it can well be the means of our destruction, unless accompanied by the Spirit of God. Paul was a university graduate, but he was a persecutor nevertheless until the Holy Spirit came upon him. Goethe once made a trenchant evaluation by saying, "They are beasts; education will make them devils." The thing that made Nazi Germany split the heart of the world was by no means a lack of formal education, it was a lack of the Godly Spirit.

And we have turned to science. That, too, was to have brought us a Utopia. And it is also not in my mind to underestimate technical skill, but that alone will never be the means of our salvation. On the contrary, it can be the means of our destruction, if unaccompanied by the Holy Spirit. Gibbons describes the Emperor Gallienus as being "The master of several and useless sciences, a ready orator, an eloquent poet, a skillful gardener, an excellent cook—and a most contemptible prince." Science has given us the atomic bomb and germicidal weapons. The scientific spirit has generated enough power to blow us off the face of the earth. Only the Holy Spirit, in the hearts of humanity, can generate the power to prevent that and lead the world in precisely the opposite direction.

And that power will come when the Holy Spirit has come upon us.

The Power to Become
John 1; Acts 2: 1-21

June 10, 1962
First Methodist Church, Sylvania, Ohio

But all who received Him, who believeth in His name, He gave power to become children of God; who were born not of blood nor of the will of the flesh nor of the will of men, but of God.
John 1: 12-13

The great psychologist, William James, claimed that people habitually use only a small part of the powers which they possess. Great unused reservoirs of power lie buried deep within us all. Every one of us has it in him or her to become a far more dynamic, radiant, useful, and happier person. In a world full of food, people starve. In a world containing so much beauty and joy, humanity kills and destroys. Instead of health, abundance, and happiness, we find millions enduring ill health, poverty, and despair.

These tense, depressed, fear-ridden millions are what they are for the most part, because of negative, undisciplined thinking. What they desperately need above everything else in this world is to be able to say with deep conviction, "I believe in the power of the living God!" Then this, "The power of the living God is at work within me now, recreating and rebuilding my life toward wholeness and completeness."

Such power-generating statements are part of a technique of creative prayer and affirmation of faith that will unlock the infinite resources that are within, waiting to be set free.

The mind is creative. Every thought creates for us good or ill depending on whether it is positive or negative. No thought can be held in the human mind for long without leaving an eternal residue. Do you doubt this? Then read the first chapter of the Gospel of John slowly and with every faculty alert:

In the beginning was the Word, and the Word was with God and the Word was God. All things were made through Him, and without Him was not anything made that was made. In Him was life, and the life was the light of men."

A word is a symbol of thought. John is saying the Infinite Mind created everything through mind. And we have minds made after Divine Image, having also the power of creation. Every thought creates!

Now, let us proceed to the twelfth verse. I found myself pondering over and over again the meaning of this verse for a day like ours:

> *But all who received Him, who believeth in His name, He gave power to become children of God; who were born not of blood nor of the will of the flesh nor of the will of men, but of God.*

This is an affirmation concerning the greatest power on earth; the very creative power of God given to people of faith; a power that enables a person to become a radiant, dynamic, loving, world-changing Child of God. This is what Jesus referred to when He said, *"The Kingdom of God is within you."*

It is tragically true that in many people this beautiful kingdom is a splendor imprisoned by fear, worry, selfishness, greed, and lust. The magic keys that unlock the prison door are two; repentance and faith. With these keys God gives us power to become His creative children, and there is no dream vouchsafed to humanity that is too high for ultimate fulfillment if we stick resolutely to the life of great affirmation undiluted by doubt or fear.

Let us then look briefly at these thinking minds. Psychologists tell us that only about one-tenth of the mind is conscious, while the other nine-tenths remains forever unconscious. The conscious mind is the part with which we reason, forming judgements and selecting or rejecting what seems to us to be beneficial or harmful. What our conscious minds dwell upon is bound to sink into the unconscious, and thence come into manifestation in our lives. If therefore, we indulge negative, undisciplined, fearful, greedy, hate-filled thoughts, these demons of destruction dominate the unconscious and manifest themselves in such a way as to make us tense, fearful, depressed and unhappy. Jesus said, *"For out of the heart* (that is the depths of the unconscious mind) *come evil thoughts, murders, adulteries, fornications, thefts, false witness, blasphemies."* (Matthew 15: 19). If, on the contrary, we train ourselves to dwell upon what is good and true and beautiful, we gradually build integrated, poised, serene, power-filled lives. Jesus referred to this truth when He said, *"A good man out of the good treasure of the heart bringeth forth good things."* (Matthew 12: 35. And then this from Proverbs, *"For as he thinketh in his heart, so is he."* (Proverbs 23: 7).

Ah, but how—that is the plaguing question. To chart a course— but to travel, there's the work! To share an idea—but to live out the idea—there's the life! We have heard the sermons, we have read the books about the good life, and the advantages of living it—but how!

One way surely is affirmative—positive. Ralph Waldo Trine put it, "Each is building his world from within." Thought is the builder. For thoughts are forces, subtle, vital, irresistible, omnipotent. And according as each is used does it bring peace or pain, power or impotence, success or failure.

Tillie Lewis, once a penniless girl living in Brooklyn, who through developing a positive outlook and attitude arising out of believing and affirming that faith, developed one of the biggest canning industries in the world. She has huge plants in Stockton and Modesto in California's San Joaquin Valley, which can over $20,000,000 worth of fruits and vegetables each year.

In 1930, she was as discouraged as anyone else. The Depression was setting in and this poor girl felt that life could never be anything but drab. Then she saw her first can of pomodoros—pear shaped tomatoes grown and packed in Italy. She took a can home, and was sure that pomodoros had more tang than our native tomatoes. They made wonderful salads, and their paste diluted with water made delicious soup or juice. An idea struck her like a bombshell: someone should grow and distribute pomodoros in America, creating a new industry that would give employment to thousands!

Although only sixteen, poor and uneducated in the ways of the world, Tillie began to dream. She went to the Brooklyn Botanical Gardens, where experts told her that both soil and climate were wrong in America for her pomodoros. Only in Italy could they be grown. She saved her money for five years, and booked passage for Italy. On board, she met Florindo del Gaiso, part owner of a Naples cannery which exported pomodoros. He was the first man to give her any hope that the luscious tomatoes could be grown in her native land. After Tillie had visited his cannery, her drive and optimism led him to give her some seeds and some old canning equipment, and to make a $10,000 investment in the new enterprise. So, she called her company Flotill- a combination of both their names.

She went to California where looking at the San Joaquin Valley in the growing season she said, "This is it; here I can build." A score of hardheaded packers turned her down when she asked if they would pack her as yet un-grown fruit. They had no faith that pomodoro seeds would even sprout! One of them finally agreed both to grow and to can 100,000 cases of whole tomatoes and 100,000 cases of the paste if she would guarantee to sell the whole lot in advance. Also, he demanded $10,000 as a guarantee against loss.

So Tillie traveled throughout the land, taking advance orders for her dream fruit, eating little, sleeping as she rode the day coaches and doing everything possible to make her expense money hold out. She sold all 200,000 cases. Her positive outlook drove down all negative arguments.

Then a heavy blow fell! The farmers who had promised the cannery to grow the pomodoros planted enough for only 700 cases of whole tomatoes and 2500 cases of the paste. But those they did grow were wonderful. The whole idea was a success. She wrote to her friend Florindo in Naples, and he sent more money and more machinery so that she could build her own cannery.

During the height of the season in Tillie's second year in the industry, her cannery's main boiler broke down. Great piles of beautiful pomodoros outside the plant would spoil within a day or two unless she could get live steam from somewhere. She would be wiped out! She went on what she called a "think walk." She walked and thought and prayed for hours. This was no time to quit! And across the fields, she heard the shrill whistle of a locomotive. That was it—get a locomotive unto a siding near her plant to produce live steam until she could get a new boiler. She did so in record time, saved the crop, and the day.

Her dream grew—new plants sprang up, more farmers grew her fruit, and the market for domestic pomodoros continued to expand. Then disaster struck again. At the height of the 1940 season, cannery workers went on strike—even in her plants where she was paying well above the average. Again the piles of fruit would spoil. Then the director of the labor union went to Stockton, spent a few hours with this honest, hopeful girl with the big dream, and called off the strike in her plants, became her manager, and seven years later married Tillie.

Back in March of 1952, Stockton observed Tillie Lewis Day—she had given California a new industry and had supplied our armed forces with a new product. The streets were lined with cheering people as her husband drove Tillie to the public auditorium. A poor girl with a great dream had had a persistent faith in its fulfillment that would not be denied!

Or again—go to Krakatoa—a verdant island lying about 100 miles off Batavia in the Indian Ocean. In May of 1883, a trading schooner slipped into the harbor of Batavia in Java and reported strange noises coming from a volcano on Krakatoa. A group of Dutchmen chartered a boat and visited the island. They heard rumblings deep in the earth and saw geysers of steam shooting up here and there. The visitors returned home, little dreaming of what was soon to happen.

Three months later, between August 26th and 28th, the beautiful island blew up in the most awful, cataclysmic contortion of the earth's crust that the world has ever experienced. Cracks below the island opened again and again, allowing ocean water to pour down into the white-hot molten lava of the old volcano until fourteen squares miles of the island were hurled into the sky. "It made," said the Royal Society of London, "the mightiest noise which, so far as we can ascertain, has ever been heard on the globe." It was a noise so great that it was heard distinctly four hours later on the island of Rodriguez, 3000 miles from Krakatoa.

Then came a tidal wave, 50 feet high, tearing across the Indian Ocean at a speed at times of more than 350 miles an hour. It destroyed utterly 163 villages and all of the inhabitants. It destroyed Batavia. It reached Cape Horn in 17 hours and on its way destroyed 5000 ships including a Dutch Man-Of-War that was carried two miles inland. The dust from the pulverized island rose 20 miles into the air and was carried clear around the earth. In St. Louis, Missouri, six months later, the sky was still green and the sun yellow because of the dust in the atmosphere.

In 1884, scientists made their way to what was left of the island and reported that the only form of life they found was a small spider, undoubtedly blown there from a nearby island. Otherwise, nothing but bleak, lifeless desolation was to be seen. Only two years later, however, in 1886, scientists found an amazing change. There were ferns, four varieties of flowers, two kinds of grass, butterflies, ants, and caterpillars, not to mention the morning glory, the mango, and the sugar plum. Birds which carried the seeds of all manner of vegetation were there in abundance, and in a few more years, the island was once again a paradise.

Now what about all of this? Simply this: An indestructible Life Principle is at work in all creation that will not be denied. Nothing has ever defeated it. For millions of years it was threatened by heat, cold, flood, drought, earthquake, and volcanic eruption. To resist, to survive, to win through is the end to which the Life Principle has ever set itself with a singleness of aim beyond our comprehension. And not only in the world of nature do we see this triumphant, on-going force, but also, and even more so, in the lives of humanity.

When a person has flooded and drenched his or her thoughts with fear, failure, despair, and hatred, that person's very soul is in danger of becoming a barren life-less desert waste—a human Krakatoa after the big blow. Then, when that person is so far down that there is no direction left to go but up, he or she is apt to begin crying out blindly for God, the infinite Love and Light Who has made all that is through creative thought and Whose very Being is shot through and through with the indestructible Life Principle. Then let that person ponder John's immortal words, *"But to all who received Him, who believed in His name, He gave power to become Children of God."* *(John 1: 12).*

Let that person repent of all sins and open the mind and heart to the inflowing of God's forgiveness, love and light; let that person dare to accept and acclaim rebirth and step boldly out upon a program of great affirmation. Let that person have the courage to start acting as if it were true here and now; and behold, the miracle will have been wrought!

Paul closed his great letter to the Ephesians with a triumphant shout, *"Now unto Him that is able to do exceeding abundantly above all that we ask or think, according to the power that worketh in us, unto Him be glory."*

When Jesus and Paul centered their teaching around faith in the power of God within, they counted on us to grasp the untold possibilities that lie dormant within us all. And not only dormant! These possibilities are smothered and killed in many millions of careless lives because of the flood of negative, defeatist, hate, envy, and greed-filled thoughts that take over the citadel of consciousness from morning until night, day after weary day. When Jesus found them thus, He said, *"No man having put his hand to the plough, and looking back is fit for the kingdom of God." (Luke 9:62).*

For those who are willing to put both hands to the plough of faith and affirm that faith, without looking back over the past—broken lives and hearts will be healed, and the hurt places of life made whole again.

Through the Valley

(Winter, Western Pennsylvania)

"The Lord looked down from heaven upon the
children of men, to see if there were any that
did understand, and seek God."
Psalms 14: 2

The Call of the Depths
Psalm 42

July 19, 1953
Concord Methodist Church, Beaver Falls, Pennsylvania

*T*he nights of this week have given to us once again that silver moonlight which touches the familiar earth and makes it a place of mystery, and lights it dramatically before us. Nature constantly is surprising us and making us gasp with childlike wonder at her striking pictures. So the psalmist of Israel went to nature for some stirring pictures that he uses with remarkable effect—and nearly all choir singers are familiar with that anthem lifted from his thoughts so long ago:

> *As the hart panteth after the water brooks,*
> *So panteth my soul after thee, O God.*

Then he goes on to remonstrate with his own oppressed heart:

> *Why art thou cast down, O my soul?*
> *And why art thou disquieted in me?*
> *Hope thou in God; for I shall yet praise Him*
> *For the help of his countenance.*
> *O my God, my soul is cast down within me:*

And then comes the psalmist's great appeal to God in nature—

> *Therefore will I remember Thee from the land of Jordan—*
> *And of the Hermonites, from the hill Mizar*
> *Deep calleth unto deep at the noise of Thy waterspouts.*

So he remembers how Jordan and Hermon had witnessed God's goodness to him—but more than that—it's an effort to lose his own spiritual vexations in the vastness and majesty of the universe. So he casts his own turmoil of spirit, the disquiet of his soul where the billows and tides are sweeping and beating across one another—realizing his part in the larger world—finding peace in its whole.

One of our thinkers gives us his recipe for calming fears, restoring order out of confusion and tension by telling us that we should take time in life for a look at the stars. Perhaps all of us know what he means as we stand a kindred spirit with this psalmist of old. Perhaps many of us know what it is to take a troubled soul, a perplexity or a confusion with us out under the stars—then gaze long upward until we fairly lose ourselves in the miracle and majesty of the universe, knowing ourselves as a part of it and finding calm and peace in the glory of this new awareness of greatness. One says such an experience as this, "fills the little with the large,"—reminds us that the small is small—lets us hear deep calling unto deep below and forgetting the small in the very greatness in which we stand.

So this phrase comes to us out of this psalm—and it speaks to us of one of our fundamental needs. It warns us of some of our apparent lackings—"deep calleth unto deep." The psalmist takes us in his own recall to the sources of the Jordan—back to Dan where with a mighty roaring as of a distant cataract, "a river springs full-born from the ground," the water rushing out through its subterranean channels, the deep below crying out to the deep above.

There is a profound responsiveness of life caught up in the words—forces in nature correspond and relate themselves one with another. Man responds to the world in which he lives, and that world to the human nature which inhabits it—and they call to one another as surely as deep calleth unto deep.

There is that bit of sculpture called *The Hand of God*—a great block of unhewn white marble—from which emerges a great hand, and the great hand holds within it the shapes of the bodies of a man and a woman—all from the hand of God. So the sculptor sets forth human greatness…so much of greatness held therein—made in the same image—the spark of divinity within humans that sets them off and far above all other creatures of earth. Creatures with a high potentiality for responding unto the God who made them, and lifted them, and breathed divinity into them. But the manner and the degree of responding determines the "worthfulness" or the worthlessness of humans. This it is that makes them at times beastlike and at other times supreme. So the world waits and calls, and humanity responds.

We know full well that in humans—and in the world about them—there are depths and shallows. Out of the deep of the world there wells up before people solemn and perplexing questions and vast challenges. On the other hand, how shallow some of the world's activity is! So with humans—what struggles within the depths of their souls, what peace may be theirs; what suffering, what joy. And on the other hand with humans, how shallow and superficial so much of their lives are—chasing shadows and frolicking even amidst the heaviest shadows.

So they stand—the world and humanity—one against the other. So they converse. So they respond one to another. So greatness emerges or is layered over with petty things and trivial affairs.

The psalmist's words come back to us, *"Deep calleth unto deep."*

So the river springing forth into light cries forth from the depths of its underground cavern to the roaring waters above. So the strongest powers of man and his soul are often brought into reality with the call of the world to face its heaviest problems or to do its largest tasks. When the world demands the very best of humans— then truly it is that "deep calleth unto deep"; and we taste of the more abundant life which our Lord Jesus lived!

It's found in the story of the life of Chevalier Jackson, world-famous surgeon at Temple University Medical Center in Philadelphia. He was a strange appearing individual in his personal appearance, so those who knew him testify—clothing never seemed to fit him well. "I always insist on a comfortable degree of oversize," he would say. His collars were two or three sizes too large, "turtle collars," he called them because of the way his head and neck could move around in the opening. He said of himself that his shoes were so long that eternal vigilance was required lest he trip over his own feet. He was a man who required room—space in which to work, and freedom in which to exercise his sensitive and large nature. To this man, inventor of the bronchoscope, they hurried the little Kelvin Rogers twelve-thousand miles across the earth from Melbourne, Australia to Philadelphia where Dr. Jackson could use his bronchoscope—which he did with no charge. And this is only one of the many deeds of kindness that he performed with his surgeon's skill as he went about, "doing good."

Deep calling unto deep is the response of the soul to the holy call of God as well. It's the experience of an Isaiah and countless multitudes since his day who go into the temples of their divine worship to stand alone and silent before God, so that when God's voice calls, out of the quietness of the depth of the soul, they hear and understand. It's the constant growing of life, maturing and enriching, as the most heroic parts of personality are touched and lifted ever nearer their creator and ever more worthy of God.

It's the way the poet beckons us:

> *Build thee more stately mansions, O my soul—*
> *While the swift seasons roll.*
> *Leave thy low-vaulted past!*
> *Let each new temple, nobler than the last,*
> *Shut thee from heaven with a dome more vast*
> *Till thou at length are free,*
> *Leaving thine outgrown shell*
> *By life's unresting sea!*
> *(Oliver Wendall Holmes)*

It's deep calling unto deep.

But we do not always live on so heroic a plane as that. There is such a thing as the deep calling unto the shallow—the high and holy things of the world crying forth, and the response received is flimsy and superficial.

The story is told that the only comment one American real estate man made when for the first time he visited the Pyramids of Egypt was, "They're certainly in a bad state of repair." One of the besetting sins of our American way of life is this failure of appreciation—he could not appreciate the glory that was Egypt, the miracle of construction of that early age, the scores of years of hard and heavy labor, the dreams of Pharaohs, the respect of people. All he could see were the cracks and the damage wrought by the years. Great truth, in a little spirit.

Or again, the story is told that Michelangelo stood with his pupil in one of Italy's old quarries, "And what do you see?" the master asked his student as he indicated a huge block of material.

"I see flawless marble."

"And I see an angel," was Michelangelo's rejoinder.

So often the great things go unused and unappreciated because of the speed and superficial character of our modern living—this deep crying forth and only shallow responding. Tennyson has Guinevere pray for release from this folly:

> *Ah, my God,*
> *What might I not have made of thy fair world,*
> *Had I but loved Thy highest creature here?*
> *It was my duty to have lived the highest;*
> *It surely was my profit had I known.*
> *It would have been my pleasure had I seen.*
> *We needs must love the highest when we see it.*

And from our own land comes the prayer of Thoreau:

> *Great God, I ask Thee for no meaner pelf*
> *Than that I may not disappoint myself,*
> *That in my action I may soar as high*
> *As I can now discern with this clear eye.*

> *That my weak hand may equal my firm faith,*
> *And my life practice more than my tongue saith;*
> *That my low conduct may not show,*
> *Nor my relenting lines,*
> *That I Thy purpose did not know,*
> *Or overrated Thy designs.*

In yet another regard of this response which exists between the world of living and the personality of humanity, there is such a thing as shallow calling unto deep. This comes when the superficial things of life lay hold of people's serious nature and their earnest desire to think great thoughts and to do good deeds. I'm not sure why I was thinking of Christmas so much this week. Perhaps such thinking began last Sunday afternoon when I stood before the large and richly colored stained-glass window in a church nearby and saw caught there by the artist, that little Bethlehem scene when love was born historically into the world. Christmas is a time when people's deep nature is stirred, when their thoughts turn Godward, and their souls are nourished in the goodness of so great a love that God would send forth God's own Son into the world to save that world. But Christmas is fast becoming a time when the superficial character of the holiday and festivities blur and often obscure the underlying nature of the event. It's a time when we are people so busy with so many things, when the world in "Christmas-keeping" beckons with so many trivialities that our own spiritual thirst goes unquenched. This is a shallow calling unto the depths, and there's a disproportion about it that is sad indeed!

But the saddest falling comes when the perversion of the good things of life comes from both ends—from the shallow things of the world calling and receiving a shallow response from people who forget their great beginnings and potential glories. Never in this relationship are the strongest powers of humanity stirred to noble activity. Small interests beset one, and one readily yields to the pettiness of the world. The world summons humans to enjoyment, and they succumb to the beckoning—enjoying to be sure—but missing the deep and underlying, and the eternal joy of a great calling and a good work. Such response as this is truly what one describes as "clothing oneself with cobwebs"—no communion rich and deep is here. We see it in our own day—when those set apart from others and held forth as honorable men do not understand nor appreciate their honor and give it up easily when the lighter pleasures of the world call. Perhaps it is some of the misunderstanding that beset Martha of Biblical fame—she was beset with all the little duties of earth and missed the great truths and the real serving. All in all, it is wearisome and weak.

So the psalmist sets our minds pondering about the responses that we make to life. He rolls forth his phrase "deep calleth unto deep" as the deep thunder of the organ strengthening life's music. And this is the noble company—humans responding with the very best of their power and skill to the very highest callings of the world about them. There is a royal retinue of the servants of the king who wait—not giving service to lesser beings—but waiting for the king himself. So those of the noble company sense the sacred in life and keep that which is sacred within themselves only for their King. No lesser lord attracts these select souls—for they are unwilling and unsatisfied to respond except where deep calls unto deep.

The religious leaders of the land point to these for example and preach with great pleading. "Wait—wait thou upon God." If you are not ready to give your deepest affections, and your complete loyalty to God, at least refuse them to any other master. None but God is worthy of our best offerings. Treasure and withhold your best and most sacred offerings until you can carry them unto the King. Wait—and surely the time will come when the call of the deep comes, and you can then make answer, for you have kept your sacred best for only the highest Lord.

So Christ who walked before us warned us, *"Cast not your pearls before swine,"* such would be to respond to the shallow calls with the deep. *"Render to Caesar that which is Caesar's and to God that which is God's."* Such is to treasure and cherish your most sacred part and to keep it for when only the highest calls.

So Jesus speaks to us, and so He lives to teach us. Men came to Him about the silly little division of inheritances and He would not waste His time with them. Nicodemus came eager for spiritual light, and Christ would sit all night and teach him. The people of Nazareth wanted to stone Him, and He quietly passed away and left them; but the cross demanded Him, and He went up to that terrible experience with a consecrated soul to endure it without sparing Himself. He understood the worth of life and lived to give His all to the highest calling. If we truly follow Him, we walk in a way of spiritual balance—unexcited over little things, not wretched over petty affairs—these are things of the moment—but already and always willing to use ourselves and to be anxious over spiritual things. Such is to reply—when the deep calls. Whether one is good and honest, whether one is growing in truth and character; whether the world is better for one's living; whether one is finding God—these are the grave and great issues which bring us unto the company of noble souls.

The words of a well-known hymn sum it up so well:

Rise up, o men of God!
Have done with lesser things.
Give heart and mind and soul and strength
To serve the King of Kings.
(William P. Merrill)

Why Do Good People Suffer, Too?
Mark 15: 34

February 3, 1963
First Methodist Church, Sylvania, Ohio

When a gambler loses his shirt, a sigh of satisfaction ripples across the community. The people are pleased that he got what he deserved. No sense of the fitness of things seems outraged when tragedy comes upon the evil man. In the Psalms it says, *"The wicked are like the chaff which the wind drives away."* When they are caught up like that and blown off, justice seems to have been realized.

But when a good person—one of high thoughts and purpose in life is struck down with tragedy—when the business falls apart, or the heart fails, or the children disgrace the home, or when death parts the family, or all the things that can plague us beset that person—then what do we say? How do we explain the intolerable agonies that make up life: sickness, suffering, tragedy, death? You cannot brush aside such things with some easy chirpy word about getting out of life what we give it.

When a good person suffers, we question the purpose of God—we ask impatiently, even as Jesus asked in that ultimate moment of inquiry, "My God, my God, why..."

Then when that suffering besets a whole people—an entire race of a faith group, the cry goes up to God a hundredfold.

A rabbi during war days told a minister that his old father had been reading of the Nazi atrocities against the Jewish people in Germany, and he was so shocked with the terror of these things that he cried out, "Abraham, when I get to heaven, I am going to march straight up to God, grab hold of His beard, shake His head, and shout into His ears—Why did you let it happen—why, why—tell me that?"

And in about the same spirit—a sense of outraged justice—James Weldon Johnson, the famous Negro poet, has the Negro preacher of his poem *The Crucifixion* challenge God:

Oh, look at black-hearted Judas—
Sneaking through the dark of the garden—
Leading his crucifying mob
O God.
Strike him down!
Why don't You strike him down
Before he plants his traitor's kiss
Upon my Jesus's cheek.

It is possible, of course, that there is no answer to why God permits these things to happen. The complexity of evil has been a subject that has always managed to stymy the philosophers. Some thinkers claim that there is no answer to the problem of evil.

There is the story of the elderly seminary professor catching a student napping, who proposed the question, "Why is evil permitted in the scheme of things?"

The student, not coming to quickly enough to realize what was going on, used the dodge, "I used to know professor, but for the moment I have forgotten."

With dignity and seriousness, the professor replied, "Students, this is a fateful moment in the history of human thought. Mark it well. Since time began only two people have known the answer to this question. Jesus, and He didn't tell, and the other is the student in our midst—and now he has forgotten!"

We keep searching for the answer to this—and whether or not we shall find the answer I do not know—I only know that we shall go on seeking.

There are those who believe that God permits evil to happen because God is vindictive. "Our God is a terrible God," they say. "God is stern, austere, and implacable in God's righteousness. God cannot countenance evil at all. The sight of it makes God sick and angry. And at every show of iniquity God's justice makes itself known. All evil must be paid for in kind and in quantity. There is no suffering which is not the result of sin, and the suffering must be extracted as a propitiation for the sin, or God is not God. In all the affairs of life, God is an impartial referee, an unpurchaseable judge, whose righteousness and justice must often decree terror and suffering even as they often give grace and love." So runs the venerable doctrine about God whose wrath is the equal of God's love.

We believe that all suffering is indirectly the result of sin in the human family. Once life did not involve suffering. Bread was not earned by the sweat of the brow. Roses were without thorns, and no weeds grew in the garden plot. Death was unknown and life was entirely without disappointment. But something happened, and as St. Paul says, *"Sin came into the world—and death through sin, and so death spread to all men because all sinned.*

Suffering comes as an indirect result of sin.

Another explanation is that God does not have anything to do with evil. It is no concern of God's. Indeed there are those people who retreat from reality, who believe that the world has long since been cut off from any connection with God. The Almighty has made us, but has long since lost real interest in the affairs of humanity.

But Christians go on believing that this is God's world and that God is vastly concerned with the suffering and grief of God's people. We believe that God is a good God who suffers when we suffer. We believe that God permits suffering not in order to assuage God's anger, but that it may serve some useful purpose in the divine scheme of things. We believe that God is vitally concerned and eminently able to deal with the problem of suffering.

Two stories come our way to illustrate this. Did you read in the papers about Beverly Smith—a little brown-eyed girl? She was a remarkable child—she never cried! Not even when she cut a gash in her head, nor when she burned a blister on her hand—nor when they gave her a deep injection of liver extract. She was a painless baby. But Beverly's mother realized that her small daughter might break a bone and no one know it. She might burn to a crisp and not feel it. She might develop appendicitis without having nature's usual warnings of pain. A life without pain would be perpetually dangerous, you see.

Then there was the man—a large handsome kind of man who was full of energy and enthusiasm for his work as crusading mayor of a city, resolved on turning out the rascals and the evils of government. Full of confidence in himself, prejudiced. He went on his way until something laid him low. Months and months of sickness and pain upon a hospital bed. And during those days, he talked with his minister who discovered certain changes coming to pass. Consideration began to replace prejudice—thoughtfulness replaced hatred—evidence of goodwill began to creep in. And when at last he died, both body and soul were different than they had been, for he had learned to love life and to respect others. Suffering had mellowed his temperament; pain had softened his brutal attitudes, and he forsook the god of Mars to trust in the Prince of Peace.

Is it not true that suffering produces a sensitiveness to life's essentials? Without suffering, all life would be crass and hard. The Negro spirituals were hammered out on the anvil of adversity and hardship. The very richness of the spiritual music is evidence of the depth of suffering which the Negro had known.

There are those literary, musical, and poetic geniuses who confess that suffering has been their great inspiration. When Victor Hugo was exiled because of his political views, his detention became the wellspring for some of his greatest works. "Why was I not exiled before?" he exclaimed.

Think of John Milton—blind, yet dictating *Paradise Lost:*

> *What is dark in me illumine*
> *And David's psalms had ne'er been sung*
> *If grief his heart had never rung.*

Helen Keller, freighted down with a multitude of limitations, overcame them all to typify the very spirit of compassion and understanding. On one occasion, she was sharing with a group of friends the rich visions she had seen even through her blindness, the music which she had heard in spite of her deafness, the aspirations which she uttered though dumb of speech. One person, blessed with sight, hearing, and speech cried out, "Not thou, not thou—'tis we are deaf, are dumb, are blind!"

We live in such a marvelous land and in such a privileged situation that it is easy for us to assume that life is "things." It is one of the nasty symptoms of the malady of our culture that we cannot dispose of the illusion that in materialism there is happiness. The very drive for success, for financial superiority, for status among our fellows, makes it difficult for us to achieve the sympathy and compassion which are gifts of suffering. I do not for one moment desire that suffering come to myself—to my family—or to you— because of what such suffering will do to us personally. That would be psychotic. But I do know that our easygoing, overflowing kind of life makes it often difficult for us to achieve that sensitiveness which is so readily grown in the rich soil of suffering.

No word concerning the problem of suffering is begun, much less continued without meditation upon that supreme Sufferer, even our Lord the Christ. His suffering gave Him an instinctive and concomitant sympathy with every person who had any kind of suffering—a broken arm, a stone-blind eye, a leprous isolation, a dead daughter. All others who suffered recognized in Him a kindred spirit. The suffering He embraced is one of the major factors which makes His life so sensitive to the needs of our spirits, as was sensed by the unknown poet who wrote these words on the walls of a hospital in Denver:

The cry of man's anguish went up to God,
'Lord, take away pain!
The shadow that darkens the world Thou hast made,
The close-coiling chain
That strangles the heart; the burden that weighs
On the wings that would soar—
Lord, take away pain from the world Thou has made
That it love Thee the more!'

Then answered the Lord to the cry of his world,
'Shall I take away pain,
And with it the poorer of thy soul to endure,
Made strong by the strain?
Shall I take away pity that knits heart to heart
And sacrifice high?
Will you lose all your heroes that lift from the fire
White brows to the sky?
Shall I take away love, that redeems with a price
And smiles at its loss?
Can ye spare from your lives that would climb unto mine,
The Christ on His cross?
(Anonymous)

The Sacredness of Life
Psalm 21

May 19, 1963
First Methodist Church, Sylvania, Ohio

Life is a thrilling thing—a gift of the great God on high to the children of earth—such is the conception of it that comes forth in our text: *"He asked life of Thee and Thou gavest it him, even length of days forever."*

This is a picturesque scene as the people of Israel gather in the presence of their king to sing forth their gratitude. They are enthusiastic for their ruler. But over all of this feeling of people for their reigning king, there is felt and sung their praise of God. From God have come the blessings which have benefitted the king in his rule. First is this recognition of God and God's goodness, then there is the proper time and place for their recognition of the king's victories over enemies and escape from troubles that beset him. Finally in a last breath of praise, the people turn themselves again unto God and sing, *"Be Thou exalted, Lord, in Thine own strength, so will we sing and praise Thy power."*

So we, too, ask of God for life; often the request is not directed unto God as a formal prayer. More often it consists of our individual participation in the vast struggle for existence—a struggle that involves our endeavors at self-support, that includes our shudders at the thoughts of dying, our gladsome experiences in the delights of living. All of these are parts of our asking for life.

And the cry is heard and the gift is given. And wrapped up in this gift are not only the powers of present being and present enjoyment, but the powers as well of thinking, feeling, loving, living so that we are attuned to the great and continuing movements of the universe The gift is not a momentary thing—but a part of the life of the universe, eternal life!

Now, we have differing outlooks upon life. There is that understanding of its full delights that Browning has the boy David sing forth in the presence of King Saul:

Oh the wild joys of living! The leaping from rock to rock
The strong rending of boughs from the fir tree;
The cool silver shock of the plunge in the pool's living water,
How good is man's life, the mere living! For fit to employ
All the heart and the soul and the senses
Forever in joy.

But not always does one content oneself with such pleasures of the sensual portion of life. There comes a time for a deeper look, for a nobler participation, for a finer appreciation of all that is wrapped in the gift of life. A time when the light-hearted indifference and casual appreciation of earth enlarges into the deeper concerns for life and what we make of it and how we use it. Unless we move into this more serious consideration of the gift, our gratitude cannot be full nor is there growth toward the nourishment and building that is potentially held for each of us. Life's living then is a mere foundation to what it might be one day—a structure fair and adequate.

So with life—a beginning that has never gone on to complete itself, character that is not developed. Oh the tragedies of these foundations of character into which maturity has not breathed a loftier living—skills unused, sympathies untraveled into the area of true interest in our comrades along life's pilgrim way, bodily vigor atrophied through lack of use in godly endeavors, minds cobwebbed with bigotries because thinking has not been energetic—life unfulfilled!

How different is the poet's conception: *"He asked life of Thee and Thou gavest it him, even length of days forever."* And they praised the king because he had used life well.

While hiding from the Nazis, fifteen year old Anne Frank wrote in her diary:

I think that God would not create a thing entirely void of beauty.
There is, I know, in everyone deep down, a lovely soul; in every soul,
however bad, some good.

It is in the spirit of Noah in the play *Green Pastures, "I ain' very much, but I's all I got!"*

How then do we rise up to the heights of living? How then do we develop our potentialities into fine expressions and noble experiences of living? How do we build so that no foundation of possibility need crumble for lack of resources? We go back to the Hebrew people again, to the people praising the deeds of their king. But as we go back, we remember that they first turned their thoughts to God. And here is the beginning if life is to move forth and unfold its true beauty—a recognition of God as the source of life and the power of growth. I believe that the world needs God, but I also believe that we affirm that need so loudly that at times we fail to realize that we are the ones who most desperately need God. The world needs God, yes; but that is a generality. "I need God," is specific and meaningful and applicable to my own life's development. And if I, that needful soul, wish to build fittingly upon the foundation, to unfold into life's higher appreciation and usefulness, then I do it best with recognition of God—and follow that recognition with obedience to God, to God's Will.

> *The sweetest lives are those to duty wed*
> *Whose deeds, both great and small,*
> *Are close-knit strands of unbroken thread*
> *Where love ennobles all.*
> *(Elizabeth Barret Browning)*

To give ourselves unto the will of God that God may do in us that which God made us for, which we ourselves but dimly understand, such is our only true completion. This submission to God is not an enslaving thing, not a concession we make, but rather the doorway toward the full and beautiful completion of life. The brush of the painter and the instrument of the musician, yea the hammer of the carpenter are nothing alone—but how useful, how beneficial they become when placed in the hands of the artist and the musician and the carpenter. The foundation of possibility is then built upon to become the completed reality. So it is with the cry of the righteous people who come to the place when their souls can earnestly say, "O Lord, not my will, but Thy will be done." So it is that I have said to you that I appreciate the earthly life of our Lord Jesus most deeply in that garden of prayer. There you see the human inclinations of self-preservation battling against the divine necessity of life's fulfillment. There you witness the high moment when decision is reached that life must move on and be complete according to the will of God. Without submission to that will, life misses the greater structure of its completion.

I believe that life's high moments come when our souls reach forth and find our God and understand God's will for us. I believe that between God and us there can be this close bond that when tempered with understanding and strengthened with constant searching after God, becomes firmer and more realistic until we have a spiritual experience kindred to the earthly experience of that pilot who climbed in his ship far above the earth until it seemed:

> *...with silent lifting mind I've trod*
> *The high untrespassed sanctity of space*
> *Put out my hand and touched the face of God.*
> (John Gillespie Magee, Jr.)

And power comes into life to help it complete itself most beautifully in all its sacred nature when we find our God and maintain a constant fellowship with God. Such power that life and its perplexities and its dangers have no fear to us. The old man put it this way, "Nothing is going to happen to me today that God and me together can't handle!"

And we find God in our seeking most intimately through that One who came to reveal God unto us. There is in Jesus that human quality that brings God so close to us, and yet there is that divine following of God's will at every step that holds Him far above us to be our constant star that doesn't fail as we follow it.

Albert Schweitzer writes of it in these words that mean so much to me:

> *He comes to us as One unknown, without a name, as of old by the lakeside He came to those men who knew Him not. He speaks to us the same word: 'Follow thou me!' and sets us to the tasks which He has to fulfill for our time. He commands, and to those who obey Him, whether they be wise or simple, He will reveal Himself in the toils, the conflicts, the sufferings which they shall pass through. In His fellowship; and as an ineffable mystery, they shall learn in their own experience who He is. God asked life of thee and thou gavest it God, even to lead a deeper life and to do greater things.*

A boy, large for his age, yet only a boy, was going to a distant city to live and work. One day before he was to leave, his mother said to him, "John, I want you to go down to the art gallery tomorrow with me and see a picture that hangs there. I want you to do this for me."

The boy did, and saw in the picture a man at prayer...Christ in the garden. What a wonderful face He had, and yet why that look of worry and care? His mother had always taught him that Christ was not afraid to die; then why that look?

"Mother," he said, "why that look of worry on His face, and why do His hands seem to be pleading so?"

"Son, He had been a teacher for three years, and there was much that He wanted to teach and to do. But now, on the morrow He was to die and leave it undone. I think He was worried with the fear that those whom He loved and trusted would forget and leave the work undone. For even now the three that He had asked to watch with Him for one hour were lying asleep at the entrance to this garden. I think that He was afraid that all through the centuries His followers would forget and leave undone the work that He, in going, could not do. I think that thing might have caused that look of worry on His brow."

For a long time the boy stood looking at the picture, his face sinking lower and lower as his eyes looked steadily into the face of the Man at prayer. Then he raised his head as he straightened his shoulders and said, "Oh, Man of Galilee, if there is anything that You have left undone anywhere that I can do, you can count on me."

And he went out, away to that distant city to work, and to live a Christ-guided life.

The Journey to Jerusalem

They came seeking...
seeking life...
and they tasted the glories of an age to come
as they left all and went without a backward look to follow—
But some turned aside!
We asked life of Thee and
Thou gavest it—a cruel cross.
Instead of torture, humiliation of final death,

A precious symbol,
a fulfillment of hope,
a sacred service and
a gateway into eternal life.
(Anonymous)

The Far Look
Psalm 121

Community Methodist Church, Whitaker, Pennsylvania, July 8, 1956

We live in a region of beautiful hills—and after one travels or lives in other parts of our country where the hills are lacking, he or she returns then with a new and keener sense of the beauty of the hills and of their physically enduring quality. Perhaps, the returned traveler really knows then the feeling of the psalmist who sought God and in his seeking turned toward the hills—for the mountains of his day were the holy places, the hills were the steps by which Deity could descend to earth. So for the psalmist and for us, the hills stand forth as being of the most permanent and most uplifting objects of the natural world. And with him we cry forth, *"I will lift up mine eyes unto the hills, from whence cometh my help?"* And then the reply comes forth—perhaps from the priest to whom the question may have been directed—and the priest knows and shares that knowledge with the worshipping poet: *"Help cometh from the Lord Who made heaven and earth."*

In the reply is the very center of the faith of Israel in the availability of divine help, sufficient for every human need. So many times in life do we have this need, and then for many of us there comes the experience of turning unto the great and spiritual "hill" which for us is God. Such lifting of our earthly eyes toward the eternal God brings its genuine rewards to our days of living.

In turning toward the great Hill from whence comes our help, we find healing for tired bodies and weary souls. The upward look restores our perspective in life and is a calming and a steadying influence on us.

There was a certain seamstress who was having skull-splitting headaches without knowing why. Finally, that seamstress went to a doctor who asked her, "How many hours a day do you sew?"

"All day," she said. "My living depends on it."

"And what do you see out of your window?" he asked.

"Oh, not much. Only some grass, and the trees, and the road and the people that pass by."

"Nothing else?"

"No, only the horizon and the line of hills."

"Good!" he exclaimed. Go back to your work, but one hour each day, drop your sewing and look beyond the grass and the trees and the people to the hills—to the hills."

There is healing in the "far look."

And for one who strives to look upward toward God, there comes a vision of greatness which serves to renew the spirit. One of our well-known pieces of sculpture, which I have mentioned before, is called *The Hand of God*. This remarkable work of art, carved from a single piece of marble, consists of a great hand, and held within that hand are the forms of a man and a woman all hewn from the same piece of material—an artist's conception of the glory that is of God present in the creation that is humanity! It's an interpretation of the possibility of divinity within that creature of creation if the created draws forth from the self all of the beauty of that divinity and all of the power of that inner glory. The psalmist sets it forth in his own enduring way,

> *As I look up to the heavens Thy fingers made*
> *The moon and the stars that Thou hast shaped, I say;*
> *And what is man, that Thou should'st think him?*
> *What is man that Thou are mindful of him,*
> *And the son of man that Thou visitest him?*
> *For Thou hast made him little lower than the angels*
> *And hast crowned him with glory and honor.*
> *(Psalm 8: 3-5)*

In such a heavenly-formed creature in whom is the breath of God, there must be the continual looking toward that source of strength and love and peace which draws forth the highest from the created being. As the hills hold within them the sources of the streams that make up the mighty waters that flow down through all the plains and bring fertility to the regions roundabout, so does the great and eternal God hold the source of spiritual waters from which we must continually drink if we are to spiritually live. Humanity, with the breath of God within, must look to God for renewal of the spirit. A deep faith in the source.

And you, o my soul where you stand
Surrounded, detached, in measureless oceans of space,
Ceaselessly musing, venturing, throwing, seeking the
Spheres to connect them,
Till the bridge you will need be formed,
Till the ductile anchor hold
Till the gossamer thread you fling catch somewhere
O my soul.
(Walt Whitman)

Dr. Grenfell, in his experience of being *Adrift on an Iceberg,* recounted his belief in a something that was physically intangible but spiritually real for him, and he resolved,

> *I am determined, God helping me, that no man shall rob me of my faith—I won't hide it away. I'll keep it right around me if I can. I will see that it gets exercise. When in real danger, if I can, I will go to someone stronger than I to help keep it safe. But when that necessity arises, to whom shall I look for help? Surely directly to Him who gave me this faith—for I know "whom I have trusted, and I am persuaded that He is able to keep it against that day."*

A beautiful comparison has been made between windows—great cathedral windows—and the soul as the window of the heart. We must—to experience God most vividly for ourselves—open those cathedral windows of the soul toward God. We must lift up our eyes to the hills from whence comes our help—we must open our hearts unto the Lord who made heaven and earth.

Then for the one who strives to look upward toward God, there comes a challenge to grow. Majestic words are used in the entitling and description of the Being whom we worship—words that in their very sound and through their very connection remind us that our God is a great and an abiding Power who is worthy of our praise and service. As we look toward that Power who made us and who gave us the breath of life, God's very greatness and God's majesty stand as a mighty challenge to our own littleness and make us "long to grow,"—to grow into more perfect beings, into more dedicated believers and followers of God's great way of living.

The little story is told and retold of the scrub tree who looked down to earth and thought, "How small I am—I must grow and see if I can reach that star." And it grew and became tall, and towered over all the trees. In our shortcomings, in our human weakness, we can look about us at the pettiness and the weaknesses of others and live content because we are as good or perhaps just a little better than they—according to our own standards—we have then a sort of false sense of our own greatness—

OR

We can look up to an ideal that is without flaw—to an inspiration that is captivating in its very purity—and we can grow...

We can grow for this is the very nature of life and the mighty challenge of our religion. The poet fervently cries forth her gratitude:

> *Thank God a man can grow!*
> *He is not bound*
> *With earthward gaze*
> *To creep along the ground;*
> *Though his beginnings be but a poor and low*
> *Thank God, a man can grow!*
> (*Florence Earle Coates*)

Life in its quality as being a gift from God, is a challenge to strive higher—to grow in all of these ways to be like God from whence the life comes.

And in our upward look to that spiritual Hill who is the source and the strength, the renewal and the way of life, there comes an insight into eternity. In turbulent and tumultuous days, there came to the psalmist a sense of the protective quality of those majestic hills. In days when so many attractions lure us and so many material glamours tempt us, in days when the temporary quality of earthly life is so evident before us, in days when faith in so many false gods has brought disillusionment, it is of infinite worth that we rest our faith in a secure Hill that will not move, that will stand forever in its protective influence over us. And to the one who lifts one's eyes unto the God who is such a refuge and such an abiding power, there comes a sense of eternity that steadies life through the storms that beat upon it, that calms life in hours of turmoil, that brings life abiding joy that comes with knowing God and turning unto God, and throws over all our anxieties the blanket of assurance that life does not end, that the great spiritual values endure, and thus gives us peace.

There are those among us this day who have found themselves in periods of physical pain, who have gone through the dark valleys of sorrow, who have known the long and bitter periods of their own weakness. There are those among us who have been overwhelmed by the confusion of a fast-moving, rapidly changing world. There are those who have been discouraged through the failures of some personal plan. To them comes the word and the promise:

> *Come unto Me, all ye that labor and are heavy laden*
> *And I will give you rest.*
> *(Matthew 11: 28)*

Here is the very real source of eternity that we find when we look upward unto God who gives life, who sustains and protects life, and who brings it home at last. For those who catch this sense of eternity, there comes deep joy because for them there has been the upward looking unto that something great which they worship. There has been the stepping forth in fellowship with their hand in the hand of God. There has been for them the firm belief in the resources that comes to one who spiritually seeks. And there has come for them the confidence that life is good because it is governed by so enduring and so capitating a Presence as is the great God of our worship, the Hill from whence comes our help.

In the words of one who has known suffering, but who believes firmly and shares that belief, I draw this resolution of faith, of renewal, of spiritual growth, and of high confidence:

> *I will lay hold of enduring things;*
> *I am wearied with the din and the noise and fret*
> *About me, close distracting things*
> *Grapple my soul—Lord help me to forget*
> *The clamor of it. Grant me the peace that stills,*
> *Deep peace of quietness and hope that cheers.*
> *I will lift my eyes to Thy strength-giving hills,*

Steeped in the light of far eternal years.
I will lay hold upon enduring things;
Faith that illumines though the eyes be blind,
And joy continuous, a heart that sings,
And love that suffers long, yet still is kind,
They are such paltry things I've bartered for
I am soul-sick with the weariness it brings.
Now with high lifted face I turn me, for
I will lay hold upon enduring things.
                    (Anonymous)

Christian Service

(Sanctuary Dedication, First United Methodist Church, Sylvania, Ohio)

"The harvest truly is great, but the laborers are few; pray ye therefore the Lord of the harvest, that He would send forth laborers into His harvest."

Luke 10: 2

On Walking Crooked Miles
Isaiah 2: 1-5

November 9, 1953
Concord Methodist Church, Beaver Falls, Pennsylvania

In our ancient churches, there were many forms of symbolic art that we seldom see in our modern houses of worship. For instance, they tell us of the triptych—a three-folded screen that used to adorn the altar of the church. The triptych was a painting that represented some sacred event. Many of them on one panel portrayed the birth of Christ and on the third panel the enthronement of Christ as King. Then the central panel revealed the way of causation, the method by which the transition was made between the first and the third phases of this sacred event.

So it is that when we contemplate the significance of a day set apart in history, it does take us back into the past as we contemplate the beginning of that day as a special event—this one being established to celebrate the armistice over the earth after the years of struggle and warfare and hatred. So a day such as this does make us recall past history. Moreover, it leads us to ponder over the future and what that future holds—in this event when and whether peace will come and if it does, whether it will long endure.

The British poet, Tennyson, in the last century gave serious thought to it, and then wrote the words of his vision:

> *For I dipped into the future far as human eye could see*
> *Saw the vision of the world, and all the wonder that could be,*
> *Till the war drum throbbed no longer, and the battle flags are furled,*
> *In the parliament of men, the federation of the world.*

Perhaps his vision was beyond our present days, for we have not yet achieved that "wonder that could be." The world in our hour is at tinder-pitch, and we are well aware that even a slight incident might become the spark that enkindles the whole into open and terrible world conflict.

So much depends, you see, upon our present conduct—upon that central panel of our nation which is the present hour—as to whether the world will progress from its warring days of past into a period of peace and good will to all..

The world's history is abundant in the examples of ways we should not choose to walk in a critical hour—and this week as I've been thinking about it, there came ringing through my head that old jingle that you know so well:

> *There was a crooked man*
> *Who walked a crooked mile,*
> *He found a crooked sixpence*
> *Upon a crooked stile.*
> *He bought a crooked cat*
> *Which caught a crooked mouse,*
> *And they all lived together*
> *In a little crooked house.*
> *(English Nursery Rhyme)*

No other house you see would be suitable—it must fit its occupants. We have seen the world distorted through the years by people walking crooked miles and attempting to fashion the world about their perverted personalities so that they themselves would feel at home in it. We are creatures of choice, and two ways of life are open to us—two sets of values—a twisted sense of values leads only to a warped world.

Georgia Harkness, noted woman theologian of Methodism, said it this way a few years ago:

> *There are two dates of outstanding importance in the history of mankind. The date of the birth of a Baby in Bethlehem nearly two thousand years ago—a date which is so important to us that we count our present time from that birth, and August 6, 1945, Hiroshima—the fate of mankind hangs in the balance between what Christ stands for and what the bomb stands for.*

It's the central panel, the one of causation, you see, that determines the future.

Let us consider briefly some of the crooked miles down which people have walked along war's roadway—these are forces which made for war:

Competition between armed states—unrestrained by consideration for international understanding, welfare competition without cooperation.

Fear in its several forms—fears of attack, fear of loss of power and promise, fears of loss of property and wealth and position.

The gigantic struggle for power by huge economic interests that consider the welfare of people only as they are pawns in the great game of monopoly building and the reaction of greater storehouses to hold the wealth accumulated.

The threat present so evidently in our day of totalitarian governments that are unwilling to come to agreement with other nations.

The threat of military domination of foreign policy in our nations—our military budgets are far out of proportion to our other budgets—we are spending more to destroy than we are to educate the world.

The fanning to flame of misunderstanding and prejudice by irresponsible citizens. We do live in a time when the principle of propaganda prevails and must be cautious against the reports we hear and the gossip we share.

Then there is across our world widespread poverty and illiteracy. There are so many "have-nots" in this world of ours and promises of better futures lure them into following any cause. Surely such a critical hour as this needs all the sound mission support we can lend to offset the hypocrisy of leaders who are interested only in their own well-being and not concerned for any greater cause such as the Cross of Christ under which our missionaries serve.

Then, too, there is present continued racial injustice and exploitation in many areas of the world. We need not go far afield to find men and women anxious to squeeze from their neighbors all that may mean a person gain.

Naked selfishness and empty promises of wonderful futures are evident in all of this perplexing picture of the crooked miles people will walk for ill-gotten gain.

If all of this is painted upon that central panel of causation in the triptych of history, then that third and final panel carries a grim painting indeed—one in which darkness prevails over the mind of humanity, education neglected, culture forgotten, Christ ignored. It's a sobering thought for our reflection upon an anniversary of the day of peace.

As well as these, there is the other way—the highway of the Prince of Peace—and our gratitude is surely due to all those who could center our minds upon that way of walking and who challenge us to His cause and to His following. There are forces available to us by which peace might be established—and so established as to satisfy the deep hungers of humanity for good will and harmony upon earth.

And the first of these is God—the great God on high who gives us all things and whose worship lifts us beyond the petty horizon of selfish living into a great concern for brotherhood under His fatherhood. The worship of God that warms our hearts and lights our lives. Faith in God that steadies us and emboldens our belief in God's goodness, in the possibilities of peace among humanity, and the Kingdom of God upon earth.

Then there is the divine availability through the power of prayer—I am sure that all of us believe in it—though I am honestly not so certain that all of us avail ourselves of its power and peace often enough in daily living. We need prayers to go forth to God in every language and from hearts everywhere—sincere prayers uttered in the spirit of the Prince of Peace.

Another hope that we have is the growing world fellowship of Christians—the new age of our Protestant branch of Christendom is ecumenicity—the worldwide cooperation of our varying degrees of Christian belief and the united action of all. The work of the World Council of Churches for peace is surely a godly force in the right direction.

Then, too, there is the hope that is in many hearts today that with the organization of the United Nations there will come the ability to deal with world situations of tense nature so that the tinder-pitch is passed and governments restrain themselves often in the face of provocative circumstances and even when contrasting policies make agreement difficult. They have proved this possibility in some instances that give us added hope for future peaceful settlements of disputes which, without the United Nations, would flare quickly into open warfare.

Walking the crooked miles, you see, is never sufficient for the followers of the Master who goes forth down the highway of the Prince of Peace—His cross is still the great way of causation by which He is established and enthroned as King over our lives—that cross that enshrines for us the beautiful example of selfless living and dying out of love for humanity. The factor of personality is the priceless element of the world, and for this Christ would give himself. It is for us to follow loyally in His train, to study His way and to make His principles the active force in our lives, and through us in the world of our living.

> *Christ stands at the bar of the world today*
> *As He stood in the days of old*
> *Let each man tax his soul and say*
> *Shall I again my Lord betray*
> *For my greed, or my good, or my gold?*
> *(Anonymous)*

We must lift ourselves out and beyond self-centered interest if this world is made better and carried further toward good will through our personal efforts.

It is essential that we aspire and sustain hope in our hearts for peace. It does not take any longer to think rightly than to think wrongly, to decide wisely than foolishly, to act peacefully rather than violently. As Christians we need to be the leaders in the prayers and plans for peace over the earth. Sensing people's distress and doing our utmost to alleviate them and to better their condition is one way fitting for followers of the Christ. Learning to love our neighbors is still part of the great commandment that He emphasized for us. Edgar Guest puts it:

231

I have a kindly neighbor, one who stands
Beside my gate and chats with me a while.
Gives me the glory of his radiant smile
And comes at time to help with helping hands.
No station high or rank this man commands,
He, too, must trudge, as I the long day's mile;
And yet, devoid of pomp or gaudy style,
He has a worth exceeding stocks or lands.

To him I go when sorrow's at my door;
On him I lean when burdens come my way;
Together oft we talk our trials o'er,
And there is warmth in each goodnight we say.
A kindly neighbor! Wars and strife shall end
When man has made the man next door his friend.

It is an anxious hour when what we write upon that great central panel of our historic moment will determine the future light or darkness of the world. Woodrow Wilson's words fall upon us with clarity in such an hour:

Men's hearts wait upon us; men's lives hang in the balance, men's hopes call upon us to say what we will do. Shall we live up to the great trust? Who dares fail to try?

And out of the Old Testament Deuteronomy comes the call to the high and holy way:

See, I have set before Thee this day life and good, and death and evil, in that I command thee this day to love the Lord thy God, to walk in His ways, and to keep His commandments and His statutes and His ordinances, that thou mayest live and multiply. But if thy heart turn away, and thou wilt not hear, but shall be drawn away, and worship other gods and serve them: I denounce unto you this day that ye shall surely perish—I call heaven and earth to witness against you this day, that I have set before you life and death, the blessing and the curse; therefore choose life, that both thou and thy seed may live.

232

Forgiveness—W. H. Davies

Stung by a spiteful wasp
I let him go life free:
That proved the difference
In him and me.

For had I killed my foe,
It had proved me at once
The stronger wasp, and no
More difference.

A Complete Offering
Acts 3: 1-10

February 5, 1969
First United Methodist Church, Sidney, Ohio

The man in this story was a cripple from birth. He had never been able to do any work so was carried to the Beautiful gate of the Temple where with outstretched hands he secured his livelihood. He begged in order to live.

It is impossible for us to enter into the experience of someone so limited. We take our health, our God-given strength and abilities for granted. We cannot imagine what it would be like to live our whole life, limited, compelled to beg.

We do not ordinarily look at life through the eyes of someone so handicapped as this, but this man, sitting at the Temple gate with hand outstretched, looked at life as a cripple must. He saw two young men coming up the steps toward the Beautiful Gate. One was the son of a ship owner, the other was a fisherman who had spent his life thrusting his hands down into the sea to lift the net to make a living.

As they approached the beggar, they paused, and Peter said to the beggar, "Look at us." He recognized a very important fact of experience. When we seek to help a person, we need his or her undivided attention. If Peter was to perform the miracle of recovery, he must have this man's attention. It is possible that through the years this beggar had become ashamed of his begging, and as people approached he dropped his eyes and would not look at those who were about to give something, but Peter said, "Look at us!"

Then, when he had the man's undivided attention, Peter said, "Silver and gold have I none."

The mind of the beggar must have been stunned. What else can anyone give to the poor? What other means is there to help? Money has amazing power since it is the most fluid instrument humanity has. We do wonderful things with money. It is a basic need in all cultures, for by the use of money people may transfer their resources of mind and skill.

✠ 235

This beggar rightfully expected that he would receive silver and gold from these two sturdy well-dressed young fellows. But Peter said, "Silver and gold I have none; but such as I have, give I thee. In the name of Jesus Christ of Nazareth, rise up and walk."

This beggar must have heard of Jesus before. This is not hocus-pocus. There is no magic in words, and it must be that the beggar had some knowledge of Jesus. There is not magic here, but there is the mystery of the power of God touching a human mind. Only as the mind of the beggar had some concept of Jesus Christ could these words have had any significance for him—"in the name of Jesus Christ of Nazareth, rise up and walk!"

Then Peter did what was perhaps the most exciting and significant thing of all. His words were important, the command was significant, and the call to the mind of the beggar was necessary. However, what Peter did is what we are thinking about in this passage. Peter reached down and grasped the twisted hand of the beggar and lifted him up. Peter became involved in this. God's involvement is through people, and God needs people's outstretched and outreaching hands. God needs a person's hand to create a needle or a locomotive. God does not create certain things without people's help. God could, I believe, but God never does. This is the kind of a world it is. God never writes a sonnet nor ploughs a field without a person's hand. This is the heart of the matter. As George Elliot has pointed out, God and Antonio Stradivarius made Antonio's violins, but God did not make Antonio's violins without Antonio!

This, it seems to be, is at the very heart of the Gospel. Not until the hand was outstretched was the cripple restored to strength. Perhaps God could do without people, but God never does. Never in all of human history have we found a product indicating that activity of the Mind except as a mind was involved. Not until the hand of Peter was outstretched, not until the surgeon's scalpel is used, not until the teacher's instruction is given, not until some act is performed by a person, does God act.

Christ and human hands are intertwined. There was the outflow of strength and the inflow of strength. As hand touched hand, the cripple was healed.

What is strength in the body? How is the message carried from the brain to the muscle? The wisest person does not really know. We know that tragic illness occurs when the message is not carried from brain to muscle, but we do not know the secret of the strength pouring through the body. We do not understand this power. There was the touch of a strong hand in this instance, after the statement, "in the name of Jesus Christ of Nazareth, rise up and walk," and the miracle occurred.

So we are thinking of this very significant fact; God has no hands but our hands to do God's work today. The ancient psalmist said, "Establish Thou the work of our hands upon us, yea, the work of our hands establish Thou it."

There are countless ways in which our hands are used. We speak of this as work. William Stringfellow, speaking at the University of Colorado recently noted that in the *Bible*, work is thought of as a curse. And he pointed out that we must re-evaluate the whole concept of work, the whole idea of the use of our hands.

The Puritan idea was that the labor of the hands had virtue in itself. This has been so deeply ingrained in me that I find it difficult even yet to think otherwise. Yet I know that some of the greatest work is being done, not primarily by physical energy expended, but by the writer's pen or the artist's brush. Peter's most important work was not in lifting the net, but in reaching down to transform a body by the touch of his hand.

We see in a moment, of course, how important the hands of Peter were. He did reach down and lift the net; he did pile the stones on the Mount of Transfiguration and say, "Let's build a monument here so we can come back and worship again." Peter's hands were used in many ways. Once his hands were used to wield a sword. He had smuggled it to the supper. Then in the garden, when Jesus was threatened, he drew forth the sword from under his fisherman's robe and struck it at the head of the high priest. But he was so inept that instead he cut off the ear of the servant of the high priest. The hand of Peter was not trained to wield the sword, but it was the same hand that now was reaching down to lift up a crippled man.

Let us think of the many uses of the hand; the surgeon's skilled hands used to carefully transplant a kidney from one body to another; and of all that is done in a hospital by the trained hands of a nurse; all the thoughtful acts of mother and father in a home—acts which bring benedictions and blessings to children. There are countless opportunities God gives us to use our hands.

Yes, hands present opportunities, but hands also present responsibilities. How shall the hand be used? The hands of the soldier were used to drive the nails into the hands of Christ. The hand of a John Wilkes Booth pulled the trigger destroying the life of Abraham Lincoln. A hand on a gun took the life of President Kennedy. The hand of a person may write lies: a few years ago, Robert Welch wrote that President Eisenhower is a communist, a traitor to his country—this same man who had used his life as a military leader and then as president. The hand of a Professor Oliver at the University of Illinois wrote that President Kennedy had participated in a plot to turn the United States to communism. Hands can be used by twisted minds to do dastardly things. There have been falsehoods written by human hands which puny minds picked up and believed, until the very structure of a nation is threatened.

The hand is supremely important in this story of the first miracle in the *Book of Acts*. It can be used for constructive healing, lifting purposes. Acts may be performed for Christ, and we must ask ourselves, each of us, continually, "How am I using my hands? Do I have a constructive purpose as I write this check, as I make this will and sign my name?" The use of the hand in so many ways determines the quality of life. We must ask ourselves, "Is this act performed in love?" For not to love is not to live since the purpose of life is love. "I live not where I breathe, but where I love," says

238

someone wiser than I. "Can I imagine Christ doing this that I now do?" This was the motivation behind Peter's act—he had seen Jesus heal. He had seen the hand of Jesus reach down to comfort. He had seen the hand of the Master used to transform human life, and so now, "In the name of Jesus Christ," he says, "Arise and walk!"

But, you may say, would Christ lash out against evil, using His hands? Do you recall that He made a whip with a rope and lashed at those who were defrauding widows at the gate of the Temple? Do not make of Jesus a pale Galilean without the capacity to react to evil. He did lash out at people when He saw their evil deeds.

We dare not make of Him a man with pale hands which signified weakness. He would attack the evil in our time. He would call people what they are because of the way they use their hands. There was nothing weak in this Man's hands. There was the strength that came through the creative commitment of His whole life to the purposes of God.

Today it is thrilling to think that all across this world there are the millions of humble tasks being performed every day by a mother, a father, in a shop or at a desk, a doctor in the office, a teacher in the school, a nurse in the hospital, a surgeon with the scalpel—a poet with the pen—millions of people performing countless acts in the name of Jesus Christ. Your hands and my hands are God's instruments if we will make them so.

The Offering:

Establish the work of our hands upon us,
Yea, the work of our hands,
Establish Thou it.

Thanksgiving

(Thanksgiving, Lakewood, Ohio)

Enter into His gates with thanksgiving, and
into His courts with praise; be thankful unto
Him and bless His name.
For the Lord is good; His mercy is everlasting,
and His truth endureth to all generations."

Psalm 100: 4-5

241

Warmth in the Winter Wind
Ephesians 5: 19-20

November 11, 1954
Community Methodist Church, Whitaker, Pennsylvania

*O*ne of the saddest afflictions from which a person can suffer is to be born without the spirit of appreciation.

> *Blow, blow thou winter wind!*
> *Thou art not so unkind*
> *As man's ingratitude.*
> (*William Shakespeare*)

Shakespeare claims that this deficiency is positively wicked:

> *I hate ingratitude more in a man*
> *Than lying, vainness, babbling drunkenness,*
> *Or any taint of vice whose strong corruption*
> *Inhabits our frail blood.*

Those are strong words, to be sure; but do we not agree with them? Remember how the Old Testament legalists constantly pointed out the keeping of the law in all the outward aspects—and constantly preached against the sins of the flesh—which admittedly are bad enough to be preached against. But remember also how our Lord Jesus came forth teaching the value of humanity's inner attitudes and how He seated the sins of humanity in its intent, in its inner nature. Surely the sins of the spirit go deeper to taint the mind and corrode the soul. By way of pointing out the contrast, consider the Ten Commandments in all their positive prohibitions—and then reflect upon the powerful beauty of the noble Beatitudes that crown life with blessings. And when Christ was most critical, that scorn was blistered against the virtuous life of the Pharisees. "*Hypocrites,*" he called them. "*Whited sepulchers!*" Sins of the spirit were theirs.

And few of the afflictions that attack our spirits can match ingratitude! The lack of appreciation, the dread habit of taking things for granted, the absence of the grateful heart. Was not the heart of the Savior of humanity made heavy indeed when He called forth to the one who returned, *"Where are the nine? Were not ten healed—were not ten made whole—were not ten benefitted? Where are the nine?" (Luke 17:17)*

Blow, blow, thou winter wind!
Thou art not so unkind
As man's ingratitude!

Now Thanksgiving Day appeals to those who do possess the grateful heart. It is a wise and beautiful tradition, our first American holiday. It comes in the heaviness and the chill of a New England November to breathe warmth into the winter winds. Keep it, we ought for tradition's sake. And keep it, we must, for our own soul's sake!

Yet, as we approach Thanksgiving, let us be aware of false paths of gratitude.

For one thing, beware of a thanksgiving which is figured from a balance sheet. "Let's see, now, what are my advantages?" That will not do! If our Pilgrim Fathers had calculated on the basis of a profit and loss statement, there never would have been instituted a Thanksgiving Day. By all the tokens which so many of us use to figure our cause for thanksgiving, the Pilgrims were pitifully in the red. They were poor, had not even had a good harvest. They were not in good health—half of them had died during the preceding winter—and their one hope was that they might survive the next that was already blowing in upon them. They had no security of the kind that so many moderns make their prime search in life. They were not safe from enemies. Even the cemetery was disguised, they tell us, lest it betray their weakness. Yet, they were the very ones who founded Thanksgiving Day. It was not done, however, by a balance sheet of advantages. We sing quite roundly: *"Count your blessings, name them one by one."* [Johnson Oatman, Jr.] Perhaps they could find just one—not a multitude such as we have in our day. Yet, they were grateful.

Now while we may count our blessings, we must remember that often we cannot recognize a blessing when we see it. It was only after a quarter of a century, looking back, that Phillips Brooks could discern the hand of God in the calamity which made him a failure as a schoolteacher. At the time it was a bane. Twenty-five years later, he discovered it had been a blessing.

And there's another side to it—sometimes blessings are not what they appear to be—wolves in sheep's clothing. Some years ago there was a winner of the $64,000 question. He considered himself very lucky, but he went out that night and spent most of what he had won in a tavern and was killed on the way home. It's the insidious thing about the love of gambling that is gripping our people today— what seems to be luck and blessing attack their souls with a "get-something-for-nothing" attitude that degenerates into a "world-owes-me-a-living" outlook upon life. And then they lack the initiative and the fortitude to stand up to life and make it the vibrant and vital thing of accomplishment that made our nation great and our people ambitious.

One of our ministers tells how he looked up the words "gratitude" and "appreciation" in a literary concordance. What author do you suppose had the most references—what author wrote most often something of gratitude? A man with a pile of money? No. A strapping, healthy man who lived to be ninety? No. A man who never knew pain or trouble or sorrow? No. The longest list of quotations concerning thankfulness and appreciation came from a man who spent most of his life in a sickbed, wracked from hemorrhages, and who died when he was 44. He was the one who wrote:

The world is so full of a number of things
I'm sure we should all be as happy as kings.

And his name was Robert Louis Stevenson.

Oh, when you make up a list, you see, often you cannot tell a bane from a blessing at short range. Sometimes we get so discouraged, don't we, as we look about our world? But it takes time to evaluate, lots of time, more years perhaps than we have to spend on this planet. Arnold Toynbee in his great work *A Study of History* looks back through the centuries to chart the slow unrolling of great good out of apparent ill, and the great evils out of what seemed to be glorious times. Blessings that often go unrecognized, you see!

Another thing that happens when people draw up lists is that they forget blessings. And the thing is that the most constant blessings are often those left out, largely because they are most constant. We take them for granted—like the sun coming up—and all the rest of dependable and everyday experiences.

Let a college president say a word here: Mark Hopkins, that amazing educator who claimed that the greatest communication came from a teacher sitting on one end of a log with a student on the other end, was president of Williams College. During his tenure, some of the buildings were defaced, and when the culprit was caught, he turned out to be a young man from a prominent and wealthy family. When this young fellow was summoned before the president, the young man haughtily reached for his pocketbook and said, "Well, Dr. Hopkins, how much is the damage? I'll pay for it."

Mark Hopkins replied, "Young man, put up your wallet. No man can pay for what he gets here. No wealth can pay for what Colonel Williams has given and half-paid professors have sacrificed to make this school what it is. Every student here is a charity student."

Consider our church in the same light. We put our offerings in the plates; do we pay for the church? Why a hundred forty some years of devotion have built this church. I am amazed constantly when I remember the sheer courage and insight and surely tremendous spirit of hope that inspired people to raise up this building a hundred years ago in this place. Beyond that, two thousand years of martyrdom and saintliness and sacrifice built the Church. Ten thousand years of moral and spiritual pilgrimage from the dark jungles of primitive man built the Church. If each one of us should put every asset he or she has into the offering, our deeds, our savings, all of it, and walk out of the church penniless, not one of us would yet have begun to pay for what the Church has given us, has given our world, or for what it means to humanity. *"Live, like the pagans you are!"*

Oh, you see, a balance-sheet thanksgiving is a false path. Our thanksgiving must be whole-hearted and spontaneous, not because of what we have or think we have, but because of what we are and what God is. Because it is a good thing to give thanks unto the Lord. Because we have grateful hearts; and grateful hearts just naturally overflow into praise—breathing warmth into the winter winds.

The other false path is a thanksgiving with an overtone of pride. Frequently, I think we are led to say, "Yes, we are grateful. We have so much more than others, more advantages, more opportunities, and more wealth," until we begin to believe we are better than others. Here again, Jesus has something to say unto us. Remember the story of the Pharisee who prayed, "God, I thank Thee that I am not as other men." Oh, you see, it ought to be a thanksgiving with an undertone of humility and repentance. Thanksgiving and honest repentance go together. The contrast to the Pharisee was the Publican who was justified—remember, "God, be merciful to me, a sinner."

Leslie Weatherhead, one of England's foremost preachers, shares a legend from the war years about the English mother who had a particularly gifted son who gave up his life on the battlefield. He was a brilliant fellow. He had led his classes in scholarship and made a remarkable record in Oxford Then he went to war and was killed in action. Afterwards, his mother had a strange dream. She dreamed that an angel came to her and told her that she might have her son back for five minutes. "Choose," said the angel. "Which five minutes will it be? Will it be in the hour of his high honor in Oxford, or in the hour of his heroism in battle?"

The mother did not even hesitate. "If I can have him back for five minutes, I prefer to have him, not when he was in Oxford, not when he was in war. I would like to have him back as a little boy on a certain day when he had disobeyed me. He had run into the garden, angry and rebellious. Then pretty soon he came back and threw himself into my arms and said he was sorry. His face was hot and red. He looked so small and so precious. I saw his love in his eyes and felt his love in his body pressed close to mine—and how my love went out to him at that moment! If I can have him back for just five minutes, let me have him as a dear little repentant boy."

No thanksgiving to God, I do believe, will reach the throne so quickly, nor touch the heart of God's vast love so surely as the humanly, strong, sturdily honest admission of repentance. That we have hated when and what we ought to have loved. That we have hurt where and when we ought to have helped. That we have blamed when we ought to have encouraged. We have withheld when we ought to have given, been cheap when we ought to have been generous. That we have not been true to Him whom we deeply adore—and that we are ashamed and sorry. And we promise a better discipleship from Thanksgiving on through forever.

The Mayflower is Still Sailing
Psalm 67

November 19, 1967
First Methodist Church, Sidney, Ohio

*T*hanksgiving is a time of looking back, a time of reflection upon the holy and heroic heritage that is ours in this fine land of America where truly "pilgrim feet with stern impassioned stress a thoroughfare for freedom beat across the wilderness." [Katherine Lee Bates]

It's a time when we might naturally go back to a small village in the east of England—Scrooby—so insignificant that to this day no railroad serves it. Yet, out of Scrooby they came in that Puritan migration—they took their religion so seriously and believed in God so deeply that they were willing to forsake their loved homes and "go out like Abraham seeking a better country where they could worship God in freedom." Perhaps Scrooby was a Nazareth which surprised the world by sending forth such a significant spiritual force. From Scrooby they went to Leyden in Holland in their search for freedom of worship. And from that place then in 1620 they set sail for the land across the sea, and with them says the poet:

> *Laws, freedom, truth and faith in God*
> *Came with these exiles over the waves.*
> *(Leonard Bacon)*

Now, New England is a barren place in November—the spring is fresh and green and welcome, the summer is delightful, the autumn is glorious beyond our human description, and the winter itself is pretty with the clean white snow reflecting the cheerful lights from the windows of the clean white houses. But November is a month between—October's glory is gone, winter's snow that covers all scars of earth has not yet come in any large amount—and the land is barren and brown. And in that particular time they had thankful hearts for a harvest which helped to soften the sorrow of that first terrible winter which had touched so many homes with its icy finger of death.

249

They brought much more than themselves and their little boatload of provisions which proved scanty indeed. They brought their spiritual truths—on a hill above Plymouth, there is a monument to the Pilgrims. On a high granite pedestal there is a colossal figure of Liberty. That figure stands looking back across the sea over which our Pilgrim Fathers sailed so long ago. One hand of the figure is raised aloft with a finger pointing into the skies—symbolic of their belief that they were God-guided in their voyage to this new land where they could be free. And then there came the time of settling down in this land upon which they had counted so heavily. One of those founding fathers describes these days. "After God had carried us safe to New England, and we had builded our houses, provided the necessaries for our livelihood, rear'd convenient places for God's worship and settled the Civil government." These things were important—homes, religion, government. Here lies a nation's foundation. On such it is possible to build a good and a free life.

Oh, truly Thanksgiving is a time for looking back and remembering not only the great day in our American calendar which those valiant soldiers of freedom gave to use, but remember them, also, for something deep and abiding—for a way of life, for a firm belief that has endured.

> *Not for battleship and fortress*
> *Not for conquests of the sword;*
> *But for conquests of the spirit*
> *Give we thanks to Thee, O Lord.*
> *For the priceless gifts of freedom,*
> *For the home, the church, the school;*
> *For the open door to manhood*
> *In a land the people rule.*
> *(William P. Merrill)*

Thanksgiving Time is a time also for looking about us. I wonder this day what impression a Pilgrim visitor would have as he steps into modern life clad in his breeches and buckled shoes. What would his opinion be of us, his debtors for a godly heritage? I think he would surely smile his gratitude when he walks through Concord—by that "rude bridge that arched the flood where once the embattled farmers stood and fired the shot heard round the world." [Ralph Waldo

Emerson] He would be warm with understanding when he sees people insisting on their rights to freedom—a cause upon which he and his company of fellow pilgrims had gambled so heavily.

I think he would be startled at the culture we have established upon those simple beginnings at Plymouth. He would be amazed at the complexity of our civilization as compared with the simple life of farming, of education, and of worship that marked the early towns of New England.

And he would be disillusioned deeply to see how we have placed the great festival of Thanksgiving upon one of the shelves of our lives, to be pulled out for a few hours, and then pushed back to rest in its forgotten corner for an entire year. Theirs, too, was a great festival that took place on a set time of the year. But more than that, it was a constant spirit of gratitude, of worship, that permeated all of religious living in that day. Surely as God does not cease God's concern and God's care over us for a day, we should never relegate our gratitude unto God to a set time and forget it the rest of our days. Keep the feast, yes—keep it with all of its historic memories that stir our hearts. Keep it in its great festivity. Keep it with all of its family connections. Keep it with its sharing spirit of concern for those less fortunate in the world's store of riches. But also, maintain its spirit through all of the days which the Lord God has given unto us.

And so Thanksgiving also demands from us in addition to the looking backward to the historic and heroic heritage of the pilgrim fathers, and the looking about to realize the bounties and the benefits which life can afford us in these the days of our living; it also demands from us that we look within—that we search deeply to know and to understand and to appreciate the gratitude that the heart can feel.

Gratitude is a child of faith. And being a child, it needs the nourishment of daily life and practice to make it grow and develop toward maturity. As one who has recovered from a suffering disease arises to new heights of happiness with recovery, there is a reason and a practice of gratitude. One lady who noticed this recovery and this gratitude blithely remarked that of course anyone would be thankful, too, who would recover from such suffering. Yet she, herself, never realized how grateful she should have been for her own health through all her days. It is easy for us to sing forth our thanksgiving for the turkeys and the special occasion. It seems harder to remember that life's daily fare and daily blessings, too, should merit our appreciation unto God. It is truly a fine habit to be thankful for life's daily blessings.

Then, too, gratitude is not genuine if it is selfish. We are extremely dependent people—no matter how we feel ourselves to be. We do not make ourselves entirely, do not rise completely upon our own efforts. Whenever such self-conceit possesses us, we do well to remind ourselves how much would be left if God took everything except what we are or have done ourselves. Civilization would be done; our cities would vanish; the sun would drop from the sky; the stars no more would shine; this earth would cease its energetic whirling about, and we ourselves would have no foundation and would find ourselves plummeting through space, helpless. How little avail, then, those bootstraps by which some boast they pull themselves up in life! How dependent we are upon the gifts of God and the use people have made of those gifts in fashioning our culture, our civilization, our way of life.

In our selfish natures, too, there occasionally comes that devilish spirit to blur our own blessings because others have seemingly greater and richer abundance than we can enjoy. So Thanksgiving dims with the jealous nature. It brightens and shines forth when we can lift ourselves to praise God for the good God has done for others as well as for ourselves.

To be truly grateful, we must think the thoughts, and sing the phrases, and practice the deeds of gratitude. It was Paul who knew full well of the suffering and anguish of this life, who went forth to admonish the people of Thessalonica that they should, *"in everything give thanks."* He went about telling his friends and his Lord how thankful he was—and you know, the more he gave expression to it, the more thankful he became. Surely God who knows the depths of our hearts realizes when we are thankful whether or not we express that gratitude. But yet it does us good to ponder and to contemplate the blessings which life does hold for us: abundant material blessings, blessings of friendships and family love, the deep and loving gifts of the spiritual realities. And it does us good to so feel in our hearts the warm expression of appreciation that the songs pour forth from our lips, and we recognize God's goodness.

The expression of gratitude is a measure of Christian growth. Moreover, it is a gateway to usefulness in the Christian life.

We thank our God best in praise and in Christian practice. There are many, many times during the passing days when we can stop to consider the goodness of God whom we worship. And with the contemplation of that goodness within our minds, we can then utter a sincere word of gratitude from the heart's depth that pleases God and lets God know that we are aware of God's bountiful provision for us and of God's goodness unto us.

Then too, we can very evidently give thanks unto God through the work of our hands. The hands of thanksgiving cannot be clenched fists, nor clasped hands of idleness. They should be open hands that are able to serve our fellowmen and fellow-women, and through serving, serve also our Father God. For truly *"in as much as ye do it unto one of the least of these, ye do it unto me."*

> *God, let me be aware*
> *Let me not stumble blindly down the ways*
> *Just getting somehow safely through the days.*
> *Not even groping for another hand,*
> *Not even wondering why it all was planned—*
> *Eyes to the ground, unseeking for the light.*
> *Souls never aching for a wild-winged flight'*
> *Please, keep me eager just to do my share.*
> *God, let me be aware.*
> *(Miriam Teichner)*

Thanksgiving is a time of looking back—heritage.

Thanksgiving is a time of looking about us—goodness.

Thanksgiving is a time of looking within us—worship.

> *Truly our hands and our hearts are full*
> *And our knees should be bent.*
> *And God shall have the praise.*

The Mayflower Compact

*I*t was on November 11, 1620 that the Pilgrims gathered in the cabin of the Mayflower and drew up the first charter of a government of the people, by the people, and for the people.

The self-discipline of these colonists has been one of the glorious chapters in human history. Their moral standards were so high that a trip to the stocks was usually all the punishment necessary to bring an offender back to orderly behavior.

It was their firm belief that laws should govern human's effort to apply moral principles to human affairs.

Thanks to these great Americans who preceded us, we have a day in November which has been set aside for us, in the tradition of those Puritans, to give thanks for all the many blessings we enjoy. A day to be observed in a becoming spirit that it may accomplish the purification and strengthening of the sentiment of nationality, which was fostered by ancestral memories, cemented by the blood of our Fathers and wrought into the structures of our country by the hand of God; evidenced by God's freedom, human dignity, and prosperity.

In the Name of God—Amen.

Christmas

(Joel Hartland as Joseph, Christmas, Tipp City, Ohio)

"And she brought forth her firstborn son, and wrapped him in swaddling clothes, and laid him in a manger; because there was no room for them in the inn."
Luke 2: 7

The Abiding Light
John 11: 1-14

December 3, 1972
Christ United Methodist Church, Columbus, Ohio

"He made the night a little brighter
Wherever he would go,
The old lamplighter of long ago."
(Jim Ed Brown)

*T*hey tell me that a tradition of the advent season in years now gone was the candle-lighting along the streets. In my own mind, I am sure that never can these neon and plastic combinations that adorn our streets at Christmastime take the place nor hope to rival the beauty of the old candles. The tongues of flame leaping up through the darkness of the night speak of Him whose life was the light of men- *"And the light shineth in darkness..."*

Here, too, Jesus associated us with Himself. *"Neither do people light a candle and put it under a bushel, but on a candlestick, and it giveth light...let your light so shine." (Matthew 5: 15).*

So we should stand forth at all times and in all steadfastness as open witnesses of our faith. Let the redeemed of the Lord say so! Let the disciples of Christ wear the insignia of Christ, always and everywhere. Put your light on a candlestick. Let it shine.

Many of you may remember the big moment in your life when you received your high school ring. You gazed fondly at the emblem of the school upon it, knowing that through the years the emblem would stir you with memories of happy days. I remember such a time—and I recall one of the girls in my class looking fondly at her ring, then turning it on her finger and realizing for the first time that the little band of gold looked ever so much like a wedding ring, And some secret desire in her heart pointed out to the group of us the similarity—how if she wanted so to do, she could go about life with her ring turned inside and reveal only the thin gold band of it that would seem to the world an insignia of her marriage. Then at will, she could reverse the ring—quite convenient, you see.

Now I suppose that such examples were prevalent in Jesus's day, too, and about Him, He could see those who took lightly their religion as a matter of convenience—there are so many such today. Surely He warns against such a flighty and frivolous showing forth of emblems only upon occasion. Religious conviction must be a more steadfast affair of life than that. Paul put it, *"I bear in my body the marks of the Lord Jesus."* His credentials were scars, and they were there to stay.

"Let your light so shine"—we were discussing the other evening something of our ignorance when it comes to election time. Often we know so little about our candidates. They tell of a national election some years ago when one candidate went out to put his light on a candlestick, so to speak, while the other hid his under a bushel. There perhaps were many people who didn't care for the light that they could see, but they preferred it to one they couldn't see and which, for all they knew, may have gone out. One candidate said to the farmers, "I'll maintain high prices for you," then to the consumers, "I'll bring prices down for you." It didn't make sense. But the other candidate only murmured platitudes like, "You and I are for a great America," with nothing concrete to offer the people. His light was hidden.

Or again, we constantly refer to ourselves as a Christian nation—by tradition and historical evidence we are a God-fearing nation. Since the first, we have opened the sessions of our Congress and the Supreme Court and other important affairs of state with prayer. I do hope this is not a mere formality, but a genuine awareness of God. I have labored over many invocations for special events, and then have felt the people relax immediately and feel that the formality was over. Yet we do at least have the form whereby we recognize our God, and it's a bitter pill to swallow when we realize that it is our official American policy to reject the use of prayer at all meetings of the United Nations—out of deference to the atheism of Russia. They surely never hesitate to bring out their candle and put it on a candlestick—and at a time when world ideologies meet, we defer and hide our own light under a bushel. It would reveal a wavering similar to that of the girl with the new class ring. It surely reveals a lack of faith in our historic birth.

Bishop McConnell, leader of our Methodist church, points out an interesting interpretation of this teaching of Jesus. In economics, he reminds us, there is the expression called place utility. This is the important function in production of the effective distribution of stock to the places where it will do the most good. A light must be in the right place to be of fullest value. The brightest light is useless under a bushel—its value depends upon where it is.

When Dr. Grenfell was converted by Dwight L. Moody, he went forward and told the great evangelist about it.

"Fine," said Dr. Moody. "Now this evening you go up into the balcony and speak to your neighbors. We were rather short of Christians up there yesterday. Goodbye."

When people criticized Jesus for consorting with sinners, He said, *"Those who are well have no need of a physician."* He was practicing place utility. He was letting the light shine where it would do the most good. It would seem that the perfect place to put one's faith in God on a candlestick would be in the presence of sin and unbelief. Where else could it be of so much value? When Jesus asked, *"Who say ye that I am?"* it was good for Peter to affirm, *"Thou art the Christ, the Son of the living God."* It was also relatively easy, for then he was among the disciples. How multiplied would have been the power of that declaration had he made it in the courtyard among Jesus's enemies. But then, of all times, he hid it under a bushel.

Finally, it comes down to this: Light is functional. It is not merely a decoration. The ultimate purpose of a candle is to dispel darkness. We are to use it, make it work for us, do things for us—and it cannot if we hide it under a bushel.

Consider this in terms of the approaching Christmas— Christmas is a light. It is happiness, good will, generosity, kindness. Put it to work. Let it shine in dark places. Scientists have invented a beam which when placed at the open door destroys all microbes that seek to enter. Christmas ought to be such a cleansing light rigged to fit us for the New Year which follows. Christmas is strategically located at the open door, to help us get rid of all the accumulated rubbish of the dying year. Through a functional application of its gentle but potent light, we may enter the New Year with clean hands and mended hearts.

Put the Christmas spirit to work. Put it on a candlestick. Aim its healing straight at hurts, its peace at conflicts, its love at resentments. Carry its carols straight to where the harmony of good relationships has been silenced. Don't let a grudge remain when the Christmas dawn arrives.

Repair those broken ties in the family circle. Here is the perfect season for such therapy; do not let it slip by unused. There will be lots of love around—take it home and stock up on it. The very air will be saturated with peace on earth and good will. Breathe it in deeply, then exhale in total forgiveness.

Christmas is a functional season. It should be used. Don't hide the light of the Christmas candle under a bushel or reduce it merely to a decoration. Put it on a candlestick. Let it shine forth into dark places. Put it to its wondrous work.

Neither do men light a candle and put it under a bushel, but on a candlestick...let your light so shine.

The Everlasting Sign
Galatians 4: 1-20

December 10, 1972
Christ United Methodist Church, Columbus, Ohio

Hark! A voice from yonder manger,
Soft and sweet, Doth entreat,
'Flee from woe and danger;
Brethren, come; from all that grieves you
You are freed;
All you need, I will surely give you.'
Come, then let us hasten yonder;
Here let all, Great and small,
Kneel in awe and wonder,
Love Him who with love is yearning.
(Paul Gerhardt)

Christmas is the birthday of a King; it is also the token and promise that the kingdoms of this world belong to that King and will one day be ruled by Him. Christmas is a divine pledge that the kingdom of God and of His Christ—for so many hundreds of years a pious Christian hope—will one day be established; that our ancient prayer, "Thy kingdom come, Thy will be done in earth, as it is in heaven," is to be fulfilled.

Measured against the long and tortuous story of the progress of humanity, we are yet but the merest step from that cradle in Bethlehem. Measured against the impatient and often critical judgement of critics, we are still in the jungle. Measured against many of the heartbreaking facts of our fear-torn world, the prospect is discouraging.

But that kingdom will come. Every year Christmas reminds us of it and renews the faith of those whose hearts grasp the deeper significance of the season. For ten thousand atomic bombs cannot smash what happened at Bethlehem; but as surely as stars shine, what happened at Bethlehem will one day put an end to the use of atomic power in bombs.

Bethlehem—

How will the kingdom come? There are suggestions in the Christmas story, especially as recorded in Luke. Mary and Joseph went down to Bethlehem to be taxed—if you have any trouble understanding the *Bible*, start reading at that verse. You will understand that. That is familiar territory—taxed!

"While they were there," the record states, *"the days were accomplished that she should be delivered." (Luke 2:6)*. Not only Mary, but the world that had waited so long—the centuries of yearning had come to the fullness of time for deliverance.

> *For unto us a son is born, unto us a child is given, and the government shall be upon his shoulders. And He shall be called wonderful, counselor, the mighty God, the everlasting Father, the Prince of Peace. (Isaiah 9: 6).*

Consider the historic hour from the standpoint of divine strategy. Rome was at the zenith of her power. Her empire covered the known earth. She was busy binding it together, building roads and communication lines, making one world out of what had been up to that time a collection of isolated fragments. If you want to mold a man, catch a child and start there. Well, here was the infant world. The crucial hour? Right then, at that point in history which we today name the first century. The chosen time had come.

Consider the place. At the crossroads of the East and the West lay Palestine—Ishmael to Egypt—Arabia to Rome. It was a vast veritable funnel for the interchange of cultures of the Occident and the Orient. Anything planted there spread everywhere. The ideal site? Where but Palestine—the chosen place.

Consider the matter of human agency. The Jews had one genius and one only—religion. Art? Music? Literature? Conquest? They possessed no special skills along those lines—only for religion! Most of the great religions of the world have sprung from that tiny strip of land between Europe and Asia. It would almost seem that the varied talents of the rest of the humanity were denied the Jewish people in order that the full power of their total genius might be concentrated on the greatest art of all—the creative gift for comprehending the nature of human and of God. The Jews were indeed the chosen people.

So time and place and people conspired. So history and geography and anthropology met one wonderful night to launch a kingdom. No wonder there was a star that made a glory in the sky. It was a spark of fulfillment!

Consider the method. *"There were shepherds abiding in the fields, keeping watch over their flocks by night." (Luke 2: 8)*. They were busy doing their regular work. Suddenly an angel of the Lord appeared and told them of the birth of the Messiah, *"And this shall be a sign unto you."* I like the way Lew Wallace describes it in *Ben Hur*:

> *the night, like most nights of the winter season in the hill country was clear, crisp, and sparkling with stars. There was no wind. The atmosphere seemed never so pure, the stillness was more than silence; it was a holy hush, a warning that heaven was stooping low to whisper some good thing to the listening earth. And the watchman who was out there guarding his sheep, came toward the fire—but paused; for a light was breaking around him, soft and white—like the moon's. He waited breathlessly. The light deepened—things before invisible came into view. He looked up; the stars were gone. The light was dropping as from a window in the sky, and as he looked it became a splendor. And in terror he cried, and the other shepherds clambered to their feet wondering, "See, the sky is on fire!"*

The light became so very bright that they covered their eyes and dropped to their knees. Then they fell upon their faces and would have died had not a voice said unto them, *"Fear not!"*

And they listened.

263

"Fear not! For behold I bring you good tidings of great joy which shall be to all people. For unto you this day in the city of David is born a Savior which is Christ the Lord! And this shall be a sign unto you, ye shall find the babe wrapped in swaddling clothes and lying in a manger." (Luke 2: 10-12).

The herald spoke not again—his tidings were told. And then there came a whole multitude of voices chanting in unison, *"Glory to God in the highest and on earth, peace good will toward men." (Luke 2: 14).*

What was the sign? Not a legion of angels. What was the distinguishing credentials of God's coming to earth? Not a procession of cherubim and seraphim. What was the evidence that the kingdom had been born? Oh, it's so warm and so human and so wonderful, *"Ye shall find the babe!"* That was all. A baby. No legions, no pomp and circumstance, no spectacle. The sign was one of the most ordinary and normal events in life. *"Ye shall find the babe."* We are told that a star guided the Wiseman, and an angelic choir sang to the shepherds there beyond the town, but the sign of the Christ, the sign of the kingdom, was *"the babe."*

How then will be fulfilled the kingdom for which we pray and sing, and toward which we strive, and of which Christmas is the sign? It will come by a process as normal as birth. *"Ye shall find the Babe."* George McDonald tells us in his poem, *The Holy Thing:*

> *They all were looking for a king*
> *To slay their foes and lift them high;*
> *Then cam'st, a little baby thing*
> *That made a woman cry.*

It will come as the harvest of the accumulated devotion of people who take the spirit of Christ with them to the shop and the office and the home, and who are busy—as those shepherds were busy—doing the job at hand. It will come through work, through effort, through the slow but sure shaping of young minds by conscientious mothers and fathers who have the deep wisdom to know that the Christian rearing of a child is the greatest, noblest, most gigantic and most vital task on the face of God's good earth. And whoever exchanges that important job for a "career" or for the social round is guilty of a bargain that echoes again the "mess of pottage" exchange which was pretty cheap indeed.

A birthright for a stew.

The sign of God's kingdom was *"the babe,"* the prospect of God's man or woman, the only material out of which such a kingdom can be built and with which God supplies us an abundant new generation every year.

The kingdom will come—the sign of it, the portent of its beauty lies with the babe wrapped in swaddling clothes, lying in a manger. A thousand babes were born that night, and likely a good many of them were lying in mangers. That wouldn't be an uncommon cradle—do not we often use baskets for our own tiny ones? Certainly all of them were wrapped in swaddling clothes. *"The kingdom of God is within you,"* said the Christ. (Luke 17: 21). So it comes quietly and persistently. There are small areas where it has already come—areas as small, and as large, as a single human spirit. In homes where love rules, in such places of earth, the spirit of the kingdom is present.

F.W. Boeham has written many inspirational books. One he wrote when he was past eighty years of age he entitled, *I Forgot to Say.* This writing represented the random thoughts that he had neglected to mention before. It represents the overtones of his life, and in them one meets God. When did God so beautifully take up residence in his soul? He could not say—he simply looked back at a late hour upon his life to discover that it had long been within the boundaries of the kingdom. Along the line, growing old, he had been growing wise. Quietly Christ had entered his heart as he entered the world at Bethlehem, and there Christ had found home. Looking back from the vantage point of eighty years, the author was glad and grateful.

It may be that in the days to come—we know not the year nor the hour—the world, a world of brotherhood and peace and contentment—will look back, will review the long record of hate and greed and bloodshed, will watch the hearts of humans sicken at it, will see the diminution of it, will witness the process of the leaven of Christ's spirit working, will trace the growth of wisdom and faithfulness, of tolerance and reverence, and know that as it should be, Christ has slipped onto the throne of the world. We do not see a tree grow each day…but it grows. And surely His spirit is present and is working even as the leaven in the lump, or as the tiny mustard seed—until one day, looking back, the world will see the great change that has been wrought because God entered history quietly and humanly at Bethlehem. Then it will be that the promise of Christmas will be fulfilled. As we believe in His ultimate triumph, so we become people with hope in our hearts. And the sign of it all—the sign that endures through the ages to be the everlasting symbol of humanity's hope in the future good—the sign was, *"the babe."*

> *Come then, let us hasten yonder;*
> *Here let all,*
> *Great and small,*
> *Kneel in awe and wonder:*
> *Love Him who with love is yearning;*
> *Hail the Star,*
> *That from far Bright with hope is burning.*
> (Paul Gerhardt)

The Enduring Word
Isaiah 55: 1-11

December 17, 1972
Christ United Methodist Church, Columbus, Ohio

"*The Word of God shall stand!*" *(Isaiah 40: 8b)*

But the word—what word?

We turn to John and he speaks it forth with rare beauty:

> *In the beginning was the Word, and the Word was with God, and the Word was God. The same was in the beginning with God. In Him was life and the life was the light of men. And the Word became flesh and dwelt among us. (John 1: 1-4, 14).*

The familiar and beautiful account of our Lord's advent is to be found in Luke's Gospel—there the record stands warm and human, and we love the words. The most scholarly account is in Matthew's gospel. John's account is entirely different from these and stands forth as the most majestic. A musician makes the comparison that Luke and Matthew comprise the libretto while John gives us the musical score. Luke tells what Mary and Joseph and the shepherds were doing that first Christmas. Matthew tells what the nation of Israel and Judaism were doing. John tells us what God was doing. "*In the beginning was the Word and the Word was with God and the Word was God. And the Word became flesh and dwelt among us.*"

The Word becoming flesh was Jesus—the historic person living among the humanity of earth—walking with them, talking, teaching, healing, lifting, loving.

But what one Word could become the adequate personification of this Jesus? The *Bible* scholars point out the similarity of this prologue to John's gospel with the Greek philosophy of the first century. The Greeks believed in a mysterious pre-existent and eternal divine substance called the logos—from their term for "word." John

267

uses this term and idea and reveals that this pre-existent divine substance becomes incarnate in Christ. The Greeks would say, "The Word was in the beginning," and John adds his brief but profound Christmas story, *"The Word became flesh."*

The Word was personified in a human who lived among us. So He becomes the language that God chose to use to speak to humanity—so we do ask, "What is the particular Word that He embodies?"

"In Him was life." "Life" could have been the Word—Life became flesh and dwelt among us—for this Christ is life. How do we describe life?

On a winter cruise to the Caribbean, people appear quite carefree lounging on a luxurious steamer—basking in the sun. "This is the life," they say.

A young mother sits in a hospital beside the bed holding her child that could not live. We must learn to take it—this is life.

A reporter back from Europe after seeing the torture chamber at Buchenwald grimly said, "The American people have to face the facts of life." Buchenwald—horror, selfishness and fear and torture—life.

"In Him was life," God is saying to the world. "Here is Life for you." We find it in Him. During the Advent season we often dwell exclusively upon what the Incarnation tells about Jesus that we miss its meaning concerning humanity. The Incarnation glorifies humanity—*"What is man, that Thou art mindful of him—Thou hast crowned him with glory and honor." (Psalm 8:4, 5b).*

Or perhaps the Word was "Light." It's a beautiful word—one of my favorites. *"In Him was life, and the life was the light of men."* It is the unknown that we fear the most, and it is light which drives out the darkness and makes plain the path. The *Bible* begins in the first chapter with God saying, *"Let there be light!"(Genesis 1: 3).* It's a sparkling declaration of the goodness of God that God would not condemn God's creatures to groping through the dark. In the last chapter of the last book of the *Bible* there comes forth the statement of faith that I have known to be meaningful to people in the hour of earthly parting when their sorrow was heavy upon them. *"And there shall be no night there; and they need no candle, neither light of the sun; for the Lord God giveth them light." (Revelation 22: 5).*

Here again the Incarnation exalts humanity, sets forth its true nature when one lives according to one's ability and to the extent of one's potentiality. The words come forth from the One who personified God's light, *"Ye are the light of the world—a city set on a hill cannot be hid." (Matthew 5: 14).* In Him was light. Light became flesh and dwelt among us.

Or to use a more complete term—the Word was "Love." God is love. It's the description we use for God as most adequate even when we are children in our beginner's and primary classes. Surely if Jesus personifies one Word, this is it. Christina Rossetti says it in one of our carols:

> *Love came down at Christmas,*
> *Love all lovely, Love Divine;*
> *Love was born at Christmas,*
> *Star and angels gave the sign.*

And here again, the Incarnation points straight to humanity, for Christmas has not only to do with Jesus—but with us as well. This is the real reason why joy should be in our hearts at the remembrance and reality of God's love.

> *Love shall be our token,*
> *Love be yours and love be mine;*
> *Love to God and all men.*
> *Love for plea and gift and sign.*

In Him was love. Love became flesh and dwelt among us.

So we begin the Advent season with a search for the Word which became alive and walked among us. What was the Word?

"Light?" "Life?" "Love?"

269

All of these it was—and many more. The Spirit that was in Christ holds good for God—the Spirit that was in Christ holds good for the universe. And though we cannot yet say that the Spirit that was in Christ holds good in the free wills of all people, we can say that it beckons to the best and truest instincts of humanity, everywhere and always.

There is a timeless quality about the spirit of Christmas—and the secret of that timelessness lies in the universality of the Word which became flesh and dwelt among us full of grace and truth. Hope is always high at Christmas that more people will find that truth and follow that way and know for themselves that come what may, the Word endures.

"The Word of God shall stand."

The Eternal Miracle
Luke 2: 1-7

December 24, 1972
Christ United Methodist Church, Columbus, Ohio

Little Tommy was one of seven children, and one day he met with a painful accident. He was taken to the hospital from a family so poor that he was hungry often and his hunger was not always satisfied. A nurse brought him a glass of milk.

"How deep may I drink?" he asked.

Tears forced back, the nurse answered, "Drink it all; drink it all!"

Christmas is the celebration of the Christian doctrine of the Incarnation. Here is the root cut out of which Christmas as we know it was born, and out of which it still draws its strength. Other pleasant and happy traditions have flowered from it, and some parasites have attached themselves to it, but the charter of Christmas was, is, and always will be, found in the beautiful and eternal words:

"For unto you is born this day in the City of David a Savior, which is Christ the Lord." (Luke 2: 11).

The range of implications is enormous. May we for a moment consider an exceedingly practical one. Dicken's *Christmas Carol* is one of the classic stories of the Christmas season. The reason, perhaps, is that it describes about as perfectly and completely as it is possible to do it, the strange power Christmas has to work human miracles. Old Scrooge was hopelessly unregenerate, grasping, selfish, heartless, conscienceless. Here is the enemy of society—the person you can do nothing with, the person who has no soul to work on—the person you cannot understand—the one with whom you cannot reason, to whom you cannot appeal, one whom you cannot trust.

But Christmas came.

The air was charged with good cheer. The contagion of this spirit, the persistent friendliness of Bob Cratchitt, and the irresistible gentleness of Tiny Tim, all worked their ageless miracle, and even old hardened Scrooge surrendered to it. Now it's just a story, yet the world loves it and understands it because its theme is true. It happens every year. It is happening this week. It happened in the life of a little girl to whom a certain minister was talking—the little girl's parents were separated.

"Doesn't your dad ever come to see you?" the minster asked.

"No," answered the little girl. Then her face brightened. "Except at Christmas—every Christmas he comes."

So at Christmas that little girl has a home and parents for that one day. The situations vary in detail, the cast of characters is different, but the miracle is the same.

Most of you who have heard it can never forget it—that Alexander Wolcott famous story from the First World War. The grim stalemate on the Western Front—no man's land between the two opposing trenches. Then came Christmas Eve, and during a lull in the bombardment, the Americans could hear the Germans singing a familiar universal Christmas carol. It's a glorious experience to hear the carols sung in their original tongues—to hear the Germans singing, "Stille Nacht," or the French their "Un Flambeau Jeanette Isabella, or to hear in the Latin the great old favorite, "Adeste Fidelis." So the Germans were singing a carol—the Americans joined in, and across that desolation of barbed wire and enmity their voices blended. The Americans sang and the Germans answered. Then one man, under a white flag, ventured into no man's land. An enemy soldier met him halfway. There they arranged a truce for Christmas Day; and the next morning saw that strange spectacle of thousands of men whose business it was to kill each other, showing each other photographs from home, acting like friends. The high command had nothing to do with that! That was Christmas at work. Gentle Season, but give it half a chance and it rips the guns from men's hands and the enmity from their hearts and puts a song on their lips.

Why?

Perhaps we may find a clue in a little poem by the African American poet Countee Cullen. He was writing about Simon the Cyrenian, who bore the cross for Jesus, and who tradition says was a black man. I played the part of Simon of Cyrene once in a religious pantomime, and it does make one humble to enter the part of one who carried a cross. The poet pictures him as a proud, independent, suspicious man who was resolved to die rather than become a slave. Yet, he stooped and like a slave bore the cross for Jesus.

Why?

Let the poet speak in the words of Simon:

> *He never spoke a word to me,*
> *And yet He called my name;*
> *He never gave a sign to me,*
> *And yet I knew and came.*
>
> *At first I said, 'I will not bear*
> *His cross upon my back;*
> *He only seeks to place it there*
> *Because my skin is black.'*
>
> *But He was dying for a dream,*
> *And He was very meek,*
> *And in His eyes there shone a gleam*
> *Men journey far to seek.*
>
> *It was Himself my pity brought;*
> *I did for Christ alone*
> *What all of Rome could not have wrought*
> *With bruise of lash or stone.*

So what is the secret of the miracle of Christmas—a miracle that touched the heart of a Scrooge and leads him forth from selfishness to service, one that touches an unconcerned father for a brief day of the year to bring him to his child's side to do for her as he should on every day, one that silences guns and kindles friendship and song, one that conquers haughty pride and bows it in the dust to serve the Christ of life? Well, it really is no miracle, nor is it a secret. It is the demonstration of an elemental principle of human relationships—the response in kind. Its unhappy operation is familiar; suspicion breeds suspicion, hate breeds hate, accusations result in counter-accusations, threats are answered with threats, force asks for retaliation.

At Christmas we catch, for a little while, the exactly opposite spirit—the spirit of the Christ. Good will and generosity become our mood, and the law still works. We send forth friendliness, and friendliness comes back to us. We forgive and find ourselves forgiven. We generate a little good will and behold—there is good will everywhere!

It works at Christmastime! The jails give freedom to certain prisoners—even healing quickens so that the hospitals can discharge patients in time for the holiday at home. It works at Christmas, you see, and it will work every day in the year if we will put it into operation every day in the year, as we do put it into operation generously and gloriously at Christmas. And then we are so amazed at the result that we term it a miracle.

Yet it is no miracle! The strange miracle is that after a demonstration so clear, after evidence so conclusive, when Christmas is over, we take down the star and store it in the attic, the songs die on our lips, we go back to our guns and threats and accusations, vengeance again holds sway, the criminal courts reopen—man's inhumanity to man becomes the way of the world. Then we wonder why the world is in such a mess and why life is so hard.

The real and unbelievable miracle is that we prefer to be groping people when at Christmas, God has given us enough light to see for a lifetime—and for eternity.

Lawrence Housman puts it:

> *Light looked down, and beheld Darkness.*
> *"Thither will I go," said Light.*
> *Peace looked down and beheld War.*
> *"Thither will I go" said Peace.*
> *Love looked down and beheld Hatred.*
> *"Thither will I go," said Love.*
> *So came Light and shone.*
> *So came Peace and gave rest.*
> *So came Love and brought Life.*

The world is infinitely improved through Christmas—and the light will continue to shine forth through the darkness, intensified through the efforts of every man and woman and child who catches its gleam and shines it forth through the days of their living.

We should be joyful people knowing the privileges and the opportunities that are ours to share Christmas and its eternal light, its enduring word, its everlasting sign, and its eternal love to all God's children, everywhere.

Following Jesus

(Sunrise over Lake Galilee)

John 11: 27

"My sheep hear My voice, and I know them,
they follow Me."

This Above All
Isaiah 53: 7-9

October 22, 1978
Tipp City United Methodist Church, Tipp City, Ohio

One of the most stirring passages in all literature is the admonition of Polonius, addressed to his son, Laertes, in Shakespeare's *Hamlet*. The young man, Laertes, had won his father's consent to leave Denmark for France. There was a tug at the old man's heart as he felt the eagerness of his son to be off to try his wings and challenge the future. Perhaps Polonius was haunted by memories of his own yesterdays as he looked into the eyes of Laertes. His counsel, therefore, was wise with the wisdom of affection and experience. "Beware of entrance into quarrel," he warned. "Give every man thine ear, but few thy voice." Then, with gentle insight, he urged,

> *Take each man's censure, but reserve thy judgement, but this above all; to thine own self be true, and it must follow as the night the day, Thou canst not then be false to any man. Farewell, my blessing season this in thee.*

So Laertes ventured into the future with the noblest advice a father ever gave to a son.

Polonius might have pointed to Jesus for an illustration of his theme: He could have said of Jesus that He rings true. Those who lived in Jesus's day said of him, "there was no guile in him." Isaiah, thinking into the future, said of One who would save Israel, *"There was no deceit in His mouth."* (Isaiah 53: 9). No subterfuge, no double-dealing, no trickery, no insincerity. Jesus was exactly what He appeared to be on the surface, and His contemporaries summed up their estimate of Him when they said with awe, *"God was in Christ."* *(2nd Corinthians 5: 19)*.

What we want to know and what Laertes needed to know is how we can be true to ourselves in the world we know and experience from day to day. We sing, "I would be true, for there are those who trust me," [Howard A. Walter] and we would be if we could. We thoroughly agree when Polonius says, "This above all; to thine own self be true." But when we find ourselves caught in the welter of contemporary life with all of its social, political, and economic pressure, we wonder how we can preserve our inner integrity and our spiritual independence.

Jesus answers quite simply, *"Follow Me." (Matthew 4: 19)*. On another occasion He remarked, *"If thine eye be single, the whole body is full of light." (Matthew 6: 22b)*. That is to say, "If your loyalty is concentrated on the highest, then the self will be true and radiant." Or, to put it another way: "Follow Me, and while you follow you can trust yourself no matter who doubts you." In short, inner integrity rests on a dependable loyalty. It hinges on faith in One who remains trustworthy, *"yesterday, today, and forever."*

Obviously, two things are involved. The first is a dependable loyalty. When Jesus says, *"Follow Me,"* can we resist following? Our era has listened to innumerable voices shouting, "Follow me!" and many people have followed eagerly. The Italians followed Mussolini. The Germans followed Hitler. The Russians followed Stalin. The eye was single in its loyalty to the man on horseback, but the body was not full of light. The object of the people's loyalty was something less than dependable. Someone says that the Pied Pipers of our contemporary world were and are blind leaders of the blind.

There is a decided difference between the raucous commands of a self-appointed leader shouting into a loud speaker, "Follow me!" and the gentle summons of the Master. In one case, a person is speaking for his or herself; in the other a Man spoke for God. In the first instance, a person points only to oneself with unfettered egotism, but in the other, a Man points beyond Himself, with the ego altogether submerged in the ultimate affirmation, *"Not my will but Thine be done."*

Jesus commends Himself to us because He points always to a power behind Him, reveals a reality within Him, suggests a reference behind Him. He spoke to His generation and He speaks to our as *"One having authority, and not as the scribes." (Matthew 7: 29)*. His authority was the authority of obedience to the will of God. So, when He says, *"Follow Me,"* we can fix our eyes on Him and follow, trusting ourselves, our judgements, our moral choices even though we meet doubt and skepticism on every hand.

There is a suggestion of what I mean in the conversation of the Earl of Kent and King Lear, wherein the King says to the Earl, "Who wouldest thou serve?" and Kent replied, "You!"

Pressing the issue, King Lear asks, "Dost thou know me fellow?" To which Kent replied, "No sir, but you have in your countenance which I would fain call master."
Startled, the king inquires, "What's that?" and the answer comes, "Authority."

So in Jesus Christ there is that which we would fain call Master. He speaks with an authority we feel instinctively is worthy of trust. He leads with an authority we know is safe to follow. He is our own fixed point in a world of change, one whose wisdom can be trusted, *"yesterday, today, and forever."* By the light of His mind, you and I can walk with integrity of spirit through the conflicting loyalties of our day without skepticism. We can challenge questionable business practices and popular prejudices in His name without self-doubt. We can be true to ourselves undergirded by the authority of Jesus Christ.

So, inner integrity depends first on a dependable loyalty, and second on the depth of the loyalty. A dependable lodestar is of little value if we ignore its guidance. It is all very well to know in theory that what is highest in human aspiration, as we see it in Jesus, is also deepest in nature and God. But inner integrity awaits our loyal response. We are forever being challenged to betray Him and ourselves as well. Like the late Senator Ashurst, we betray ourselves under pressure. Pressed by the party leadership on one occasion to shift his stand on an issue, the Senator was congratulated by a colleague for "having seen the light."

"I didn't see the light," the Senator replied, "I felt the heat." On another occasion, he supported a bill he inwardly opposed with the comment, "Certainly I was for it as soon as I saw it was inevitable."

"This above all: to thine own self be true." It is the ultimate "above all" demand of the spiritual life. But to be true requires, first, a basic faith that Jesus spoke as *"One having authority,"* when He called, *"Follow Me,"* and second, faithfulness in following. Fix your eyes on Him and trust yourself even when all others doubt you. You may "feel the heat," but you will cling to the light. You may feel the inevitability of an event you oppose, but you will remain, if need be, a minority of one against it.

There is then, a second admonition that flows from the mind of Christ to us who would be true to ourselves. Jesus put it simply when He asked, *"What shall it profit a man if he gain the whole world and lose his own soul?" (Mark 8: 36).* Profit and loss are not the final arbiter of our souls. Indeed, Jesus seems to be saying, "Set your mind on God and treat both success and failure as impostors. As Kipling has it:

> *If you can meet with triumph or disaster*
> *And treat those two impostors just the same.*
> *Then you'll be a man.*

But what is more, you will be true to yourself.

Now one of the striking things about the Master's triumph is in the fact that He was not taken in by that triumph. He seemed to feel that the triumph was an episode. Momentary popularity with multitudes casting palm branches in His way, was by no means the test of His authority. Success in winning the plaudits of the multitudes was no adequate criterion of His message, and triumph was no assurance of wisdom. A person can crystalize and popularize what people wish to believe and conquest is easy. But popularity is no test of prophetic wisdom, and Jesus knew that full well.

Jesus was not deceived by triumph, nor was He deceived by apparent defeat. As Isaiah said, *"He was despised and rejected of men." (Isaiah 53: 3).* What is more, He was oppressed and afflicted—and in the end He carried a cross on that sad journey to a hill called The Place of the Skull to be crucified between two thieves. But neither the cheers of Palm Sunday nor the jeers of Good Friday were the arbiters of His destiny. Both of them were incidental responses to the integrity of His own spirit. Both the triumph of Palm Sunday and the disaster of Good Friday were impostors—they were irrelevant to the judgment of history and God.

You and I had best remember that, and keep our eyes fixed on God and not on the crowd. No person can be true to self while playing to the galleries. No person can be true to self if he or she sets too high a value on what we commonly call "success," for both success and failure are impostors. What seems like success may be abject failure; and what seems like failure may be triumph of the first order.

The great and enduring satisfactions of life do not arise from petty conquests on the field of self-assertion. The abiding gratifications of life grow from the virtue of doing right by the right principle. An ancient sage remarked wisely, "Pity the man who knows no happiness but the fulfillment of his own greed." Success and failure both are liars in the final summing up. Certainly that is the message of the defeat of the cross and of the triumph of Easter, too.

But we forget, and in forgetting betray ourselves. Dorothy Sayers asks thoughtfully, "Do we admire and envy the successful because they are rich, or because the work by which they made their money is good work?" If we hear that Old So-and-So pulled off a smart deal, do we say, "Old So-and-So is pretty smart," or do we feel a sense of shame both for ourselves and him? Do we see a motion picture whose theme is woven around empty-headed people lolling in luxury, and feel envious, wishing we could share their life? Or do we return to honest toil and little homes with grateful hearts, not wanting what we have seen?

There is a bit of sober wisdom in the words of Moses to his brother, Shendi, in Christopher Fry's play, *The Firstborn*. Shendi has become a tool of the Egyptians, a captain in Pharaoh's army. Moses, troubled, wishes he would abandon his success on the altar of justice for his oppressed people. But Shendi indignantly rejects the suggestion of his brother. Then Moses says:

> *Make yourself live, then Shendi;*
> *But be sure it is life. The golden bear success*
> *Hugs a man close to its heart; and breaks his bones.*

So success and failure are impostors in the alchemy of life, and in the long run nothing really matters but this:

"This above, all, to thine own self be true."

That is the supreme enterprise of life. *"What shall it profit a man if he gain the whole world and lose his own soul?"* It is better, under God, to be despised and rejected, oppressed and afflicted for Jesus's sake than to betray one's soul.

That leads us to a third implication of the Master's life and teaching. Let me put it this way: Link your life to the lasting, and let all others count with you, but none too much. To be sure, Jesus cared deeply for people, for friends and foes alike. But, as somebody observed, He never gave His mind over to any save God. He was not deceived by His friends when they tried to keep Him from danger in Jerusalem. He was not crushed when those He loved most, His own family said, "He is mad." He was not awed by Pilate nor was He awed by the Pharisees. He stood on the integrity of His own soul before God. Quite simply, His life was not linked to the lasting values of our heritage. He stood His ground with His feet planted on the eternal, on values that could not be shaken because they are rooted in God. He knew that love and truth, goodness and integrity are not elective courses in the University of God. They are required as foundations upon which the future can be built. They are permanent necessities undergirding life. Jesus linked His life to them and became a vehicle for their expressions in His time.

No person can be true to self except as he or she links his or her life to lasting, enduring values. As Paul said, *"There are things that are eternal and things that are transient." (paraphrase: 2nd Corinthians 4: 18).* You can link your life to one or the other. Philosophers say some values are "instrumental" and other are intrinsic, and again you can link your life to one or the other.

But the difference between them is significant. Instrumental values are not valuable in themselves, but rather serve as a means to something else. Your watch, for example, has instrumental value. It is valuable because it keeps time. If it won't run, it has no value except perhaps for the gold, or platinum, or diamonds on it. And they are valuable only because you can sell them for something else. Your automobile has instrumental value as a means of taking you where you want to go. It may be instrumental, also to the buttressing of your pride. But in and of itself, it has no value. It is useful as an instrument. Money is instrumental, and so is your house, your refrigerator, or almost anything you can mention. But notice, if you will, that instrumental values are not lasting. They are the *"things that are seen,"* and transient.

On the other hand, there are intrinsic values—values in themselves. There is love, for example. To be sure, it may have a degree of instrumental value. It may get you a diamond ring, a big house, and a mink coat. On the other hand, it may get you none of these things. It may get you only a coat from the bargain basement, housemaid's knees and chapped hands. It may get you drudgery and worry and the necessity for sacrifice. Nevertheless, love is good no matter what it gets you. Love is good in and of itself and not because of anything it gets you or accomplishes for you. It is good even when it costs a crown of thorns and a cross.

Or there's truth, another intrinsic value. It is good in and of itself no matter what it gets you. It may result in increased business responsibility and salary as your reputation for loyalty to truth inspires confidence in you. It may bring you a degree of fame as when George Washington could not tell a lie and confessed to chopping down the cherry tree. On the other hand, truth may be costly, as when Jesus challenged the Pharisees with the truth. It may be costly to the politician who sticks to the truth in spite of the heat. It may be costly to the businessman who stands by the truth despite the half-truths of the competition. But truth remains good whether it gets you what you want or costs you what you want. Its value is intrinsic, permanent, lasting, no matter what its consequences may be.

Truth and love, goodness and integrity are intrinsic values, implicit in the nature of the universe. They are expressions of the life of God in the life of humanity, for God is truth, God is love, God is good. So, when we link our lives to the lasting, intrinsic values of our common life, we link our lives to God. We are true to ourselves. Jesus was oppressed and He was afflicted, nevertheless, He did not protest in fear. He endured in obedience to the truth and was sustained by it. He allowed no violence in His defense, but in loyalty to the lasting He prayed, *"Father, forgive them."* There was no deceit in His mouth, but rather a great commitment of His life and His lips to the enduring values He knew were rooted in the will of God.

Link your life to the lasting values that are expressions of the life of God in you. Your devotion to them is a token of your loyalty to your essential you. It is evidence of your will to answer the summons of Jesus, *"Follow Me."*

This above all; to thine own self be true,
And it follows as the night the day,
Thou canst not then be false to any man.
(Shakespeare)

I heard Him call,
Come, follow; that was all.
My gold grew dim,
My soul went after Him,
I rose and followed.
That was all.

Who would not follow
If he heard Him call?
(Leonard Ravenhill)

The Value of Venturing Forth
Genesis 11:31-12:9

Christ United Methodist Church
July 8, 1973

*F*rom the moment we are born until we take our last breath on earth, we are confronted with a certain dilemma—do we stay where we are, or do we move out into the unknown? At just about every stage of life we face the choice of growing or shriveling as persons.

None of us can avoid the dilemma—the youth leaves home for a new adventure, college or service or work; and responsibility falls upon him or her. Or the young couple starts out in life together and plans for the care of their families with all the choices that career presents. Or middle-age comes upon us with its changes in activity and routine and home habits; or retirement with its choices and its change.

Really, it makes little difference who or what we are. Each of us in our own lives faces the same problem of new responsibility. The trimmings of civilization have not altered in the least the venture of becoming a person. The choices—to grow or to shrivel—are age-old. Abraham, you remember, was called to leave the security of the past for the uncertain possibilities of the future. To do so, he had to journey through all that anxiety of the present. Abraham is known as the father of the faithful precisely because he responded to the summons to fulfill his destiny. It is to him we look in our attempt to understand our encounter with new beginnings and the ventures of life.

Abraham lived in Ur of the Chaldees. Culture and religion thrived there in the midst of economic prosperity. Ur stands for all that is safe and comfortable and stable in life. Here we see our hard-won accomplishments and security; a nice home, recognition, a thriving business, mastery of a special job, a small circle of friends, and the satisfaction of having arrived at a firm faith.

In the midst of such safety, Abraham heard a command rising out of the ground and source of his being. "Get out—leave your land, your relatives, and your father's house." To become aware of life's possibilities means cutting ourselves off from the past. No longer can we complacently accept what has been. Awareness of potentiality destroys the status quo. New beginnings mean giving up the security we have acquired; the accumulation of accomplishment and the prop of family protection. One of America's noted artists describes the beginnings from which emerged her genius—following the promptings of a persistent instinct, she writes, "I turned my back on all that I had done and faced the dark."

When we get into new situations, we want to cling to the past. It isn't easy to give it up. The school-age child may revert to earlier behavior—baby talk and such. Whenever we find ourselves in a new group, we gravitate as quickly as possible to the same familiar faces. Because we are uneasy about meeting new people, we hang on to those we already know. In one way or another, each of us uses our past as a security crutch in the uneasy present. But growth and creativity mean giving up the status quo. They mean leaving behind what we have cherished from childhood.

Awareness of unrealized possibilities not only destroys acquired security, it also drives us to create new patterns and qualities of life which we only partially can conceive. After telling Abraham to throw off the past—his land, his relatives, and his father's income, God tells him what he will receive in return: "*The land that I will show you.*" And as the *Book of Hebrews* puts it, "*He went out not knowing where he was to go.*" To turn our backs upon the past is to face what that noted artist called "the dark." We move from a certain and secure yesterday into an uncertain and insecure tomorrow. Real growth brings apprehension.

Possibilities only become actualities, expectations only become realities, dreams only turn to facts, by our passing through this experience of anxiety. In short, to begin any new adventure in life is to become anxious. It is to feel the tension between what is and what can be; between stagnation or growth. The Danish philosopher, Kierkegaard, saw it: "to venture causes anxiety, but not to venture is to lose oneself."

So, like Abraham, at the promptings of the center and depth of our souls, we open up to new beginnings. A new class, a new job, a new relationship, a new responsibility is created. However, something often happens. Abraham's father had started out for the unknown. Then we come to these tragic words in the Biblical narrative: *"But when they came to Haran, they settled there." (Genesis 11: 31).* None of us escapes the temptation to give up the struggle for the sake of security.

You know what it's like. You can hardly wait to start something new. You are all keyed up. The first few days or even weeks you are conscientious. Everything is done perfectly and on time. Distractions are ignored. Then the first flush of enthusiasm fades. You begin to take a more realistic view of life. After all, why kill yourself? What isn't done today can always be done tomorrow. Only tomorrow never comes.

This is the tragedy of so much of life. We do begin on something creative, but the pressure becomes too great. We want to give up and settle down. As students, we might find it hard to ignore the attraction of writing several term papers on the same subject. "After all," we rationalize, "one ought to try to do a thorough job." How convenient it is to discover we can read the same book for different courses. That gives a chance to really understand it. The professor or the teacher wrestles with the temptation to use the same course outline and the same lectures without revision, "After all," we say to ourselves, "facts are facts." In our relationship with others we keep to the same little circle—someone calls it a cage—of friends and acquaintances. Newcomers are greeted politely and left to go their own way. We take a tentative step into the unknown. Then we quickly settle down and build a fence to protect us.

We embark on the sea of life, launching out into unknown beginnings. But the perils of the journey frighten us. We long to return to the safety of pleasanter days. When we pull back, the security of the past is no longer safe. To give up the struggle would mean being "sucked down" into quicksand. Spiritual death would result.

There are perils and uncertainty in moving forward. There are greater dangers, though, in abandoning the venture. What we need to do is just to keep moving. As you well know, there will be moments when you wonder if you can create anything of significance, whether it be a term paper or a friendship, or a family life, or a vocational opportunity. When Agnes DeMille was in a time of agony, she asked her friend, Martha Graham, "Practically, Martha, what do I do tomorrow between waking and sleeping?"

"You make yourself a program of activity, and you do not stop once. You keep going—that is your only responsibility."

Whenever we feel the tendency to settle down in Haran, we ought to remember those words—"You keep going—that is your only responsibility."

As we continue reading the Biblical account, we discover God did not let Abraham rest comfortably for long. Abraham pulled up stakes. He left security and comfort for the land of promise. But that Promised Land of fulfillment is not as we might expect it to be. We are told Abraham journeyed there as in a foreign land, living in tents.

When we begin to find ourselves and our potentialities, we shall be in strange and unfamiliar territory. There will be no permanent landmarks to guide us and no places to settle permanently. A movie director came across the following introduction in a script: "Words fail to describe the scene that follows."

"That," stormed the director, "is a great help!"

But whether we like it or not, that is the way of the Promised Land. Words fail to describe our experience in it, for we sojourn as in a strange country. To become a person is to experience freedom. Yet freedom is expansive. There is a constant movement and no arrival. Words fail to describe what lies ahead.

In the adventure of life, we are never finished. As someone once remarked, "Life seems to be all road and no arriving." Only as our achievements become spring-boards to further accomplishments will they gain significance. For example, a couple grows in their marriage partly because in their younger years they began to move freely and easily into an increasingly wider and deeper friendship with members of both sexes. When you stand at the altar and promise to love and cherish each other, you are beginning a journey into a strange land. You will never know completely where your path of beginning is going to lead. It reaches out beyond the horizon of your immediate understanding. The rainbow of promised fulfillment is something that is never fully grasped. It always lures us onward, for freedom is expansive. We never arrive. We only journey as pilgrims in an unfamiliar land.

Up until now, we really have been looking at the problem of new beginnings from a partial and distorted vantage point. We have seen that growth brings an awareness of possibilities. The acquired security of the past has to be discarded. New patterns have to be created. There is no way to avoid the anxiety of the uncertain future. None of us escapes the inclination to abandon the struggle. Yet if we are to become purpose driven persons, we shall live in that blessed state as in a strange place. There will be no secure conditions or places or relationships.

To complete our understanding of the experience, we need to see the perspective of the Biblical narrative. We are told Abraham was empowered to face that task because of faith. It was *"by faith"* that he left Ur, not knowing where he was to go. We, too, can venture into an uncertain future with the confidence of Abraham. Faith is simply trust in God as we know God in Christ. Faith gives us an inward certitude and firmness in the face of the anxiety of possibility. We believe it is Christ Himself who makes us restless. We can trust the creative impulses and urgings within our hearts. These come from Christ who is the ground and source of our lives. The summons to pull up stakes and forge new pathways is not simply the result of our own uneasy spirits. The source of dissatisfaction without security is rooted in that which is ultimate. Wherever we are, whatever our circumstances, Christ calls us to leave past certainty to live in the uncertainty of the Promised Land. Christ strengthens us for the venture. Christ gives us faith and trust in His promptings and guidance.

George Newmark said it three hundred years ago, and it is just as true today:

> *If thou but suffer God to guide thee*
> *And hope in Him through all thy ways,*
> *He'll give thee strength whate'er betide thee*
> *And bear thee thro' the evil days;*
> *Who trusts in God's unchanging love*
> *Builds on the rock that naught can move.*

Gleam Following
John 1: 1-18

June 8, 1986
Urbana United Methodist Church, Urbana, Ohio
Retirement Sunday

Follow, follow the gleam,
Standards of worth o'er all the earth;
Follow, follow, the gleam
Of the light that shall bring the dawn.
(Bryn Mawr Silver Bay Prize Song, 1920.)

Light is found throughout the *Bible*. Indeed, the first command of creation was *"Let there be light." (Genesis 1: 3)*. This was the light of day. In Moses we have the Light of the Mind. In the prophets we have the Light of the Spirit. In Jesus is the Light of the Personality: *"For in Him was Life, and the Life was the Light of Men." (John 1: 4)*.

From the first, humanity has been on the great quest for light. Sometimes it seems only a "spark in the dark." These were the words spoken of a lighthouse keeper who every night kept sending out his "spark in the dark," and never knew whether it was seen or not.

A spark disturbs our clod
Nearer we move to God.
(Rabbi Ben Ezra)

Isaiah puts it, *"The people that walked in darkness have seen a great light: they that dwell in the land of the shadow of death, upon them hath the light shined." (Isaiah 9: 2)*.
This was a burning vision—one vast and engulfing experience.

The quest for light can be a long, long quest. In the last century, Cardinal Newman, sick in body, sick in soul, was on a ship which met a dead calm. He could only pray for light and guidance. And out of that experience came a living personal fellowship with a living personal God, and the hymn written of the struggle:

Lead, kindly Light, amid the encircling gloom,

Lead Thou me on.

The great need of the soul is the need for light.

A bishop faced with a request from a church board to remove a minister from that congregation said, "Now, I want to know the truth about this preacher. I have to move him from every church at the end of his first year. I want you to be frank about him. He's the best prepared man we have in the conference. He has six degrees, including a Ph.D. He is a college and seminary graduate. He is one of the finest minds in our denomination."

An old board member replied, "Bishop, what's the use o' havin' a pedigree, if you ain't got a hoss?"

Words spoken without the light of Christ's spirit are empty words indeed.

A farmer fell into an old well. That well was thirty feet deep, slippery and steep. When he realized how dangerous the spot was, he was at first paralyzed with fear. He yelled for an hour, but no one heard. Then he began to get chilly and numb. For the first time since he had fallen into that well, he looked above him and saw a circle of light. Above that light was shining a star, for the depth and darkness of that well made it possible to see the star in the daytime. Then, when he saw the circle of light and that star, he knew that there was only one way to go—that was toward the light—that was up! So for five hours, he dug steps in the soft wall of the slanting cell and climbed to safety.

Art and literature takes us on this journey of moving from the darkness, up to the light. In Dante's *Divine Comedy* is found a path that led directly to the stars. Beethoven, in his *Ninth Symphony*, fourth movement, shows the search of the composer to find the one note that gives unity to life, attempts to get a tune; and then leads to *Ode to Joy*. And Job in his own deep well of suffering, says with confidence and faith, "*I know that my Redeemer liveth!*" (Job 19: 25).

Light can be reflected from us to others, but we often fall woefully short of the task.

A disgruntled diner complained to the waiter, "Say, waiter, I ordered strawberry shortcake and you brought me a plate of berries. Where's the cake?

"Well, suh," responded the waiter, "that's what we is short of."

A little daughter said to her mother, "Why is Father singing so much tonight?"

The mother answered, "He is trying to sing the baby to sleep, dear."

"Well," retorted the little girl, "if I was the baby, I'd pretend I was asleep!"

One of America's great ministers had been a coal miner before he came to the U.S. He was what they call in England a "breaker boy." This boy had the job of driving a mule in the mine. The stubborn mule pulled the boy and his coal car through the dark tunnels past an intersection that was a very dangerous spot, for it had a steep incline. At that steep intersection more than a few boys had been killed when a runaway car would smash into another car.

On his first trip, the boy was behind the mule riding a big load of coal, and approached that intersection with anxiety and fear in his young heart. He had heard so many stories of boys and mules being killed at that spot that he was frightened terribly. His legs went cold; his body trembled so that he could hardly hold the reigns over the mule's back. He thought he heard the thunder of a runaway car coming down the incline toward that narrow dark place where the two tracks crossed. There were no signals then as there are in modern coal mines; a fellow just had to take a chance. Then, just as he turned the corner and approached the dangerous intersection, he saw a tiny gleam of light, and when he reached the intersection he brushed a tear from his eyes with his dirty sleeve, making a smear across his cheek. He smiled then as he looked up, for there stood his own father, a coal miner, with a lantern in his hands. He had thought of the boy's danger and fears on this first trip toward the dangerous crossing. "That was the most beautiful light I ever saw in my life, and my coal-smeared father was the handsomest man I ever saw, as he stood there in the dim light of that lantern, waiting for me with a big light on his face."

So this world would be a dark place, if it were not for the lantern-bearers who stand with their light in life's darkest places. Here is a grave need that we must fill. And we must fill our lanterns full of light for ourselves.

There is a striking legend about the Golden Palace. This palace was said to contain everything that would please the heart of any child, and all children everywhere tried every day to do good things that would earn them the key to the palace. "What shall I do to earn the key to the Golden Palace?" asked one little girl. "I have brushed my hair until it shines like gold in the sun, and I have woven many yards of linen—all for the key, and no one has given it to me."

"These do not count," said the old doorkeeper. "Do something each morning for somebody else, and thou shalt earn the key."

So the child searched to find someone to help. She found an old beggar and ran to him with all the coins she had been saving for many weeks. "Now," she laughed. "I have earned the golden key."

"Try again, child," said the doorkeeper.

So the child was disappointed and went back to the city, where she saw a poor lame woman who was climbing the hill painfully and dragging a heavy bundle upon her back.

"I'll help her. That will surely be enough to earn the key," she thought.

So she helped the woman and ran off for the key. But the old gatekeeper said, "You must try again, child."

But the child was discouraged. She walked home slowly and decided to give up the work for the key; it was impossible to earn it. Then passing through a section of the woods, she heard a faint cry. She listened and realized it must be a little dog. Such it was, caught there in the trap of a hunter.

"Oh," she cried as she knelt down and tried to unfasten the trap. She pulled at the heavy spring until her fingers were bleeding. But finally, the dog was free and licked her hand and whimpered. She tore some bandages from the skirt of her dress and bandaged the wounded paw. Then she picked up the little dog and carried him homeward.

Suddenly, there appeared before her the old doorkeeper, holding out to her the key to the Golden Palace.

"Oh," she said, surprised. "The key is not for me. I did not help the little dog for the key. I forgot all about the key."

In the eyes of the old man there were tears of joy. "You forgot yourself, dear child. The key is for those who forget themselves."

If the light is in us, it cannot be contained.

How dull it is to rust unburnished,
Not to shine in use.
(Alfred, Lord Tennyson)

A certain nurse in an American hospital always seemed able to bring cheer to the suffering and discouraged soldiers. One boy who had lost his legs, waited all through the day for that nurse to come on duty. One night, just before she was to leave the ward, that boy called her over to his bed. And when she looked down on him, he said, "I like you best of all the nurses."

"Well, why is that?" she asked surprised. "There are a lot of fine nurses in this ward."

And he answered her shyly, "I like you best because your face shines."

"Then I'd better go powder my nose!" she replied, laughing.

"On, no," replied the boy. "I don't mean that—it's a light from inside that shines in your eyes."

In the *Bible* we have the story of the first Christian martyr, Stephen, who died with a shining face.

Real beauty is spiritual.

John Masefield in his play, *The Faithful,* describes the scene where the mother is at home alone and the enemy attacks. She resolves that they would not enter her home—and so she used her body as a shield and kept the door.

"Did she die, Father?" asked the child.

"As far as such souls, die, she did."

Our task is to be one with the light. Alfred, Lord Tennyson puts it, "One far off divine event, to which the whole creation moves."

St. Paul wrote, *"I am one with Christ. Christ liveth in me."*

And then this from *Pilgrims Progress:*

The Man therefore read it, and looking upon Evangelist very carefully said, "Whither must I fly?"
Then said Evangelist, pointing with his finger over a very wide field. "Do you see yonder Shining Light?"
He said, "I think I do."
"Then," said Evangelist, "keep that Light in your eye, and go up directly thereto, so shalt thou see the Gate; at which when thou knockest, it shall be told then what thou shalt do."

Hold high the torch!
You did not light its glow
'Twas given you by other hands you know.
'Tis your to keep it burning bright,
Yours to pass on when you no more need light'
For there are other feet that we must guide
And other forms go marching by our side.

Hold high the torch!
You did not light its glow—
'Twas given you by other hands you know.
I think it started down its pathway bright,
The day the Maker said, 'Let there be light.'
And He once said who hung on Calvary's tree—
Ye are the light of the world…
Go…Shine…for Me.
(Anonymous)

James Robert Hartland began serving his first church in 1945 while a student at Mount Union College. Over the next 41 years, he served churches in Massachusetts, Pennsylvania, and Ohio. After retirement, he served as a nursing home and hospital chaplain, pulpit supply and interim pastor, and visiting pastor for various churches. He also served as lead chaplain for Civil Air Patrol well into his eighties. "Pastor Jim" blessed all who knew him with his wisdom, inviting smile, and empathetic nature. He entered into Glory on Sunday morning, February 10, 2013.

Marilee Hartland Lake was a teacher for thirty-six years. She and her husband Rick have two sons. This is her second book. The first book, *Nana's Cookbook: A Celebration of the Life of Helen Jane Croft Hartland,* tells the story of her mother. Marilee is active in her church and in the drama/music group LightReaders. Marilee has traveled to Central America on several mission trips. Proceeds from this book support Bradley's House of Hope, a therapy center for handicapped children close to Managua, Nicaragua. Website: www.MarileeLakeAuthor.com.

Made in the USA
Middletown, DE
30 May 2016